STASH

STASH

My Life in Hiding

Laura Cathcart Robbins

ATRIA BOOKS

New York   London   Toronto   Sydney   New Delhi

ATRIA
BOOKS

An Imprint of Simon & Schuster, Inc.
1230 Avenue of the Americas
New York, NY 10020

First Atria Books hardcover edition March 2023

ATRIA BOOKS and colophon are trademarks of Simon & Schuster, Inc.

For information about special discounts for bulk purchases, please
contact Simon & Schuster Special Sales at 1-866-506-1949 or
business@simonandschuster.com.

The Simon & Schuster Speakers Bureau can bring authors to your live event. For
more information or to book an event, contact the Simon & Schuster Speakers
Bureau at 1-866-248-3049 or visit our website at www.simonspeakers.com.

Interior design by Kyoko Watanabe

Manufactured in the United States of America

1 3 5 7 9 10 8 6 4 2

Library of Congress Cataloging-in-Publication Data has been applied for.

ISBN 978-1-6680-0533-0
ISBN 978-1-6680-0535-4 (ebook)

For Miles and Justin

AUTHOR'S NOTE

In 2008, I ended a marriage, got sober, and fell in love all within a ten-month period. An avid reader, I scoured bookstores for memoirs during that time, desperate for stories like mine, written by women who looked like me.

I found none.

I wrote *Stash* to make sure that the next person going through any of that, or all of that, finds themselves in the pages of a book. I wrote *Stash* for my sisters, brothers, and others of all backgrounds and colors who are scared to be themselves.

Writing about addiction, especially one like mine, can be a tricky thing. Because my drug of choice often impaired my ability to remember precise factors like dates, times, and numbers, I sometimes relied on my journals, pictures, and old day planners to interrogate my memory. For someone who has always taken a lot of pride in her recall, discovering that I'd misremembered things about certain events was a tough pill to swallow (pun intended). That said, the book in your hands is as accurate as possible. However, I have intentionally left out or changed certain names because it felt like the right thing to do. And I also changed a few locations too, for the same reasons.

Stash takes place at the intersection of race, privilege, and addiction, but it's important to know that I am in no way trying to speak for all Black people, all privileged people, or all addicts. What you're about to read is simply my experience as I remember it. To be Black and privileged in this world has meant that I needed to become a seamless code-switcher in order to survive. As you will see in the book, my inner voice and outer voice often come from two very different lexicons. Although I am most comfortable with the words of the culture in which I was raised, the lexicon of privilege and of the addict are also both familiar and authentic to me.

Lastly, this recounting of my experience is not meant to villainize anything or anyone. In the writing of this story, I really tried to stay true to the pain and shame that I felt back then. Pain that mostly allowed me only to see where others were wrong. Writing *Stash* helped me gain some perspective on this part of my life.

With gratitude,
Laura Cathcart Robbins

Stash

For years I've prided myself on keeping it hidden.

I hide it in decoy pill bottles in our guest bathroom, I hide it in my coat pockets and my makeup bags. I hide it in the toes of my rain boots and two rows behind the vanilla extract in the kitchen cabinet. I keep copious, coded notes in journals and my Filofax, writing down dates and places. I keep the journals hidden in a rusty locked trunk in our attic.

Refill days are like the Fourth of July, or better yet, Christmas. The joy of driving out of the pharmacy parking lot with a full bottle! I sing along with Beyoncé or Gwen Stefani at the top of my lungs as I fly down Ventura Boulevard, smiling back at guys in their cars at stoplights.

Why not? Life is frickin' dope right about now.

Got me lookin' so crazy right now, your love's got me lookin' so crazy right now . . .

The moment just before I take the first one is always so sweet. I fish the bottle out of the bag and hold it lovingly in my hand before giving it a little shake.

The weight is good. Thank you, God.

I feel like the fact that I can tell how many pills are in a bottle just by weight is a rare skill set, but I've never quite figured out where it would be most useful—a carnival perhaps?

Give me a bottle, any bottle, and I'll tell you how many pills are contained within.

I brace myself for the endorphin rush that I'll get just after popping the childproof cap. It's so instant and powerful that it reminds me of the brain freezes I used to get when eating snow cones too fast. At the same time, I am already fearing the moment my beloved bottle is empty again. And that moment seems to come sooner and sooner every time.

PART ONE

Circling the Drain

CHAPTER ONE

Nightmare on Field Street

Six twenty a.m. March, 2008

Last night I told him I want a divorce, and now I'm trembling in our toilet closet. He's leaving town soon, so the timing of telling him was tricky. For weeks I'd been putting it off because I was so scared of what might happen afterward.

What if he said I had to pack my stuff and get out immediately? What if I realized that telling him was a huge mistake and wanted to take it back? What if I didn't have enough pills to kill the pain after the words were out of my mouth?

But I think he read my journal a few days ago. The journal where for the last year I've chronicled my Ambien use and written freely about how unhappy I've become. If he read it, he knows. And if he knows, it's just a matter of time before he calls me on it. The jig, as they say, is up.

I can't even remember what he said after I'd finally blurted it out. All I remember is sitting across from him and feeling hollow, trying to summon the tears that ought to have been there. After we finished talking, I went into my stash and immediately knocked myself out with three Ambien and a few swigs of Baileys (nasty stuff when it's warm). And then it was morning, and he was asleep in the guest room, and the boys were sleeping with me.

Oh fuck, oh fuck, oh fuck. I can't remember what happened when I told him. Was he mad? Was he shocked? How did we leave it?

I strain for the memories of last night, grasping and clutching faint images and sound bites, but everything is watery mud, nothing emerges clear.

Once again, Ambien has stripped me of my recall.

I have to get the boys ready for school soon, and I can't bring myself to open the door. I feel like I'm in one of those nightmares where you know that you're dreaming, but no matter how terrifying it is, you can't wake up.

"Wake up," I whisper, squinching my eyes shut.

I can taste dread in the back of my throat, along with last night's pills. My eyelids are fluttering slightly, an embarrassing side effect of benzo dependency. When I open them, I'm still in my bathroom, staring at the inside of the closed door. I strain my ears hoping to hear any sounds, movement maybe? But all I can hear is my heart trying to punch its way out of my throat.

What the fuck have you done?

February, 2008

A few months ago he rented an apartment in Hollywood, explaining that he needed to work at night to get his movie done on time. He still comes home for dinner, but two or three nights during the week, he heads back to his place after, leaving me with the kids. If I wasn't so eager to knock myself unconscious every night, I'm sure I would have questioned this arrangement, maybe insisted that he stay home with us. It's amazing, though, what you accept when all you want to do is check out.

If I'm honest, I've gotten so used to his absence that now I've started to prefer it. But being without adult supervision means that my addiction is having several field days. And these days when he comes home in the mornings to find me wobbling around, he's starting to give me the side-eye and question how many pills I'm taking.

However, he shouldn't be so quick to throw shade. These pills lull me into a state that has allowed me to accept the unacceptable. His apartment, the fact that we've become strangers, the fact that I can never tell him the truth. Whenever I'm awake or connected to what's going on, I'm in a full-blown panic because my racing mind screams at me on level ten.

You're forty-three years old. This is it. If you're not happy now, it's only going to get worse. What are you waiting for? One of you to die?

But the notion of separating, even for a short while, makes me want to weep. Just the idea of our kids becoming THOSE kids. The "I'm with my dad this weekend" kids. The kids who show up for school on Fridays with a bag packed to go to the other parent's home. The two birthday parties, two Thanksgivings, two summer vacations kids. The kids everyone feels sorry for and whispers about.

There have been so many times when I've wanted to do the humane thing and put our marriage out of its misery. Because, instead of taking care of each other, he and I have spent the last few years taking turns, frantically performing chest compressions on this third presence in our relationship—the marriage. Him showering me with expensive gifts and prioritizing couples therapy over his production schedule. A fact that I honestly found to be more irritating than sweet as it seemed to be solid proof that he was more devoted to the cause than I was. Me making crib notes of interesting subjects to discuss at dinner, and surprising him on Valentine's Day with a luxe, two-week cycling trip through Italy (I'm not a cyclist at all, and I'm no big fan of Valentine's Day). But everything has been about the marriage, saving the marriage, nurturing the marriage, staying in the marriage.

Add to this that the pressure I feel in our home is so very desperate, the only way I can get through the day is to numb. Take away the pills and I can't fake it anymore. The fucked-up truth is that being loaded is the only way I can continue to show up for my family. Loaded equals numb.

And numb makes me bulletproof.

I can feel the weight of his anguish when he looks at me. He acts like he thinks I'm having an affair. Double-checking my stories, obviously hanging around to listen when I get a phone call. In a way, I guess I am; the withholding of love, the secret phone calls to my doctor and clandestine trips to the pharmacy, the heavy distance between us. Add that to the fact that except for my kids, I have never adored or wanted anything so much as I do the feeling I get when I take my Ambien.

But my pill cravings far exceed the amount legally allowed to one person by California law, which means I'm always running out, which means I'm almost always in withdrawal or detoxing. And unless I go the drug dealer or black-market route, I don't see any end to this cycle.

———

It's Monday night, and I've been pacing around the bathroom for about an hour with a near-empty pill bottle, sweating and quivering.

This is the last one. There are no more refills until next week.

I plead with myself not to take it, to save it, to give my body a chance to flush itself out a bit, so the Ambien actually puts me to sleep. I know that I need it to slow my heart rate so I can get the click I've been chasing ever since I ate that first one six years ago. The one that pulsed through my body that night and filled me with warm velvet before sending me into a blissful, silky eight-hour sleep.

Finally, I hold the small white oval between my fingers and snap it in half. I tell myself that I'll take half now and half tomorrow. But as soon as I've swallowed the first half, my right hand tosses the second one in my mouth, and I eat it dry.

I am possessed.

I wanted to save it for later, but my reptilian brain has other ideas. I stand there motionless, my whole body clenching, waiting. I need that hint of the heat behind my eyes to let me know it's working, but there's nothing. The ten-milligram Ambien is no match for the adrenaline that has been coursing through my system since earlier that day. Defeated, I spread a towel on the bathroom floor and curl up in a ball. The cold marble seeps through the towel and soaks into my bones. I am reminded of the time I went camping, and the temperature dropped below freezing. Rocking back and forth and biting my fist, I lie awake like this all night, getting up at six forty-five to get the boys ready for school.

———

Miracle of miracles, today I woke up feeling kind of normal.

All week long I've been inching my way through the most hellish withdrawal I have ever experienced. I've been taking three showers a day to wash the ever-present slime of detox from my skin, and I'm downing handfuls of ibuprofen to combat my throbbing head and body aches. After the kids went to sleep last night, I read Carrie Fisher's *Postcards from the Edge* in the living room until my eyes burned. These days, I startle when someone calls my name or touches my shoulder, I am a live nerve ending searching for an endorphin rush that may never come.

But today is Friday! And it feels like I might have finally gotten to the other side.

Maybe I'm through the worst of it, perhaps I won't pick up my refill at the pharmacy next week after all and just get this shit out of my system for good.

Maybe all of this was the only way to get free.

———

Or so I thought. I felt so great today! Driving Jacob to his basketball tournament, I found myself checking out his game face in the rearview mirror and smiling at the sight of him in his uniform. It was the first genuine smile I've given in ages. After a whole week of shivering, sleeplessness, sweating, and body aches, I was so proud of myself. I really thought maybe I might be in the clear. Maybe I could quit for good this time.

I remember with aching clarity the precise moment it happened. A kid named Tommy gets a bloody lip on the court, and I jump up to comfort him, and then everything goes dark. I wake up in the back of an ambulance, coming to as the young, white EMT calls my name, asking me questions.

"Laura, do you know what year it is?"

His voice is so kind that I want to climb out of the cushioned abyss into which I've fallen.

I'd like to give him the right answer so that he will know this is all a mistake. I can't go to the hospital. My son's team is playing for the championship. I want them to turn the ambulance around and let me out.

Is it legal to just let someone out of an ambulance?

When I give him the year, I watch him glance at his partner with concern.

"Do you know who our president is?"

Ronald Reagan is the only name I can summon, and I cringe when I hear my voice answer him.

"Ronno Ray-gunnnn."

Oh shit, I'm slurring, oh shit.

"Close," he says gently. "It's George Bush."

"W," I say triumphantly, and I feel my lips curling into a smile. "That's right."

Everything goes dark again after they wheel me into the ER.

It turns out I've had two grand mal seizures. Even now, it hurts to type these three words.

Grand. Mal. Seizure.

———

My mother is there when I come to this time. I see her and start to sob. I am panicking, not because I am scared for myself, but because of how afraid my children must be.

"Oh my God, Mommy. They must be terrified! Oh my God, oh my God."

"They were on the other side of the court, and they didn't see anything," my mother assures me. "We told them you'd just fainted, they're okay. I told them we'd call them soon."

Shame is a tidal wave that envelops me and sets my lungs on fire. My brain is scrambling to retrieve memories from earlier in the day. I have to reach through thick blankets of fog to locate my words, and each time I am struck with a bolt of pain searing through my temples. I force myself to exhale and allow my arms to rest by my side.

Maybe I'm dying. Perhaps that's not the worst thing.

The following day I'm still in Sherman Oaks Hospital, and I'm waiting for a doctor to discharge me. Meanwhile, the questions.

"How old are you? Have you ever had a seizure before today? Does epilepsy run in your family? What drugs are you taking? How many drinks do you have per day? When was your last (Ambien, drink, pain pill . . .)?"

I am as baffled as the lab coats are as to what caused those two seizures. I want them to hurry up so I can go home to my kids. My head is clearer now. I'm starting to feel quite panicky that they might have other reasons for trying to keep me here, like admitting me to the psych ward or sending me off to rehab. I go into battle mode. After all, I have a refill coming up on Tuesday.

"I'm forty-three."

"No, no seizures before today. No epilepsy in my family."

"Yes, I take Ambien, one at bedtime, as prescribed by my doctor."

"No, I wouldn't say that I'm much of a drinker, in fact, I rarely drink at all."

"My last Ambien?" It feels good to tell the truth here. "Oh, it must have been a few days ago, I'm not sure."

I dig my nails into my palms under my thin hospital blanket. I hope that my face is giving them "sympathetic mother who needs to get home to her young sons" instead of "desperate drug addict trying to throw them off the scent."

—

I've got a golden ticket, y'all. I am a FREE WOMAN!!

My hospital discharge prescription has a lot of doctor's scribble. Still, it's the six words printed at the bottom in a clear, bold hand that make me want to bounce out of my hospital bed to do the running man all the way out the automatic double doors.

EARLY REFILLS ALLOWED, MULTIPLE REFILLS AVAILABLE.

Thank you, Black baby Jesus, for the negative tox screen! The withdrawal had been so hard that I knew I hadn't taken anything, but with my fucked-up memory, I just couldn't be one hundred percent sure. But now all these nosy muthafuckahs can see that I had no detectable toxins in my system. That means no drugs, no booze. The lab coats determine that the seizures were caused by a lack of sleep and sudden withdrawal from sleep medication. The way I read it, this gives the pharmacist permission to override California sedative dosage recommendations and give me whatever I need. Whenever I want!!

No more hiding. This means I can show this get-out-of-jail-free card to him when he sees me getting up in the middle of the night to take more or when I need a quarter or a half a pill to calm down during the day.

Doctor's orders, BITCH!! Whatchu got to say now???

But suddenly the gravity of what happened smacks my ass back down to the ground.

I had two seizures.

I could have died.

And then that middle-of-the-night voice presents itself. I try to block it out, but its insistence is impressive, like electroshock therapy or, better yet, like a Taser to the back of my skull.

Buzzzz

Hey! You know why I'm here, right?

Buzzzz

You take the pills so you can show up for this marriage. If you leave the marriage, then maybe you won't have to take the pills.

And maybe you won't die.

Buzzzz, Buzzzz, Buzzzz . . .

Hey! You hearing me?

But I'm swarmed by feelings of guilt and confusion. He's never beaten me, cheated on me, or mistreated me. He's provided an amazing home and lifestyle. He's a hard worker, loved and respected by his colleagues and friends. He's a great son, a great brother, a great uncle, and an incredible dad.

Can I leave someone like that? What grounds do I have?

When people talk about enduring it's usually in an admirable way. They bravely endure the pain of childbirth, or they endure poverty or hunger. The goal is to make it through these types of things and come out "stronger," right? I've seen people endure unhappy marriages for years, justifying their cowardice by saying things like, "it's too complicated," or "it's better than being alone." Then they stay until they're too old to find love again or until they die. I've been blaming the demise of our marriage on my addiction, which blew up spectacularly this year. But if I'm being honest, we've been unhappy for longer than that. I feel as though I've been hanging onto a window ledge for the past two years and now my fingers are starting to slip. All this time I've been so terrified of the fall that I haven't even dared think about where I might land. But what if I've been afraid of the wrong thing? What if it's not where I land that should concern me but why I'm still hanging on?

Then again, what if I get out and, too late, realize that this was happiness?

CHAPTER TWO

Run, Run, Run,
as Fast as You Can

My parents were hippies who, despite their African American heritage, had done the very Scandinavian thing of continuing to parent me together after their divorce. In fact, they were so taken with the idea of a freer society, such as the ones described in Sweden and Norway, that my mother and I briefly moved to Copenhagen right after their divorce was final. But a few months later my dad had moved to Nashville to start medical school, and my mom and I moved back to the States and settled in Cambridge, Massachusetts. I missed my dad terribly, but it was comforting to hear the two of them talking "long distance" on the weekends, catching each other up on me.

I was only five when my mother remarried. She and my stepfather, Kenny, were artists, and our lives were filled with colorful canvases and the intense conversations of "conscious" Black men and women. I remember sneaking into the living room after I'd been put to bed for some of their late-night gatherings. Joints were being passed while Marvin Gaye's *What's Going On* played on the HiFi. I knew that as long as I remained silent, Kenny might not notice. So I would crouch down in a corner somewhere and become a statue, breathing as shallowly as possible, thirstily absorbing every word and sound.

I knew how to stay out of the way. I had already mastered the art of hiding in plain sight.

If Kenny caught sight of me, and he was really fucked-up on weed, his instantaneous rage was like standing in the eye of a Cat 5 hurricane. My efforts to defend myself made him roar even louder, so eventually I learned to take the opposite tact. By the time I was six it was a standoff: he would bellow and I would stand there mutely and unbudgingly, lips pursed with my fists at my side until, exasperated, he'd send me to my room. Looking back, I think he resented me on sight, maybe even hated me. I can also see that my motivation for staying small was my fear of making things worse. If I didn't agitate him, he was less likely to go off on me, and life was easier for me and my mom.

It didn't take long before I learned to gauge how fucked-up he was in order to know how to be. Two joints in, he was a straight-up monster. His energy was palpable, heavy and menacing. Even when we weren't in the same room, I could still feel him lurking around, just waiting for me to make a mistake. The sound of him calling my name made my whole body seize with panic. The sight of him all scowly and red-eyed rendered me completely silent and shut down. Holding my fork wrong at dinner was like lighting the fuse on a keg of dynamite. Mouthing off to him added more items to my punishment/chore list, which already included scrubbing the toilet bowl on Fridays with my bare hands.

When my mom was around, Kenny could be charming. He would often put his arm around me affectionately and tease me about how much TV I watched or about how I always had my nose in a book. But when he and I were alone, it was like those horror movies where suddenly everything goes dark and the characters can see their frozen breath. I thought about telling my mom, and my dad, but I was afraid it would be my word against his. Plus, I hated him so much that I was damned if I was going to let him know he was getting to me.

For my ninth birthday I'd asked for dangly earrings. After waiting for my mom to take her nightly bath, Kenny gave me a beautifully wrapped toilet bowl brush. He smiled at me as I unwrapped it and didn't move until he saw my reaction. I felt my lower lip trembling and almost crumpled right in front of him, but then something intervened. A notion popped into my head that would change how I operated forever.

Give him nothing.

I was around ten when it became clear that his high days were starting to outnumber his normal ones. And no matter what I did, me being me just set him off. At night in bed, I shut my eyes and would pray for sleep, but my mind seemed to be in a constant state of alertness, something I understand now to be hypervigilance, a symptom of PTSD. I was always scanning the house with my ears, listening for his footsteps in the hallway or for the incrementally heightened tones of him taunting my mother, which inevitably led to one of their late-night verbal brawls.

Banging, screaming, pleading.

It's crazy how even now my body still reacts the same way to these sounds. A raised voice, a bang of a fist, or a door slammed in anger. These responses are still stored in my body, in my spine, which flinches and rounds, in my hands which tremble and fly to cover my mouth. My ears are always wide-open on high alert, listening to all the sounds around me at all times.

Helpless.

One day I came home after school and he was yelling at my mother and waving my beloved one-line-a-day diary. When I heard her yelling back at him, defending me, I froze. I wasn't sure if I should go inside and rescue my mom or run away and go and live with my dad. But I couldn't go to my dad's. I couldn't leave my mom alone with him.

"I hate him, I hate the way he talks to Mama. I wish he'd die," I'd written in tiny letters. "I'm going to call the police and tell them about his shoebox of weed and have him arrested."

After that I started writing in code. If I were his prey and he were the hunter, then I was going to make myself much harder to catch. That same thought ran through my head on a loop.

Give him nothing. Give him nothing.

Eventually it got so that there wasn't anything I wouldn't do to avoid attracting negative attention from anyone. I lied whenever the truth might get me in trouble, I hid bad report cards and pretended to be sick on exam days if I hadn't studied. And because dissociation seemed to come naturally to me, I genuinely felt as though I were bubbly and carefree. No one worried about me because no one knew there was anything to worry about.

As the only Black kid in my class and at one point in my whole school, even when I was little, I always felt the burden of representing Black excellence, a theme which still follows me to this day. I assumed that, academically, I had to be as good or better than my white class-mates in order to be "part of" and/or admired. And while this was fine when it came to the subjects that came naturally to me, like reading, writing, and drama, my failures in all things math and science were mortifying, and I did whatever I could to hide my incompetence in those areas.

I was twelve when Kenny accepted a job offer in Berkeley, so we had to leave Cambridge, which meant I had to leave my beloved school and be sixteen hundred miles farther away from my dad, who had moved to Florida and opened his practice right after med school.

I found Berkeley to be dreary and depressing, all the homeless people, all the clouds, damp, and gray. The only bright spot was I was going to get to attend Berkeley High, my first-ever public school. My mom and dad were on board, but Kenny didn't have any confidence in my being able to make it there.

"You're actually thinking of sending her to a public school with three thousand kids?" he said, shaking his head and lighting a joint.

I hated him.

But he had a point.

I had barely made it in my little school with only ten kids in a class.

But this is different, I'll be older. That was grade school, this is high school.

I can do this.

But it turned out I was wrong.

Predictably, academically, that first year was horrific. The teachers would dismiss the class and I would sit there at my desk shielding my notebook from the eyes of my classmates as they filed past so they wouldn't see that I'd written next to nothing. All the other kids seemed to have received some "how to be a high school student" manual that I'd somehow missed during orientation. I watched the students who raised their hands, the ones who had read the material and understood it, regarding them with awe and wonder. I was drowning and too embarrassed to cry for help. I was determined to figure out how to do better without alerting anyone that I was failing.

But socially I was thriving.

On day two in the cafeteria, I fell head over heels in love with a handsome running back named Michael. Being with him was simple, no matching of wits, no need to protect myself. It was a much-needed break from the constant cat-and-mouse game I had to play at home. Sometimes he would take me behind the JCPenney and kiss me urgently while slipping his hand up my shirt. Later, on the F bus home, I'd be smiling like an idiot and smelling of his Pierre Cardin cologne.

I'd started my sophomore year with fresh resolve to really pay attention and study, but geometry proved to be even more mysterious than algebra, and try as I might, I could never seem to find more than three of *Catcher in the Rye*'s five life lessons. Soon, I gave up trying to focus in class and started writing little stories to pass the time until the bell rang. When my teachers started getting wise, asking me to stay after the bell or to see my work, one by one, I stopped going to each of their classes. Even though on some level I was always scared that someone might discover my secret, I took absolute pride in my ability to fool everyone so completely.

If hiding in plain sight were an Olympic sport, I would be a gold medalist.

There was a certain peace that stole over me once everyone was fooled and my secrets were safely tucked away. Only then did I feel secure, knowing I alone had control of the narrative.

But then one morning in March, one of the many notes my counselor had been sending home, which up until then I had been success-fully intercepting, slipped through with the day's mail. And just like that, it was over.

I have a hazy, shame-filled memory of sitting in the counselor's office with my stunned mother and a beady-eyed Kenny, categorically denying all the evidence the school had against me.

"You mean she hasn't been going to class at all? For the whole year?"

I wanted to tell them what happened, but I just couldn't. And now it was so much bigger than just keeping up with the white kids or hiding it from Kenny. I had told all my friends that the reason they didn't see me in any of their classes was because I was taking all honors, and no one ever questioned it because why would they? I was smart, put together, and going with the star running back. But now it was all crashing down around me. Some of my teachers didn't even know I existed; others had a vague recollection of a shy Black girl who sat in the back. My friends would all be shocked. My football player boyfriend was going to be majorly confused.

This is a nightmare.

So I sat there with my arms folded, staring ahead blankly while they all spoke. The counselor proposed a strategy to help me catch up, a plan that included remedial classes and summer school and ended with me graduating a year after my classmates. But taking this "deal" meant admitting to everyone that I'd been lying, and that I was too dumb to make it without special help.

No thanks.

Give them nothing.

Turns out there weren't very many job options for a sixteen-year-old dropout, so when I heard they were hiring banquet waitresses at the local Marriott, I put in an application.

It was around this time that my mom and Kenny finally got a divorce. And after he moved back to Cambridge, it was just us two women in the house.

I actually liked working, clocking in, clocking out, and getting a paycheck. I felt very adult among all the older college students who worked there to make pocket money.

During the day I was busy at work, but in the middle of the night I'd often wake up in a panic, flooded by waves of regret and shame. I thought I'd be that playwright kid or that girl being recruited by English departments all over the country because of her brilliant skills with a pen. What I was missing out on danced around in my head like ghosts, mocking me: pep rallies, hanging out in the quad, college tours. Sometimes when it was really bad I would get up and quietly draw a hot bath in our old claw-footed tub and sob quietly while the water made steam clouds around me.

I won't go to prom. I will never walk across that stage. I'll never move into a dorm.

When all my friends were seniors and taking their final exams, I enrolled in a couple of day classes at Merritt College in Oakland. I thought maybe a junior college would be the education hack I was looking for, but it turns out I couldn't keep up there either. It took me three times as long as my peers to do the simplest arithmetic problem, and I didn't know anything about grammar or syntax, so I secretly dropped out three months after enrolling.

But during my second week there I met a group of Black women who literally invited me in out of the rain one day to join them in the dining hall. These girls were nothing like me or my old friends. They were kiki-ers and cacklers, embarrassingly loud and hilariously fearless. They had names like Tiny, Big Gina, and Jazzy.

After hanging with them for a few months, we started calling ourselves the FLIES (First Ladies in Every Situation) and it was like I had finally found my people. I had always endured being the only one, the only Black kid, the only Black friend, the only Black coworker. But with them I was genuinely part of, indistinguishable from the others. They took me to Black clubs, brought me to Black church and hair salons, and introduced me to all these little soul food joints in Oakland. They taught me how to talk Black, sing Black, and dance Black.

With them I was the happiest of sponges, absorbing every inflection and gesture they made. Hanging with them took me back to those late-night gatherings growing up in Cambridge.

The Black education these wonderful women provided me with was invaluable. Soon I found myself spending all my free time in Oakland.

At nineteen, I met an older pimp and drug dealer named Vegas and started a yearlong affair with him. Vegas was one of those brothers who wore fur, always carried a pager (only doctors carried them then), and was never without his purple Crown Royal bag full of dope. He wasn't young or particularly handsome, but he had a way of making me feel like the baddest bitch in the room. He also liked to freebase on the weekends—that's smoking a chemically pure form of cocaine, and eventually I found that I liked it too. About six months into our affair I started disappearing for days at a time, showing up at home in the middle of the week, always ravenous and exhausted. After failing to pick up my mother at the airport one day because I was holed up smoking with Vegas, my mother and father intervened. With my father on speakerphone from Florida, the two of them decided that instead of sending me to treatment they wanted me to attend twelve-step meetings. Only, I was not down with that at all. I thought they were overreacting to a situation that was perfectly manageable, so I gently assured them there was no need for such drastic measures.

"I get why you'd be scared, but believe me, it's not that big a deal, I'll take care of it."

I stopped hanging out in Oakland that same day and started dodging Vegas's calls. And after my parents' little "intervention," I never touched another freebase pipe again. The sense of pride I felt in not needing anyone's help to quit was tremendous, on a scale with Fuji or Everest. To me, the world was divided into two categories of people: failures, aka folks who were stupid enough to let other people see that they needed help, and successes, aka self-reliants like me, who would die before they accepted help from anyone.

After a few months passed, I figured that whole "year of basing" thing had been an experiment, and now it was in the past. But without Vegas kicking me down cash, I needed money, so I took more shifts at the Marriott. Meanwhile, some of my high school friends were starting to graduate from college and taking jobs.

By twenty-two, I really hated putting on that uniform every day. The stiff black polyester pants and apron, the shirt that smelled like food no matter how often I washed it. When I looked in the mirror I no longer saw a bright-eyed, chubby-cheeked teenage face peering back and was scared that I was going to be some random, no-education-having, stuck-in-Berkeley-forever career waitress. A voice began screaming inside me, urging me to do something before it was too late. I should be commanding the room wearing red lipstick and power suits. I should be a boss like Clair Huxtable from *The Cosby Show*, or Teri from *Soul Food*. I shouldn't be serving shit, I should be running shit.

This isn't the story I'm supposed to have.

———

When I impulsively moved to LA in the late eighties, I got a job working as a receptionist for Todd Synderman, an A-list commercial director. On my second day, I ran a delivery over to his home in Brentwood and a liveried housekeeper opened the door and asked me to take it up to his office. As I climbed the wide, curved staircase, I paused and took everything in. The place was exquisite, unlike any home I'd ever seen. Gorgeous art on the walls, gleaming dark wood floors that went on forever, expensive-looking patterned throw cushions on luxurious cream-colored furniture. Working for Todd over the next few months, I was exposed to a world in which people did things like check their bedsheets for thread count and purchase resort wear for winter vacations. Growing up, most of the people I knew had patched-up, mismatched quilts and bedsheets. And if we were lucky, a vacation was maybe one or two nights at a Holiday Inn. Here in this new, luxe world, every day something else clicked into place.

This, and this and this. I need all of this in my life.

At twenty-four, I switched jobs and went to work on reinventing myself. I read the *Wall Street Journal* in the mornings before my new job at The Baird Company, a corporate entertainment PR firm. I shopped vintage stores for the pieces like the ones I found in the pages of *Vogue* and *Women's Wear Daily*. I studied women whose careers I admired, watching how they conducted themselves, how they made an entrance, listening for their cadence and tone when they spoke. But as I worked my way up the ladder from assistant to publicist, I was desperately afraid of any part of my history or person being scrutinized, lest someone, my boss, a client, a friend, or a boyfriend, discover who I really was underneath it all—a no-education-having imposter. It was like I was building this stunning home on top of a shoddy foundation, and only I knew that it would never pass inspection. But as it happened, I was really good at my job. Eventually I wasn't just handling my assigned clients, I was bringing in some big names of my own, so I opened my own PR firm. When I had finally built up enough credit to get myself a green American Express card, I knew that my worlds, the made-up one, the pedigreed, college-degreed shot-caller and the real one, the poor kid, the liar, the cocaine addict, were finally converging. Opening that envelope, I fingered the hard, mint-colored plastic rectangle in disbelief.

I've fooled them all.

That card became the triumphant symbol of my new identity. The one that I had curated so carefully: the uber-cultured crackerjack publicist who owned her own firm. The lady who lunched, the Clinton campaign volunteer, the mentor to young Black women. Finally, this was my moment to shine, and I was determined not to let anything dim my light.

CHAPTER THREE

Boy Meets Girl

I was twenty-eight years old when I met my husband. At that point, to make extra cash, I still had a Friday-night side gig at the Roxbury, a very, very happening Los Angeles supper club. He and his friends were A-list regulars there, so we would exchange a friendly "hey" or "how's it going?" as I unclipped the velvet rope for him and his crew. There was this one night when I was out to dinner with some girlfriends at Cicada (another happening spot), and he and some other white people were sitting at the table across from us. He stared at me all through dinner and then left without a word.

"He can't remember how he knows me, y'all," I told my friends. "And I'll bet it's driving him crazy."

My friends and I were laughing when the maître d' came over and said that there was a phone call for the Black girl in the leather jacket. I turned to give my friends a wink before following him to the front.

"Hi," I said, when I got to the phone. "Did you figure it out yet?"

"Huh?"

"My name."

I was between boyfriends and was well known among my friends for exclusively dating the chocolatiest brothers I could find. I had never dated outside my race before and had never even thought about dating a white boy, but for some reason with this one I was curious.

So when he asked me out on a date, I was coming from that same place of intrigue when I said yes. He was an actor coming off a hit show, but he was already starting to direct. I remember sitting across from him at our first dinner while he talked about the films he wanted to make. I heard him speaking but was mesmerized by his mouth, thinking, *Those lips are going to be on mine soon.*

During those first few years it was so easy, he and I were instant allies. Sure he was a white boy, but being from Brooklyn, he had flavor, that East Coast swag. He was the kind of white boy who would blast hip-hop in his car and hoop in the park with the brothers on the weekend. And I found out later that prior to meeting me, he was also the kind of white boy who liked dating sisters, Black girls.

I assimilated into his world the same way I had into everything else—by being a quick study. The first time we went to dinner at the Ivy I was incredibly intimidated by the sea of forks and glasses on the table.

Are these all for two people, for one meal?

But instead of letting him see my confusion, I glanced surreptitiously around at the other diners and copied them.

I was going all out, in full hair and makeup auditioning for the part, but the problem was I'd never read the whole script. I had no idea how much of myself I would replace or erase to nab the part.

I remember being excited to walk into an event beside him, feeling all eyes on us. We were that young, interracial Hollywood power couple—the TV star and the publicist. He and I had our own shorthand that our friends envied and admired. One look from me at a party and he knew it was time to rescue me from a conversation. One sideways glance from him, and I knew when it was time to go home.

Sometimes I would marvel at how we just GOT each other, could finish the lyrics all the way through to "Children's Story" or "Big Poppa." We could recite the same lines from *The Godfather* or Eddie Murphy's *Delirious*. I was dating this powerful man, and he really believed in me. Not the dropout, former druggie Laura who'd been emotionally scarred by her stepfather. He believed in the Laura who had been reborn the day she'd moved to LA. The classy, educated business owner with whom he was proud to walk the red carpet. The adorable doctor's daughter who'd never been skiing but was dying to go to Sundance. So when he asked me to marry him three years after our first date (Hawaii, Christmas Day, string quartet, the works), I was faced with a major-ass dilemma. Here was a man who had unwittingly fallen for this persona that I'd carefully honed and crafted, saying he wanted to spend the rest of his life with her. I loved him, and I loved being with him, but I knew deep down I could never be who he believed me to be—and I could never, would never, admit that she was a fabrication.

He had no idea about the walls I had to build to survive my child-hood. The "year of basing" was a secret I was determined to take to my grave; no one but my parents could ever know about that.

I call it "shide." A deadly and debilitating combination of shame and pride that has plagued me since I can remember.

It was shide that prevented me from telling my mother and father about how Kenny'd always had it in for me and wouldn't let me ask my Berkeley High teachers for help. The same shide that made me drop out of community college and resign myself to working as a waitress. I loved him and was so afraid of losing him, but my fear of being exposed eclipsed everything.

The man I love wants to marry me and I'm terrified.

What's wrong with me???

Maybe nothing.

Is it possible I'm making too big a deal out of all this? This is a really smart, discerning man. If he loves me and he thinks I'm good enough for him, then maybe I am. After all, it's not like I lied to him about my past. He just made a few assumptions, and I let him believe them. Everyone has secrets, right? Maybe marriage isn't "tell me everything there is to know about you," but rather more "I love you just as you are, so no need to go digging up the past."

And we do love each other.

So I said yes.

We were married by Rabbi Alan Weisman at 6:00 p.m. on August 17, 1997, in front of 125 of our closest friends and family members. I was thirty-two years old and wore a princess dress and white satin Manolos. I was Cinderella at the ball, only I would not be running home when the clock struck twelve.

I would never have to run again.

———

Turns out there's a big difference between a wedding and a marriage.

A wedding is a celebration, a party, a declaration of love between two people in front of witnesses.

Marriage is a lawful contract.

There are legalities, licenses, and vows. And because of his Jewish faith, we'd also signed a ketubah in a temple. I'd understood that our union would be a binding agreement, in fact, I counted on it, as it would make it that much harder to get rid of me. But what I hadn't foreseen was that there was an unwritten addendum to the contract— the director's wife clause. Contained within were all types of things. Things I loathed, things that bored me to death, things I sucked at, and now it seemed I was expected to seamlessly incorporate these items into my normal day-to-day life.

I had figured out how to take care of myself all right, but I had no clue how to take care of a home and manage housekeepers, gardeners, and handymen. Somehow, I hadn't gotten the memo that not only was I the one assigned to vacation planning, making dinner, and decorating, I was actually supposed to ENJOY doing all these things.

So I started studying the women in our circle. When we went to dinner at a friend's home and he admired the wife, what she was wearing, cooking, how she wore her hair, spoke, etc., I took note. Conversely, when he talked shit about someone on the ride home, I stored that information too.

A little leg is nice, a little cleavage is nice, but don't do both at once.

Good hostesses always ask "Can I get you something?" even when the guest is a pop-in. Good mothers don't let their nannies raise their kids. Gold fixtures? Hideous. Gold jewelry? Beautiful, but must be worn subtly. Always have a good, detailed answer to the question "What's the plan for today?" Vacations are: full of playful adventures such as zip-lining, helicopter rides, and scuba diving. Vacations aren't: lying around the pool all day and reading. Be up on all the latest designers but don't be pretentious. Never talk about money, even with family. Never tell anyone how much he makes.

Got it.

In less than a year, I'd filled a notebook with all the dos and don'ts because I was so terrified of getting something wrong and exposing myself as the imposter that I was.

Baby and bridal showers

Forget just sending a gift, not only are you going to have to attend them but you're also going to need to get really good at throwing them.

Spa days and shopping sprees

Turn that frown upside down and pretend like you can't wait to join the rest of the girls.

Children

Who cares if you don't like kids? Have at least two and then become the queen of playdates and birthday parties.

Entertaining

It doesn't matter that you're perfectly happy with mac and cheese every night. Hire a chef to teach you how to cook at least twelve of his favorite dishes and then dazzle him by making them on your own. Also, learn to decorate a table and entertain properly; you need to become the consummate dinner-party guest and hostess.

Home decorating, housekeeping, gardening (In other words, all the things that make you feel like a failure)
Figure it out, bitch. You need to become proficient at all this shit and learn to love it quick.

And oh yeah, directors are away on film shoots for weeks and sometimes months at a time, so get used to being alone a lot. Directors' wives are thin. I'm talking white-girl thin; Pilates-spin-class-juice-cleanse thin. So you'd better get yourself a personal trainer if you want that whittled waist and those amazing arms. And they all play doubles on Tuesdays, so sign up for tennis lessons. Directors' wives support other directors' wives by going to their homes for jewelry shows. They chair school committees and they're named parent association president. Directors' wives do lunch at the Ivy and have personal shoppers at Barneys.

In order to be what I thought he wanted, I had to split into two people. One of me was still happily married to my soul mate, loving and being loved, being that other half of that "don't be jealous but we just get each other" perfect couple, the beta to his alpha.

And then the other me, the lone wolf, the pre-makeover me, was always running slightly behind, wanting to veer left or right and struggling under the weight of all the "shoulds" I was carrying. And as time went on, the distance between those two mes was just too far to bridge.

While we were dating, I had presented him with this carefully curated, feminized version of myself—one that I thought he'd be most likely to marry. I didn't know much then about assigned gender roles or fluidity. I thought there were only two parts available: the wife of or the husband of. As a cis-hetero woman, I understood I was expected to embrace all the feminine tropes associated with the wife-of. I was supposed to be smart but not smarter, reliant but not helpless. When we didn't agree in front of others, I was the one who was supposed to yield. The challenge was that I was (and am) the one who automatically heads to the fuse box when the power goes out, and I'm the one who likes to order food "for the table" when we go out to eat. I'm the one who prefers Adidas to Alaïa and enjoys handling the finances.

I'm the one who likes to call the shots during sex.

Shortly after the wedding, perhaps in a last-ditch effort to reclaim some part of myself, I submitted *The Unveiling*, a four-hundred-page novel I'd been writing since my twenties, to Ms. Hope, an editor at Doubleday (a friend of a friend of a friend). Miraculously, she read it and returned it to my friend with a cover letter that made my heart soar. It was full of phrases like, "a realistic love story that sucks the reader in, I honestly cried during her graphic descriptions of grief," and "loved this intimate examination of true human emotions." But my heart dropped again when I got to the end of the letter, where the rejection was lying in wait, hidden in the final paragraph like a tiger in the brush.

"Sorry the second half of this book didn't work for me," and "best of luck finding a good home for this!"

Sending out the manuscript was me asking the universe: Am I enough?

I'd told myself that if Ms. Hope liked my book, I could allow myself to think about pursuing a career in writing, and then maybe married would just be something else that I was, not the only thing I was. But I had my answer now, and I was all at once both despondent and terrified.

With a quickness I resigned myself to focusing on becoming the best "wife of" I could be. After all, professional writers had MFAs and read books by literary heavies like Dorothy Parker and Hemingway, not *Vogue*s, Judy Blume novels, and *Archie*s. Writers were generally not Black, former cokehead dropouts.

Boy, I was lucky she sent me that rejection, because it allowed me to see what was real. And what was real was how lucky I am to be his wife. I know how many women are already in line to take my place, just waiting for me to slip up.

If I had shared these thoughts with someone, anyone, maybe they would have told me that it was all bullshit. Maybe I would have listened.

But I didn't—I couldn't risk it.

And now after years of being deceived, it feels like he's getting wise. Like suddenly he's always trying to peek behind the curtain to see what I'm hiding. That's probably why he read my journal.

So, the need to throw him off the scent, to guard vigilantly against any hints of discontent and imperfection, was paramount. Otherwise, he might start asking questions that might expose me as the phony that I am, and I wasn't ready for that.

It never occurred to me I could level with him about any of that shit, and he'd still love me, want to stay married to me. So I became Michelangelo, always chipping away at everything that wasn't what I thought he wanted, and became a new and improved, more acceptable version of myself.

CHAPTER FOUR

Babies

Three years and two kids later, I started to become unhinged.

Our boys were little; Jordan was nearly two and Jacob was a newborn. And as predicted, I was completely out of my depth with all the new-mom stuff. My husband has this huge family; they'd all grown up together in Brooklyn in adjoining brownstones: no privacy, no closed doors. And when his father moved out to Los Angeles to act in the early eighties, they all moved too. I found the way they lived to be loud and invasive, and I was bewildered and resentful that he seemed to want that lifestyle for our kids. His family was well-intentioned, but they were always around, watching me, coaching me, "helping" me parent. They made it sound like they were all "Team Family," but to me it felt like they were all on his team. I don't have a big family, so I begged my mom to move down from Berkeley. Not just so she could help me with the babies but also so that I would have a team member too. When it was just me and his family, I felt hopelessly outnumbered; my opinions would get drowned out among the cacophony of voices offering me helpful parenting tips.

And then there were all my other "director's wife contractual obligations." No one had ever told me otherwise, so I assumed that even though I'd birthed two babies in under two years, I was still expected to keep it all up: the dinner parties, the tennis lessons, lavishing him with the same level of love and affection I'd given him pre-babies.

I was beyond exhausted, and yet I couldn't sleep.

At first I wasn't sleeping because I was constantly seized with worry that my boys might wake up and need me. But eventually I couldn't sleep even when I tried; my childhood hypervigilance had returned, and it felt like a switch in my brain had been permanently placed in the "on" position. My eyes would pop open at the slightest sound from the kids' room. I felt as though I always had to be alert, like I couldn't let my guard down even for a minute or something terrible would happen. So more and more I would just lie there on the daybed in the nursery so I could be near Jacob in case he woke up. I could tell that my husband felt betrayed by my lack of interest in him (or anything other than the kids), but I couldn't help it. Whenever he tried to move me into our bed in the middle of the night, I'd have to talk myself out of flinching from his touch. And then, keeping one eye on the clock, I'd wait for him to fall asleep so I could go back and check on the boys.

Thank God for my friends after Jordan was born. These women and I were all in the same social circle, our husbands were all friends who worked together or grew up together. These gals and I did everything together—it was all very *Sex and the City* (if Carrie, Samantha, Charlotte, and Miranda had all been Black and married with babies). You know when you see a group of women and there's a certain synergy and energy, a bond between them that changes the molecular structure of the room? Maître d's rush over to seat them, men openly admire them, women want what they're wearing.

That's how we were.

These women were my ace boon coons, my lunch dates, my "I know it's late but can you meet me for a quick drink?" girls. The ones who knew I hated those dreaded spa weekends but laughingly made me go anyway. They'd been my bridesmaids, thrown my baby showers, and I'd thrown theirs. Now that I was a mama too, I listened intently when these friends spoke. When these women "got real" they talked about being jealous of their nannies or joked about wanting sex more often than their husbands. They talked about counting down the days until they could go back to work, and about having crushes on their kids' hot teachers.

Normal stuff.

Meanwhile, I was constantly scanning the conversation for any evidence that even one of them felt like everything other than their children was just one huge inconvenience. When it became apparent that I was the only one who'd rather sleep with her kids than her husband, I decided I'd better keep that bit of information to myself. I quickly learned to mimic them and say the kinds of things they said, so I wouldn't be exposed as a failure.

Lie: "Sorry I'm late, the boys had a meltdown just when we were leaving."

Truth: I had a meltdown about leaving the boys.

Lie: "We're trying to break the boys of co-sleeping now."

Truth: I love it when the boys sleep in our bed.

Lie: "I wish I could go tonight, but honestly, it's getting harder and harder to leave while they're still awake."

Truth: I don't want to go anywhere, ever.

To be honest, I was quite relieved that I actually loved my children.

I wasn't sure that I would, and I had taken a huge gamble on my maternal instincts kicking in once they were born. But there were times that the sheer quantity of love I felt for them was so overwhelming that it scared me. I couldn't understand what had happened—how had I gone from someone who didn't care if she had children to someone who was so obsessed with her kids that she couldn't stand to be away from them even for an hour? I was vaguely aware that my love for my kids was laced with something else, something urgent and compulsive. I felt as though I was the only person who could keep them safe. I protected this peculiarity by disguising my vigilance as maternal superiority. People thought I was an amazing mother because I never wanted to be away from my kids. No one ever saw it as a bad thing because I hid it the same way I'd hidden away everything all my life—in plain sight.

———

At my six-week appointment after Jacob, my OB gave me the go-ahead to have sex again. When he offered to answer any questions, I timidly asked him if I might be suffering from postpartum depression.

"I don't know what's wrong with me," I whispered, scared that someone outside the exam room might overhear and judge me. "Ever since Jordan was born, I feel like I'm on the edge of a collapse. And I don't want to be touched by anyone except my kids. I mean ever. And I feel like my kids are alternately the best and worst thing to have ever happened to me. Also, I know you said I can have sex again, but I've never felt less sexy in my life."

"What are they, two years apart?"

"Twenty-one months."

I was still sitting on the edge of the exam table, my paper gown scratching my raw, bare breastfeeding nipples. He waved away my concerns and told me to try an evening glass of wine.

"All women go through this at first," he said with a smile. "Your body just needs to heal from those back-to-back pregnancies, but don't worry, you'll be back to yourself in no time."

After that, everything felt like that disposable gown, scratchy, raw, and painful. I resented the doctor for dismissing me so easily. I resented my husband for not understanding what I was going through.

But I was also angry at him for leaving me alone so quickly when I asked him for some space.

Even still, I tried to be a better wife.

And although every fiber of my being screamed out in protest, I forced myself to buy fancy lingerie at La Perla and book a weekend getaway for us up at Ojai. On Saturday nights I made sure that the nanny was on and planned double dates with other couples at Capo and Dan Tana's. I did my absolute best to act the same way my friends did. Friends who actually (and mysteriously) seemed to enjoy spending alone time with their men. Soon, I started to inwardly rage at the fact that he was happy with this fake life I was serving him, this life that I hated, the life that wasn't me. Over the next couple of years, I stuffed that anger down and doubled down on really turning myself into the kind of wife and mother I thought he wanted, thinking that might make both of us happy. But my great-aunt Ruth was right when she told me, "If you don't dump your garbage, you're going to stink." A few months after Jordan turned three, all those repressed feelings started to erupt inside me, and I felt myself going down hard.

Added to this was Jacob's and Jordan's middle-of-the-night wakings getting worse as they got older instead of better. They felt orchestrated, like some evil ghoul was torturing the three of us. One of them would scream at the top of their lungs until I would come tearing down the nine-hundred-foot hallway to scoop them into my arms. Jacob was usually first. The sight of him whimpering and wet in his crib always made my heart ache and cut through my exhaustion. Then as soon as I got him back to sleep, Jordan would start—pounding on the gate of his toddler bed, shrieking, standing on his tiptoes in his onesie and demanding tearfully to sleep in our bed.

Wash, rinse, repeat.

By the time daylight pushed its way through the cracks in our blackout drapes, I would be weepy with despair and frayed nerves.

I had to get some sleep.

Not trusting my OB-GYN anymore, I went to Dr. Linbaum, my regular doctor. As soon as I sat down, I felt my eyes betray me by filling with tears.

"I don't know why I'm crying," I said apologetically. "I'm not even really sure why I'm here."

"When you called you said that you haven't been sleeping and that you felt like it was killing you," he said.

"Oh yes," I said, trying to laugh it off. "That was clearly 'new-mom hyperbole.' I don't really believe lack of sleep could kill me. I mean, it can't, can it?"

"Let's get you sleeping again," he said grimly. "And then we can see if there's anything else going on that we need to address. The way you're going, you may be headed for a breakdown, so let's reset your system."

He handed me a prescription. I looked at it but didn't recognize the name.

"What's this?"

"Ambien. It's a mild sleep aid. It should do the trick. One per day at bedtime, okay?"

Ambien.

I folded the paper in half before putting it in my purse.

"Thank you, Doctor."

That night, I tentatively removed one pill from the bottle he'd prescribed. I considered breaking it in half but decided instead to chance the whole thing. I had clocked out for the night, as it were. My mom had moved down (finally), so she came over to spend the night and run interference with the boys. My husband was away on a shoot, so I had the bedroom to myself for a few nights. But even with the safeguard of my mom in place, the idea of my kids waking up and me not being the one running to soothe them made me queasy.

I took the Ambien with a full bottle of water and then picked up the book on my nightstand. Too edgy to read for long, I turned off the light, pulling the covers up to my neck, and waited with my arms stiffly at my sides.

How will I know it's working? Will I feel something first or will it just render me unconscious? I should have asked Linbaum.

I was just about to get up and reread the prescription bottle when I felt it—that heat glowing behind my eyes like a furnace, making me instantly light-headed. The ferocity of it scared me.

OMG, it's happening too fast.

And then I felt my neck muscles relaxing in a way that made me want to groan out loud, like I was getting the most amazing massage.

Sweet Jesus, what sorcery was this?

Suddenly, warm golden oil coated the insides of my throat and chest, separating my head from my shoulders. Gratitude gushed into my mouth like bile, and I wanted to get up and run down the hall to my boys. I wanted to grab them and tell them how sorry I was for being such a crazy mom these last few months. I wanted to assure them that everything would be better from now on.

Oh, if I could only feel like this forever. THIS is nirvana. This is all I would ever want.

The next thing I knew, it was morning. And as soon I opened my eyes, two words sprung to mind immediately.

Again, please.

I had a feeling that what I'd experienced the night before should have scared me. The fact that I'd blacked out and had absolutely no memory of what happened between the time I took the pill and when I woke up should have made me recoil as if from a hot flame.

But I wasn't recoiling. I wasn't scared. I was thrilled.

Those pills were the gateway to a world where the pains of perpetuating this double life didn't exist. Where I had no responsibilities, no one to impress, no one to deceive or please. I could just sink into these squishy, gorgeous technicolor Ambien dreams and wake up feeling ready for the world. Those pills were the only lover's arms I wanted to be in, and I knew that if anyone found out about their power over me it would be a wrap. So, I put the pill bottle away in the back of my medicine cabinet and rationed those thirty pills out over a six-month period. These pills were my reward for being a good mom, a good wife.

After basketball practice on Saturday I can give myself a treat and check out for the night. Or, no one will fault you for falling asleep early after a day at the pumpkin patch. Let the nanny put them to bed tonight.

The next bottle lasted about half that long. Within the year, I was taking a single Ambien a night, all with my doctor's blessing.

And why shouldn't he endorse it? It wasn't like I was snorting cocaine or something. I won't need the pills once the boys start sleeping through the night. I will stop for sure as soon as they're both sleeping in their own beds all night.

But I didn't know that a pill a day would turn into two, then three.

And by the time the boys were six and eight, as many as I could get my hands on. And I didn't know that eventually, the only relief from the pain, shame, and embarrassment of being an addict would come once I was asleep.

———

Ever since I told him I wanted a divorce I only have two speeds. Nervous as all fuck or completely numb.

Numbness is different from oblivion. Oblivion is seductive and dreamy. It's that place you sink into while counting backward from ten when they put you under—the place heroin addicts chase. But every time I knock myself out with drugs and then snap back to consciousness, this terrible numbness is the first thing I feel. It's not that my body is numb, like during those Cambridge winters where I'd sit by the radiator after playing in the snow. This numb is an absence, a soul sickness. It's a thick plexiglass wall between me and everyone else. When something happens that requires an emotional response, I can feel the semblance of a familiar warmth making its way up from my toes to my abdomen, but it always stops around my thighs and then drops back down into an unreachable place. When my kids hug me, if I fight hard enough, I can grab hold of it for a little while, even pulling it up into my chest sometimes, but then it drops again or evaporates as soon as they leave the room. The effort to feel anything is exhausting, and yet I can't sleep. And because I keep running out of pills, I've also been experiencing rebound insomnia. That's a fancy term for when the sedative you're abusing turns on you and makes you into a shaky, sleepless zombie. Often, this condition is so profound that my mind spins demonically for hours or until I feel the heady warmth that tells me my pills are working. But since my seizures, I need so many Ambien to sleep that I often lose track of how many I'm taking. Sometimes I need half of one just to chill ever so slightly before my tennis lesson, other times I need two, maybe three if I'm going to get myself back to sleep in the middle of the night. Yesterday morning I found myself back at the pharmacy six days after getting a refill of thirty pills.

"Mrs. Robbins, I need to know. Are you taking these as prescribed? One per night?"

Herman, the pharmacist, looks at me over his round, rimless glasses. I am temporarily mesmerized by the harsh overhead lights dancing around the top of his shiny bald head.

The doctor's note I fish out of my purse compels him to fill my script anyway, but even through my drug haze, I make a mental note to be more careful.

I need to start getting my refills delivered.

I can't afford to raise any red flags. If the pills were to be taken away from me, I could never leave my house; I'd be all twitchy and weird and unable to look anybody in the eye. Actually, doing anything outside my house is a nightmare lately. I spend hours huddled over my Filofax every night, agonizing over which of the next day's activities I can cancel without raising suspicions. I write my excuses down (in code) because I have to keep track of which I use and with whom. When it's something school-related, I have to make sure I tell the mom wanting a playdate and the teacher wanting to know if I'll cover snack the same thing. When it's a friend, it depends on how long it's been since I've seen them. If it's been too long, I have to put on my dark glasses and power through lunch or dinner. With my trainer or tennis coach, I can almost always safely use an injury of some kind. The back pain I invented to get a doctor to prescribe Vicodin for me in 2006 comes in handy here. It's easier to be dishonest when the lie is so believable that even I believe it. I've been pretending I have a back injury for so long, sometimes I actually feel it flaring up. Some of my lies are so interwoven into my real life that they get baked into my memory as though they really happened. The real trick is to be so impossibly put together all the time and to exude enough confidence that no one dares question anything I tell them.

Even though I get through each period of withdrawal when I am waiting for a refill to come in, wishing I would die and vowing to never take another pill, Ambien is STILL the only thing I ever look forward to. And it's not just Ambien anymore; because my tolerance level is so fucked, they won't even work without booze and/or Benadryl. No Ambien means I won't have patience for bedtime stories. No Ambien means that I can't silence the alarm bells that are constantly ringing in my head. It means no steady hands for my nail appointments. I NEED these pills to help me through this divorce.

The TV remote has become my new best friend. I pass out while clutching it like my life depends on it. I come to cradling it like a baby. Anyone who dares take it away from me faces ferocious and instantaneous rage. I remind myself of a wounded animal protecting the area where it's chosen to die.

Leave me alone, please, everyone.

———

People are surprised to find out that he didn't move out after I told him I wanted a divorce.

I understand.

Every book I've read, every movie I've seen, when someone says they want a divorce, the next scene is either them or their spouse moving out. But it's just not that simple. When I first said the words, I think we were both in shock and just went on for a bit as if things were normal (for us, anyway). Looking back, I might even say that during those few days, we were kinder toward each other than we'd been in a long time. There were a lot of affectionate-sounding "I'm sorry, excuse mes" as we passed each other in the hallway at bedtime, and "No, no, you go first" when we tried to figure out who would drive whom to school in the morning as the boys went to school at different times. It was after he came back from his trip that everything changed. Our conversations suddenly had an edge to them, one that was unusual for us. I felt as though overnight we had become two predators, holding eye contact and circling each other, waiting for the other to make the first move. I also found myself becoming increasingly embarrassed when anyone happened to see this new, contentious dynamic between us—we'd never before argued in front of anyone, even the kids. I had been smug about our perfect-couple projection and was terrified of anyone finding out it was an illusion. As usual, the shide demanded that I control the narrative.

So I try to make it sound all *New Adventures of Old Christine* or whatever, explaining that we feel like we're doing what's best for the kids while we figure things out. But in reality I think he and I are playing a game of chicken to see who leaves first. We haven't been romantic in months. In fact, he's been sleeping in the guest room for over a year. It started innocently enough when he had the flu and didn't want to get us sick. But then he got well and just never came back, and I didn't ask him to. But I feel our housekeeper Maria's judgment every time I walk past that room and she's making "his" bed. Her look says, *Bad girl. You're failing your husband.*

Sometimes I consider heading to a hotel during fits of desperation, but I saw on an episode of *CSI* that when one parent packs a bag and leaves the house, they can be charged with abandonment, and I can't risk that.

I mean, didn't anyone ever tell him that when your wife tells you she wants a divorce, it's only polite to pack up and leave the premises immediately?

His staying here feels like an act of aggression, and I am thoroughly confused by it. I thought he'd be relieved that I'd pulled the trigger, because now I could be the one to blame. By asking first, I took all the onus off him, made him the victim and me the bad guy. I honestly thought he'd be happy to be free of someone so depressed, someone who doesn't want to be touched, someone who slurs and stumbles around during the day and passes out midsentence at night after taking her "medicine."

But maybe he's staying just until he's given me enough rope to hang myself. I wish I knew for sure that he'd read my journal, then I could be certain that he knows I'm an addict. I've spent night after night trying to piece together the conversation from that night, and I can't remember anything he said, not one word. They say trauma is a thief, I know this to be true. Thanks to Kenny's reign of terror, I have blank spots the size of craters in my childhood memories. Thank God I kept journals from the moment I could write or else I might never know what happened to me. But Ambien is also a thief, keeping my memories from me, always just out of reach. What if he's pretending like he doesn't know how bad my addiction is just so he can build a case against me? Then once he has everything he needs, he'll expose me as a junkie, take the house and the kids, and leave me with nothing.

Now that I've said the word *divorce* out loud, some part of me feels like the hard part is over, and I find myself just biding my time, hoping he'll leave without fanfare. On some level I'm expecting that he'll just take care of everything like he's always done, splitting everything between us, handling all the legal stuff, making it easy.

Every day I write "hire a divorce lawyer" on my to-do list, and every day it remains unchecked. Meanwhile the tension in our home is so oppressive that even though it's freezing, I've started sleeping with the windows open. There are some days where our situation is so fucking weird that I wonder if I even actually asked him for a divorce that night. Every day is a nightmarish blur of dropping off, working out or playing tennis, then getting just loaded enough, half an Ambien chased down by a few sips from a travel mug filled with a screwdriver, to meet a friend or with the contractor who's working on the kitchen, and then pickup. Terrified to give him more ammunition, I vow to do better at keeping it together during the day, rationing my Ambien and timing my outings, so I don't start detoxing on school grounds or at lunch. I am petrified every time I step out of the house, and each lunch date, committee meeting, or even snack drop-off requires herculean effort from me in order to appear halfway normal.

I want to run screaming into the house when I get home, lock the door, and eat handfuls of Ambien, but I can't give him any more evidence against me in case he's setting a trap for me by staying. I can't risk him stopping home unexpectedly at four to find me passed out, as still as the dead.

A couple of years ago, my friend Connie, who has twins in the lower school, found herself in the middle of a nasty, very public custody battle with her studio-head husband. When she asked me if she could co-room mom with me, she explained that her attorney had advised her to become more involved.

"You don't have to be the best mother," he'd told her. "But you need to look like the best mother."

At the time, I judged her harshly for weaponizing something sacred like motherhood. But now I find myself admiring how calculated she was. If the end game was to stay in her kids' lives, really, is there anything, any strategy, that's off-limits?

So I decide to do more volunteering at the Ashley School. First, I offer to help with the end-of-year gala, and then, when they accept, I begin staying on campus after school a couple times a week for committee work. At the same time, my bandwidth for all nonessential obligations is diminishing, and I feel myself pulling away from my *Sex and the City* girls. Those friends are too close, they know me too well. Worse, they're starting to ask too many questions.

CHAPTER FIVE

Black in Malibu

April 2008

We have a second home in Malibu, which I know I'm supposed to love, but it reminds me too much of Berkeley with its cloudy mornings, and all the cold and damp. He's always loved being near the ocean, so at first I went along, thinking I might grow to love it too. Originally, we were just renting for a few summers, and I thought maybe he'd grow tired of it. But then one day he came home with "a surprise." He'd bought a house in Point Dume—for us, he said. I tried to remember my face and not let my anger/disappointment come gushing out all over the floor between us.

Dude—this surprise is not for me.

Even though Point Dume is less than an hour away from our Studio City house, I find it to be terribly isolating and excruciatingly homogeneous (white). Add to that the fact that Malibu is home to the most problematically-named gated community in Los Angeles (The Colony). When we're out there it's like I've been reduced to some brown, two-dimensional version of myself. A Black character on a page, smiling and nodding to all the happy, tanned blond people at

Zuma Beach and the Country Mart. But over spring break I started spending more weekends there, and when he's working, it's just me and the kids. The bonus, though, is that it gives me a great excuse for not calling people back ("Sorry, we were down on the beach all day"), and literally puts distance between us and anyone who might want to pop in. My white neighbors there are friendly, but they leave me alone for the most part. Our golf-cart-to-golf-cart banter during our morning Starbucks runs is peppy, light, and polite. The boys and I are the only Black faces around for over a mile, and I know that this fact isn't lost on the folks there, as they've gone out of their way to make us feel part of the community.

I've always lived like a chameleon, doing my best to make my brown skin blend in with my white, pink, and golden surroundings. Long before the word *fetishized* was in my vocabulary, I knew I was considered exotic. To the white folks who delighted in my articulateness and easygoing nature, I was the "right kind" of Black. And even though admitting that fills me with shame, the truth is there are times when I enjoyed that "chosen one" status among them.

At the Ashley School, there are only a handful of Black moms, and they typically fall into one of two categories: the overly grateful scholarship moms or the militant Jack and Jill moms. Because I don't fall into either of those categories, I've been able to be friendly with everyone without any allegiance to any one particular group. A position that has afforded me the ability to always fly a little below the radar.

Which is why, when our head of school knocks on my car window at drop-off one April morning and asks to see me in her office, I am shocked—and simultaneously filled with dread.

We've never had anything more than a passing conversation. Why does she want to see me?

I pull into a parking space and sit wringing my hands for about fifteen minutes, on the verge of tears.

I smell an ambush.

I feel trapped, like that day in tenth grade when my counselor called me in and my mom and Kenny were waiting in her office.

Fuck, fuck, fuck! Somebody told on me.

There was that mom who saw me in the liquor store the other day at nine a.m. buying a pint of vodka. I tried to act casual and make small talk, but I saw her notice the bag and then look at me. What possible excuse could anyone have for buying a pint at nine a.m. on a Tuesday? Or maybe it was Miss Carter, the art teacher. I dropped a full Ambien bottle in the girls' bathroom stall two weeks ago and the pills went everywhere. I was on my knees, sweating and shaking while picking them up when she came in. She seemed flustered, mumbling something about how she'd be back, and then left.

The head of school wants to see me because she knows that I'm a spy living a double life. They all know that one day, I'm an ordinary Hollywood mom, waving hello to someone in the pickup line and the next, I'm some pathetic junkie fishing an undigested pill out of her own vomit.

Oh God.

They're going to kick us out. They're going to ask us to leave. They can't have a drug addict mom here. Oh my God, my poor kids.

I duck down in the car and snap a pill in half and wash it down with a few sips of Jordan's after-school Gatorade. Then I steel myself and cross the parking lot toward her office. She smiles widely when she sees me approaching through her picture window, waving me in and indicating the seat across from her.

"You probably know why I've asked you here today."

Oh, maybe not. God, I hope not.

"I don't think so." I force a thin smile.

"Well, there's been much deliberation, but we've all met and discussed it, and I have to say the decision was unanimous."

I hang my head.

Maybe the floor will open and swallow me whole.

"Laura, we'd love for you to be our next parent association president."

Say what?

She tells me that everyone's been raving about me, saying what a big help I've been with the gala and last year's fair. Now she's smiling at me, waiting for a response, but I'm torn.

On one hand, I know that being in such a tremendous leadership role would be my biggest command performance to date.

Can I pull it off?

I won't be able to fly under the radar any longer, I'll have to work closely with her and a whole committee. I'll have to get far more precise with my pill timing and managing my detoxes because I can't afford to let anyone get even a whiff of addiction. I'll have to really fucking have my shit together.

On the other hand, being named PA president in the middle of this mess could be the best him-trying-to-paint-me-as-an-addict-foiling ever. I could crumble his case against me in one magnificent move.

Him: But your honor, my wife is a drug addict, she's unfit to raise our kids.

Judge: But she was just named PA president at your children's school. How bad can it be?

If I do this, I'll have to maximize my hiding-in-plain-sight skills. Leveling them up to flawless, become a master of deception.

It will be a full-time job.

Connie's words ring in my head, *You don't have to be the best mother, but you need to look like the best mother.* And something inside me clicks into place.

"I'd be honored," I say.

Word of my new appointment spread quickly on campus. I am the first Black PA president since 1972. Soon after it was announced, one of the militant moms hemmed me into a corner and warned me (with a finger wag) not to mess this up.

"You know you're representing all of us now, right?"

I wanted to tell her to get her finger the fuck out of my face, but I knew she was right. Officially, I am the new PA president, representing all the parents at Ashley, but unofficially, I am the new HNIC (Head Niggah in Charge), and the official delegate for all the Black faces at our school.

In my new role, I have to show up at countless meetings and lunches with Maybach- and Bentley-driving, white committee moms, and I've heard firsthand how they trash-talk the parents who have fallen from grace.

"Did you hear that Parker's mom is having an affair with Mr. Tow-alski?" Or, "I heard, Bryce's dad lost his job. He may have to switch schools."

But the most scandalous subject of all, the one they huddled excitedly over Bellinis to discuss?

Rehab.

"Did you hear that so-and-so went to Hazelden?? Her poor children. Her poor husband. I heard he had to hide her keys so she wouldn't try and drive the kids to school drunk."

I would sit there looking from one white face to another hoping that I was giving them "horrified at the scandal of it all" instead of "terror-struck about what you'll say about me behind my back when it's my turn."

All the more reason why they can never find out that I, the Goldilocks of Black moms, am a drug addict. If I were ever exposed, I would take every other Black mom down with me into ruin.

CHAPTER SIX

Nancy

am like one of those runaway freight trains in movies speeding toward a brick wall.

Soon, I'll either derail and be utterly humiliated or crash and be completely eviscerated.

I know that it's just a matter of time before he pulls at a thread that unravels all my secrets. But I'm petrified every time I consider the next step: hiring a divorce attorney, filing, making it official. There's still a part of me that wants to keep going as we are, hoping that maybe he'll just move out and split everything fifty-fifty, and I won't have to take any legal action.

But yesterday I walked into the bathroom and saw that some things in my medicine cabinet had been moved around, like they'd been taken out and then hastily returned. Some bottles were turned the wrong way, others had been shuffled around. After I checked to make sure nothing was missing, I went in the bedroom and noticed that the lens of his Canon Point & Shoot was peeking out of his nearly shut nightstand drawer.

That's odd.

As quietly as possible, I peeked into the hallway before sliding the drawer open and fishing out the camera. I held my breath as I quickly scrolled through the pictures on the viewfinder.

He took pictures of everything.

There was my addiction in living color; the pills, my Ambien pill bottles, close-ups of the labels, the old empty Vicodin bottle from under the sink, the Gabapentin they'd given me for the seizures, the instructions from the hospital after the seizures. He'd taken pictures of every label and then emptied the bottles out and taken pictures of the pills on the counter.

He's gathering evidence.

Someone must have told him to do this.

With trembling fingers I slid the camera back in the drawer and sat on the bed with my face in my hands, rocking back and forth.

Does this mean he's hired someone? Oh God. What if I'm too late? I should have filed when I told him. I'm such a fucking idiot. Oh my God, I really fucked this up.

—

When our neighbors got divorced last year, everyone on our block felt so bad for the wife; the shame of having her husband leave her, the pain of breaking up a family, the harsh realities of shared custody. Now I wish I'd paid more attention when she was crying about it, instead of being glad that it was her and not me. I can't risk anyone finding out that I'm even contemplating a divorce, so how am I going to do this?

How do you find a lawyer without your husband finding out? How much do they cost? I've heard that the husband pays for the wife's legal fees, is that true? What's a typical settlement?

I finally take the plunge and email both her and Connie for a lawyer recommendation (for a close friend, I say).

Nancy is near the top of both lists.

"She's the best, but she's hella expensive," my neighbor tells me.

"She's a fucking shark," emails Connie. "No one wants to go up against her."

But despite finding those pictures, I still don't know if a shark is in order.

I mean, I don't want a war.

I'm not trying to fight this man. We have so much love and history together. And the boys! We made these two beautiful boys.

So I (cautiously) poll more divorcées from school and get five other attorney names. I pull over on Valley Vista after drop-off each morning, taking notes with pencils stolen from the boys' backpacks on glovebox Starbucks napkins. I made all six appointments for one day. I know if I take more than a day to hire someone that I'll lose my nerve, and if he hasn't already filed, I might still be able to get the upper hand.

—

The clock is ticking for me as I can only hold it together for so many hours before my addict slip starts showing. By the time I push the elevator button in Nancy's imposing Century City office lobby for my sixth and final appointment, I am in full-blown, gut-wrenching withdrawal. I catch a glimpse of myself in her reception area mirror and I can practically see the hysteria seeping out of my pores like steam. The receptionist seems unfazed as I give my name and proceed to burst into ugly, unladylike sobs before collapsing in a nearby seat. In an instant, a petite blond woman wearing a blue pinstripe pantsuit is sitting on the arm of my chair with a bottle of Evian and a box of tissues. My shoulders stiffen as she starts gently rubbing my back with her tiny, manicured hand.

"Hi, hon. I'm Nancy."

The shark!

"Where does your husband think you are right now?"

Huh?

"Shopping with a friend."

"It's after five thirty."

"I told him we might grab a bite afterward."

"This friend, she's trustworthy? She's covering for you?"

"Yes."

"Good. Who else have you met with, honey?"

Why?

"I'm only asking because I looked your husband up. You don't have a lot of time to mess around, my dear. Powerful men like him don't become powerful by waiting for someone else to make the first move. Now mind you, I'm not suggesting you do this, but a lot of women in your position find it helpful to contaminate the lawyer pool as quickly as possible. This limits your husband's choices in representation."

I'd read about conflicting out, consulting with different attorneys so your spouse can't hire the most competent and experienced lawyer. I'm pretty sure Nancy can't ethically recommend it to me, but I don't really care right now. The skin on my face is smoldering like it's being burned with a hot iron, it's all I can do to keep from screaming out loud.

I need to get the fuck out of here NOW.

I rattle off the attorneys' names I'd met with earlier and notice that a young Black woman has appeared out of nowhere to take notes. Nancy starts to break down the divorce process for me, but ten minutes in, I feel like I'm going to lose my shit.

"Look, I don't want a big dramatic court battle, I just want to divide everything up and have this be over with as quickly as possible."

"Of course," she says with a smile. "That's always the best course of action."

"Okay," I say, taking a big swallow of the Evian. The glass bottle is chilly and moist. Briefly, I hold its cool smoothness to the side of my face. I stand up and extend my hand toward her.

"Can we discuss all this stuff later? What do I need to sign to get started?"

I'm nauseous on the drive home. Not just because I'm free-fall crashing now but because I feel so powerless. Nancy had handled me back there in her office (literally), and I let her because I'd run out of time. I glance at the amount on the signed paperwork on the seat next to me and feel my stomach wrench up sharply.

Twenty-five K.

Fuck, fuck, fuck.

—

Nancy has me seriously paranoid.

She's warned me repeatedly about the importance of keeping a regular routine now that I've filed. I am instructed to open a secret bank account, buy a secret cell phone, and open a secret PO box for my mail. She tells me to get my journals out of the house and give them to my mother, as the contents could be used against me in a custody hearing.

"And keep up appearances," she commands. "We need you to look sympathetic and courageous, be admirably cheerful despite the circumstances, but never too upbeat. You also need to be everywhere, omnipresent. Every day someone somewhere should have a 'what a great mom Laura is' story. Do you understand what I'm saying?"

I know what she's saying.

She's saying that I can't cancel my appointments anymore, because I can't risk someone noticing that I've missed a workout, a tennis lesson, or a PA meeting. She's saying that she wants people to say what a brave person I am when they find out that I'm getting a divorce.

I come close to telling her about the pictures, but I can't tell her about the Ambien—yet. Telling her might mean giving it up, and I'm just not ready to do that. But I do let her know that he's developed a new habit of leaving for work and then returning ten or fifteen minutes later to grab something.

"Why do you think he's coming back?" She looks concerned.

"I'm not sure."

"I want you to start depositing as much money as you can into the account every week without tipping him off," she continues. "He may have hired a private investigator, so better to leave any receipts and the PO box key with your mom too. Also, forget your male friends for a while. In fact, unless it's your brother, you don't even stop to talk to a man on the street until this divorce is final. You must *not* give him any reason to want to come after you. The worst thing we can do is trip this man's ego."

My head aches when I think about how messed up this whole thing has become. When I am visibly loaded (wobbly, slurring, distracted), his antipathy is palpable as he stalks around the house. I do my best to avoid him during these times, which is why I really try to wait to eat my pills until everyone has gone to sleep. He has yet to catch me taking them during the day, but I know it's coming. I feel as though he and I are playing some elaborate game of cat and mouse, and one day he's bound to catch me with my hand in the cookie jar.

Last week he nearly did.

That morning, I'd watched his car drive out the gates from the closet window as usual. Then, because I had an uneasy feeling, I waited for an extra five agonizing minutes before grabbing my pills out of the bathroom.

I'd been sneaking a couple of shots of vodka in my vanilla tea. Morning vodka was no longer just an every-once-in-a-while thing. It was now as essential as oxygen. I was just lifting my Smirnoff Vanilla out of one of my tall boots when he strode into our walk-in closet like the Terminator and scared the shit out of me. I bit my lower lip so hard to keep from screaming that it bled in my mouth. Shifting to auto-pilot, I carefully lowered my vodka back into the boot, praying that he hadn't clocked what I was doing. I willed my voice to remain steady even though my nervous system felt like a bird in a lightning storm.

"Forget something?"

I looked up at him as casually as possible, letting the pill bottle drop, slightly behind me, out of my hand into my robe pocket. The rattle it made might have been dishes breaking, but by some miracle of God, he didn't seem to hear it.

"I forgot that script I was reading. Have you seen it?"

His eyes were daring mine to meet his, but instead, I bent down and grabbed my tennis shoes. My stomach felt like it was full of bees as I opened a drawer filled with workout clothes.

"No, but try the family room. I need to get ready for tennis, and then I'll help you look."

His face hardened into a mask of angry disapproval as he watched me fumble around for a tennis dress.

55

That look.

I know that the more he finds out about who I really am the more disappointed he is. I know he will always be baffled by my desperation to escape from our privileged life. That he will never understand that my existence these past few years has been one gushing wound, and these drugs are the only things that seem to stop the bleeding.

Now our days start to blend into one agonizing, terrifying Ground-hog Day. It used to be that I was relieved when he was out of town, because then I could knock myself out at the end of the day, no questions. But now, even when he's out of town, I jump out of my skin every time I hear a car go by or a creak on the stairs. I'm peeking through the curtains to see if someone might be watching me with a telephoto lens.

When he's home, it's worse. We barely speak, and when we do I feel as though I'm in the witness chair, being cross-examined.

"Earlier you said you picked them up from school and then went to the grocery store. But now you just said it was the other way around. Which was it?"

My memory is getting so much worse that it's gotten to where I'm afraid to say anything for fear of sounding like I'm lying.

I am no longer able to hide in plain sight. He's spotted me just fine, and it's clear he's not happy with what he sees.

———

Shelly brought her girls over to play today, and we sat in the kitchen while the kids jumped on the trampoline in the backyard. Shelly is light-skinned, tall, and beautiful with short brown hair and a sprinkling of freckles across her face. When we're out in the world, people mistake us for sisters. We call each other sister, her family is like my family, her mom calls me her "other" daughter. And even though Shelly and I are aces, it was still so strange having someone from the outside world in the house. Someone who wasn't walking on eggshells, someone who wasn't high or angry, with a normal life and normal energy.

"How are you?" she said, looking concerned. "Cause you look exhausted."

"I'm okay," I said cautiously.

"How's your reign as PA queen going? And when does it end again?"

"Next spring," I said. "Only . . ."

"What?"

"Only, they just asked me to join the board."

"You've got to be kidding me. What did you say?"

"I said yes."

"What? Don't you think you should get yourself divorced before you take on anything else?"

You have no idea.

"My attorney told me it would be good for my profile. Apparently, I need to bolster my résumé. I need to keep looking like the model mother."

"Is he here?"

"Back any minute," I whispered. "He's coming home to pick something up."

"Why are we whispering?"

I heard the front door slam and bugged my eyes out at her. We both fell silent and braced for impact. He strode purposefully into the kitchen and then stopped short, looking back and forth between the two of us wordlessly before remembering to say a quiet hello to Shelly. As soon as she started making small talk, I got up and went outside to check on the kids, making sure to come back only after he'd left.

"Is he gone?" I said, looking around.

"He just left."

I clenched my body to keep my eyes from filling with tears.

"What the fuck!" she said, after checking the driveway. "You guys live like this? Is this how it is all the time?"

"Pretty much," I said, shrugging. "I mainly try to stay out of his way when he's home."

"This is so fucked-up, Laura. You guys can*not* live like this. Why doesn't he just move out to that apartment he rented?"

"I don't know. I don't even know if he still has it. I think he only rented it for six months. He spends some nights at the Malibu house though."

"How can you not know if he still has the apartment?"

"We just never talk about it. We never talk about anything except the boys."

"And what about the boys? Do they know? This can't be good for them."

"They don't know anything's different. I mean, I don't think they do, they haven't been asking any questions."

"When are you planning to tell them? I mean, you've got to tell them something, right? You can't go on like this forever."

"Not forever. Just until we know what we're doing, where he's going to live, where I'm going to live. We don't want to blow up their world without a plan in place."

"Okay, girl, but you guys need to hurry up and finish this divorce, this is not healthy."

"I know."

—

Nancy introduced me to partners today. There are four of them, all white women in power suits with firm handshakes.

"This case is a slam dunk," she says, pacing in front of them like a general. "You all have the dossier."

I look around and see that each woman is holding a binder. My throat closes suddenly as I see *Robbins v. Robbins* under the clear plastic cover.

"They've been a couple for over fifteen years," continues Nancy. "Married for nearly twelve. Laura gave up her PR company to stay home and raise their two sons, eight and ten."

The partners murmur words of approval here.

"What we have here is a woman who gave up her career to raise their children and is now entitled to be supported in the manner to which she has become accustomed."

Up until this point I'd found myself nodding along, mesmerized by the story of this amazing woman.

Entitled?

Suddenly I can hear my heartbeat in my ears.

I'm not entitled to shit. You don't even know—I'm the Talented Mrs. Ripley.

But Nancy believes me to be the gold standard wife and mom, and I feel like now is the time to tell her about the Ambien, just in case. I know she looks at me and sees the model client, the dutiful mom and wife, involved in the school community, well liked by her friends. But what she doesn't know is that every day, while I'm getting my kids ready for school, while I'm dropping off daily hot lunch, while I stand at the podium or sit at the board table, all I'm doing is thinking about pills. Pills that I have hidden everywhere; the center console of my car, in my purse or my pants pockets.

Can I take one now? Is it too early to take a second one? Did my noon dose fall out of my pocket when I read to Jacob's class?

Also, she doesn't know about the pictures.

Mustering up my courage once we're back in her office, I tell her that we need to talk. I'm not going to tell her how bad it is, but I need to let her know enough so she won't be blindsided if someone drops those pictures on her desk one day.

"What's wrong?"

Nancy's whole deportment has changed and her voice levels up with concern.

"Um, I need to let you know that with all this trouble in my marriage, I've had a hard time sleeping."

Lie number one.

"Yes, *and?*"

Nancy's face is ashen now and her eyebrows are arched inquisitively. She's perched on the edge of her desk chair like a panther waiting to pounce.

"And I may have developed a slight physical dependency on a sedative, for sleeping, since I've had trouble, I mean . . ."

Lie number two.

"Oh, thank *God*!" she screams. "I thought you were going to say you've been having an affair."

"Oh, no. Not an affair. I mean, but you don't think this is—bad? I mean, for my case?"

"Not at all," she says, giving me a dismissive wave, picking up her phone. "In fact, maybe I can use that. Your marriage is so toxic that you're under a doctor's care for duress. He drove you to it."

"Would you say that's true?" she pressed. "That he drove you to it?"

My stomach flutters. I still can't believe I actually told her about the drugs. No one knows about the drugs.

Also, wouldn't a caring person have asked me if I was all right? Or if I needed help?

"Sorry?" She looks up sharply as she sets her phone down.

Did I say something out loud?

I swallow hard and decide to keep going—*fuck it.*

"Yeah, I guess you could say that. He drove me to it."

Lie number three.

Tell the truth, Laura. Sweet Jesus, be honest about something.

"The only other thing. This bit about me giving up my career and being entitled to his money. I don't know if it's fair to make it like he's some bad guy here that deserves to pay. The way I see it is that my marriage is like a sinking boat. And for the last few years, he and I have both been busily punching holes in the sides. And I'm sure, if you ask him, he'll say I've punched more holes in it than him."

"Look, honey, that earnest 'we are the world' thing you've got going on will come in handy if we have to go in front of a judge. But right now, especially with this new information about the sleeping pills . . . What kind of pills did you say?"

I hadn't said.

"Ambien," I say.

"Never heard of it. Is it new?"

She continues before I can answer.

"Anyway, we need to play hardball now. This was a long-term marriage in a no-fault state. Whatever you think about what's fair, you are entitled to half. And I can assure you that he's gonna do whatever it takes to hold on to his assets."

Oh, but she doesn't know him. I'm the mother of his children! Whatever she may think, he'll want me to be okay.

I open my mouth to tell her so as she shuffles some papers on her desk, but she cuts me off before I can speak.

"He hired a lawyer, Laura. A tough one. Soon he'll be coming after us with everything he's got. I expect his response to the filing by the end of day tomorrow and . . ."

She's still talking, but suddenly everything's gone white, and a high-pitched humming fills my head.

He hired a lawyer.

This is really happening.

CHAPTER SEVEN

Doctor Shopping

Too much Ambien and I'm sloppy; slurring, confused, and forgetful. Not enough and I can't make eye contact, my voice gets too loud, and I'm easily agitated. So now I'm a chemist, looking for that precise formula that allows me to operate out in the world as inconspicuously as possible. I know I can't keep this cycle up much longer, but today is very important. I have to convince Dr. Linbaum to approve my second refill override, the override that the ER doc wrote for me after my seizures only four months ago.

I'm wearing my hair in a neat bun and have on gray Theory stretch slacks and a black Stella McCartney bodysuit. I've found that if I look put together enough, people tend to overlook how jumpy I am. But now I'm sweating under my aviators and I'm afraid it's a tell. I think about removing them, but I'm scared that Dr. Linbaum will see how dilated my pupils are. And I know that my inability to make eye contact is not typical for someone who is taking her medication "as prescribed."

"Mrs. Robbins."

He barely looks up from the chart he's reading as I sit down at his desk.

Uh-oh—bad sign.

"Hello, Doctor."

He seems to startle at the sound of my voice. Self-conscious, I clear my throat and concentrate on de-amplifying it.

"How are you, Doctor?"

"Mrs. Robbins, do you have any idea how much Ambien you're taking?"

My brain revs to full speed and I'm suddenly grateful that I've kept my glasses on.

He knows! Oh Jesus, he knows.

I fight the instinct to grab the prescription pad on his desk and make a dash for the parking lot. But I'm a rabbit with her foot caught in a bear trap. I have to stay and see if I can find a way to wiggle out of this, even if it means leaving something behind.

Give him nothing.

I try to keep my face composed as I search for the right answer. I have a few top-notch excuses, but I can't remember which ones I've already used with him. I decide I don't have a choice, so I switch to a casual tone.

"Oh, are you talking about that replacement refill I got a couple of weeks ago? That's actually a funny story. You see, we'd gone to our Malibu house that weekend because our Studio City house was being tented. I won't bore you with the details."

I laugh a little, to test the waters. He's stone-faced, steady reading my chart.

"Anyway, I'd left all my prescriptions in Studio City by mistake, and of course we couldn't risk going back because of the gas, so I had to get everything replaced."

Lies, lies, lies.

I fold my trembling hands on my lap out of sight and dig my nails into my palms. Dr. Linbaum flips through ten or fifteen pages of scribble. His brows are furrowed as he mumbles, running his index finger down each page.

"Your last scan showed that your brain activity is normal. No more seizures since February."

"Yes," I say, forcing cheer into my voice. "The neurologist said everything looked good. He gave me clearance to drive again."

"But here's the thing, Mrs. Robbins. Two weeks ago, a pharmacist called your insurance company. He was concerned about the amount of Ambien he was dispensing to you."

Herman, that nosy fucker, I should have known he was going to dime on me.

"Mrs. Robbins." He closes my chart and leans toward me across his desk. His eyes are tired and kind, but I'm still braced for the worst.

"I'm afraid we're going to need to discontinue the Ambien. Safely, of course. The nurse will give you tapering instructions. And I'll see you back here next month."

I'm paralyzed as a massive earthquake roars through his office. I look around to see if the diplomas on the wall behind him are crashing down, but everything is still. I fight to gather up my face so that he can't see my panic.

Tapering.

He's cutting me off.

"Now, I'm not accusing you of anything."

Yes, you are.

"But you've got to understand that if you're abusing this medication, I could lose my license for prescribing it to you. I know you've been having a rough time, and I'm sorry to hear about your divorce. But believe me, this is the best course of action."

Shit.

Back home, I'm staring at my death sentence, aka my tapering instructions, with dry, burning eyes. The nurse's neat printing looks innocent enough, but each word is a knife in my stomach.

Thirty Ambien, refill three times only. No early refills.

That's ninety Ambien for the rest of my life.

I feel sweat dripping from my temples as my mind starts racing.

I was counting on refilling my stash today.

I open my coded Filofax.

Next month on the fifth I might be able to get the extended-release tabs refilled the neurologist from the ER prescribed for me again, but that's only twenty. And I still have that prescription from that Dr. Styles, the psychiatrist I saw last year, I think that one still has refills.

My medicine cabinet bottle has only thirty-four pills. Let's see, I need at least nine pills to get me through the night and two at the minimum to get me through the day. That means that thirty-four pills will only last me for three days.

Fuck!

Even if I boost each pill with booze and a Benadryl it's still not enough. I'm looking at days of painful, humiliating withdrawal.

My heart is pounding so hard now that it pulses my tongue against the roof of my mouth.

I go into the bathroom and lock the door and throw open the cabinet under the sink. Way back behind a bag of Epsom salts I find an old bottle of Tussionex, my favorite hydrocodone cough syrup. It's so strong that I have to give an Oscar-worthy coughing performance in order to convince Dr. Linbaum that it's warranted. And I can only ask for it, say, twice a year without raising drug abuse suspicions. But when I can get it, Tussionex is sometimes even better than Ambien. It's the smoothest, dreamiest, most euphoric, best-tasting orangy elixir ever. I usually drink a quarter bottle a night whenever I have it. There's just a little left in this one, so I tap the opening on the tip of my tongue to drain the last drops into my mouth. Then I lick the tip of my pinkie finger after wiping it around the contours of the inside of the bottle. Finally, sucking on the cap to get the very last vestiges, I start my pill inventory. I've taken my slacks off, so now I'm kneeling bare-legged on the marble floor. I spill my pills out and then count and recount them with trembling fingers.

Thirty-four.

I gather them all lovingly into three piles, six for today, sixteen stay in the bottle, but the rest need to be hidden so I don't take them by mistake in a brownout. I stash some in the toes of random pairs of shoes in my closet. I make a note in my Filofax so I know which ones once I'm lucid enough. L for Louboutins, G for Gucci, and so on. I save one to take in the pickup line a little later. I have it timed so that it kicks in just as I am arriving home with the boys.

—

The Ambien hasn't kicked in yet and the boys and I have been back for almost an hour. I have to save the rest of today's rations for tonight or else I won't sleep at all.

I'm so fucking fucked. I need to find another source and I need it now.

I'm trembling so hard my shoulders are shaking as I quietly close the bedroom door. The kids are having a snack downstairs. I sink down to the floor and pull out my phone, scrolling down until I find the number of a doctor in our neighborhood, Dr. Nelson. He's an orthopedic surgeon whose kids go to school with the boys. I made an office appointment with him almost two years ago in the hopes of getting a friendly, neighborly Vicodin prescription for a fake back injury, but he wouldn't play ball. However, at the end of the visit, he did question me about my sleep and asked if I had enough Ambien. This gave me hope that maybe he'd be willing to prescribe it for me someday. Someday when I was really desperate.

Like now.

Pros and cons of bringing Dr. Nelson into my little drug shell game:

Pro: I'll have a second Ambien source while I'm tapering.

Con: It's literally too close to home. I'll be shitting where I eat and risking exposure.

I can see my heart pounding through my bodysuit as I push the Call button.

What if Dr. Nelson mentions my call at his daughter's birthday party next week? Or what if he reports me for drug seeking?

I panic and hang up quickly before anyone answers.

"You don't have a choice," I hiss to myself, pinching my upper thigh until I feel it starting to bruise.

"Make the call."

I check the hallway before I call, praying that by some miracle a nurse answers and just offers to give me a prescription.

I know I'm playing Russian roulette here.

A "no" is a bullet through my skull. A "yes" is a stay of execution.

I hit the green arrow and the phone rings.

Jesus fuck.

When she answers I use my best white-girl voice to explain that we're headed out of town and my regular doctor is away for two weeks.

"Would Dr. Nelson mind just calling in a refill for me this one time?"

I think maybe she's hung up on me, but after a couple of excruciating seconds of silence, she asks me to hold on. I pace in a circle on the carpet, praying, praying, praying that I get that stay of execution.

Yes or no? Yes or no?

"Hello?"

"Yes?" My heart stops beating.

"He'd like you to come in for an appointment."

A gun cocks in my head.

"Since it's been over a year since you were last here. Can you come in Wednesday morning?"

Boom.

FUCK!

I can't see him for an office visit! He'll call Linbaum for my chart, and then I'm done.

Why does he have to be all doctorish? Why can't he just do a sistah a solid?

I sit on the bed and deflate like a day-old helium balloon.

I know what I have to do now.

———

He's sleeping here this week, so I wait until I'm sure that everyone is in bed before sneaking into my office, which is nestled upstairs between the boys' rooms, and bringing up the website I've been secretly cruising for the last two weeks.

Zolpidem, brand name Ambien.

I have a three-hundred-pill bottle in my cart. Three hundred pills might last me twenty-five days if I can regulate myself. I've been here before, but I'm always too chickenshit to hit Buy. If I get caught ordering drugs off the internet, there will be no more claiming I'm taking these pills as prescribed, no more blaming my grogginess on lack of sleep, or brushing off my manic behavior as simply being overcaffein-ated. I will have lost all semblance of credibility, and he will have won everything.

I hit Continue and go to the next page, extending my ears out like power antennas, listening for movement in the dark house. I'm wait-ing for that creak of the floorboard, the shadow in the doorway, that hand on my shoulder. I have to keep wiping my sweaty fingers on my pajama bottoms between entering and reentering the number of the debit card from my secret lawyer-ordered bank account. On the next page, I cheat off a crumpled-up Post-it Note from my robe pocket as I enter the address of my secret PO box.

If he were to walk in now, he'd have everything, the internet drugs, the secret account, the secret PO box.

My eyes scroll up and down as I frantically search through all the words on the next screen for a delivery date.

How long till they get here???

I freeze as I hear a clicking sound somewhere behind me.

Was that a footstep? Was that downstairs?

Shit, shit, shit.

I clench my jaw to keep my teeth from chattering as my eyes scan the page one more time. Terror begins to derail my ability to concen-trate, so I click Confirm, click off the site, and click to clear my history.

Click, click, click.

I turn to face outward in my swivel chair. I'm straining to listen with every orifice I have: my ears, my eyes, my mouth, my nose. Sud-denly, I jerk around because for a second it looks as though there is a shadowy figure just behind me.

Running on tiptoes down the hallway, I pass the closed guest-room door where I hear him snoring softly (thank God) and enter the haven of my bedroom. As usual, the boys beat me there. Their bodies are crisscrossed on top of the covers, one's head sleeping on the other's ankles. I gently move one moist body over so I can slide in beside him and pull the covers up to my chin.

Safe.

CHAPTER EIGHT

Rock Bottom

As I'm walking in the house, I hear the family room TV blasting. I drop my keys in the bowl by the door and quickly round the corner into the long hallway that leads to the west side of the house. I call Jordan's name, but he can't hear me over the TV. I can see him and Jacob lying on the big sofa, arms and legs akimbo, chewing on the collars of their respective school shirts with their eyes fixed on the screen in front of them. I open my mouth to call his name again, then stop in my tracks.

Oh my God, it's the wedding scene.

They're watching *Skirmish*.*

"I think about you all day long. When I'm not near you, all I think about is being near you. And when you are near me, I feel like I'm finally at peace with the world . . ."

Nearly three years ago, my husband was directing what was sure to be the biggest blockbuster of the summer, starring the hottest male comedian to hit the silver screen in decades. Right in the middle of filming he came home late one night to tell me they'd been stuck on

_____
*Fictitious.

a scene. The scene where the title character, Skirmish, recites his vows to the woman he loves.

"I love the wedding vows you wrote," my husband said. "Would you mind if I used them for this scene? We need him to floor her, floor the audience. Nothing the writers are coming up with is close. Maybe it's because I keep comparing whatever they write to yours. Will you?"

I was flattered, honored, but more than that I was confused. I felt like we'd been tiptoeing around each other for months, or at least since he'd started shooting sixteen weeks earlier. There had been lots of fumbling kisses at the door, quick, platonic calls from the set (mainly about the kids), waking up to find his side of the bed empty after a night shoot. I decided that the absence of adult conversation from our day-to-day was my fault, so on shoot days I'd started writing out cheat sheets of interesting things to discuss with him when he called or came home:

The Pussycat Dolls and Snoop Dogg winning Best Video
The PATRIOT Act (Maybe you can explain it to me?)
Israel's PM suffering a stroke (Not sure what this means for the Middle East.)

"Of course," I said. "That would be amazing."

All at once, I was inundated with equal parts guilt and hope. Guilt because part of me had already given up on my marriage and had been kind of relieved. Hope, because perhaps his asking me meant something.

He could have asked anyone in Hollywood to write this for him and he asked me. Maybe he's read my thoughts and this was his way of saying, "Don't give up on us yet."

"Mommy."

Jacob spots me and lights up, holding his arms out in my direction. "Come here and watch *Skirmish* with us, Daddy got us the new director's cut."

Even though I'm starting to dissociate, I can still vaguely feel their warm arms and curly heads curving around my shoulders and chest as I sit down between them.

"Watch, Mommy."

The comedian is in his fat suit reading his vows to his thin, beautiful bride, but all I see is me in my princess dress, on the cliff overlooking the valley at sunset. I can picture our hands clasped together, and me looking into my husband's eyes, waiting to say the words. Words I'd worked on for weeks, crossing out, rewriting, adding, reciting to Shelly over drinks, saying out loud in the mirror. Words I kept on a folded piece of paper in the breast of my Vera Wang corset top until Rabbi Weismann turned to me and nodded.

"The only thing I really want to do is spend the rest of my life making you as happy as you've made me."

"Hey," I say abruptly, starting to stand up. "I'll be right back, okay?"

"No," yelled Jordan. "The best part is coming, Mom. Just wait."

I can feel the pressure behind my eyes, like a garden hose that's being stepped on while the water runs. Any second now it's going to blow.

Who did he marry that day? Some con woman? An imposter who duped him into believing her hustle?

"I know that I'll never have to ask God for anything, because with you in my life, I have everything I ever wanted."

Tears are streaming down my face now.

No, this wasn't any hustle.

I meant every word. Our wedding day was the happiest day of my life. Not because of the whole Vera Wang-martini-bar-bride-fairy-tale wedding-ness of it all, because that's not really my gig. But because I was marrying HIM. I loved him so much.

"Hey, guys . . ."

"Mom! Just stay, *please.*"

It was me I didn't love—at least not enough. I didn't trust that he'd still love me if I came clean about who I was. So the relationship was doomed from the start, wasn't it? The day I said those words to him, I buried the real Laura, having no idea about the price I would pay for that act.

I sniff and wipe my eyes with the back of my hand.

Jacob looks up sharply then. "Why are you crying, Mom?"

Jordan laughs out loud, "Mom, you cry at everything! You can't cry at *Skirmish*."

They're both laughing now, and I force a smile through my tears.

"Yeah, silly Mommy," I say.

——

My internet delivery was a nightmare.

One day while in full jittery withdrawal, just as I was opening my secret PO box to see if the pills had arrived, someone tapped me on the shoulder—my husband's assistant, Charlie.

"Hi," she said brightly. "What are you doing over here?"

I jumped then. Partially for joy as I could see that my package was inside, but mostly from fright, as not only had she startled me, but whether she knew it or not, she'd busted me cold.

I managed to smile and come up with a quick lie. Saying that I was checking a friend's PO box for them while they were out of town. But I saw a look of concern flash across her face while I was speaking, and I knew that this would be the last time I could visit that PO box, which meant no more internet deliveries, as I could never risk getting deliveries at the house.

And now all those pills are almost gone.

The math makes sense though, right? Three hundred divided by thirty is ten pills a day and tomorrow it will be thirty days.

Just as I'm about to get sucked down a junky-mom rabbit hole of self-deprecation, my three ghoulish allies—minimization, justification, and rationalization—step in to argue my case.

Your Honor, ten pills a day may sound excessive to a person who has never dealt with chronic early insomnia, but let me assure you, these pills are medically required and were originally prescribed by a doctor (or three).

My mind feels sharp now and I am longing for that Ambien fog, because I can't get another refill for three days. I took one and a half this morning, left the rest at the bottom of a Tylenol bottle in Studio City, and then drove out to the Malibu house earlier this afternoon. It's July fourth, and I've got to keep it together because he's out of town on a shoot and the boys are excited to see the fireworks.

But it's been six hours without an Ambien now, and my head is exploding. Sharp, metallic pins pierce deeply into my temples, gums, and jawline, causing me to grind my teeth. My plan was to hold out from breaking into my Malibu stash until after bedtime, but I can feel the pain coming for me, roaring into me like a thunder cloud. I'm going to need to knock out before it gets any worse, and to do that I need to be alone. My best idea is to feign a headache and ask the neighbors if they'll take the boys to watch the fireworks. The amount of effort I have to put into sounding effortless on the phone drains me of my last bit of strength. Moments after watching them pull out of the driveway, I'm in the closet with a shoebox in my hand. I reach inside and thank God out loud as my fingers find the precious sock-wrapped pill bottle. Quickly, I tiptoe into the kitchen for the vodka in the freezer. I empty three pills into my palm and my ears start ringing like I've been slapped across the face.

Only three?

The familiar blanket of fog rolls in, preventing me from recalling the events of last weekend. I fight to retrieve the first memory, and my mind hits a dead end. I feel a scream rising from my chest.

HOW CAN I ONLY HAVE THREE LEFT?????

My throat is so dry that it's hard to swallow the three pills, even with the gulp of vodka. Pushing my hand into the fleshy part of my chest to calm my fluttering heart, I can picture my adrenal glands pumping epinephrine into my system at full speed.

Ffft Ffft Ffft Ffft

Floating above my body, I watch it sprint back to my closet and open another shoebox, then another. I hear the sound of my panting as I stuff my fingers into the toes of each pair over and over. Soon the closet is littered with open shoeboxes and shoes.

No extra stash.

My knees seem to be missing their ligaments as I wobble into the bathroom. I open the medicine cabinet, grab three Benadryl, and wash them down with more vodka.

Oh, please God, let me feel something. Please, please, please.

Suddenly my legs give way, and I sink to the floor with a thud. The grout between the cold quarter-size porcelain floor tiles beneath me feels smooth under my fingertips. I claw at the tile pieces until my skin starts to separate from my nail beds.

A sob starts to form in my throat then disappears. It's dark in the bathroom, but I can see my silhouette in the full-length mirror.

Another sob evaporates as I push myself off the floor.

It's time to give up.

But then I'll have to call him and tell him how bad it is. And if I tell him, it's over. He'll send me to rehab. He'll change the locks. He'll tell everyone that I'm an addict. He'll get full custody of the boys.

It might just be easier to die.

A tear pushes through the numb and falls on my collarbone. I crawl my way into the bedroom on my wobbly knees. I pass the shameful closet scattered with shoeboxes and tissue paper and collapse into a heap next to my bedpost.

"Please."

At that moment, a slow fade of heat begins rising past my ears and spreading through my head. My eyelids soften, and I feel the corners of my lips curving up ever so slightly.

The pills are working.

Finally, I can taste that wonderful chalk of the Ambien in the back of my throat. I raise my eyes to the ceiling.

"Thank you, God. Thank you, Ambien."

Being high—really high—is like being completely submerged in viscous fluid. Every movement is slow-motion wondrousness, and every sound is magnified like in a giant echo chamber. The bedside clock ticking above me is a fetal heartbeat ultrasound on subwoofers.

Boom-boom. Boom-boom. Boom-boom.

I've rammed my elbow hard against the bedpost, but I don't feel it now. The floor is made of sponge, the bed a cloud of cotton beckoning me to sink into it. I reach for it twice, but it fades like a mirage, and I misjudge the distance, falling on my face the second time I try. I burst into laughter as I roll onto my back, wiping traces of blood and saliva off my lower lip.

Scared to lose my buzz, I slide under the covers as quickly as I can. The nightstand clock looks blurry, like it's got Vaseline rubbed all over it.

Eight fifteen p.m.

My pillow.

Nine ten p.m.

My eyes pop open. It's pitch-black.

For a moment, I don't know where I am, I don't even know if it's still the same night. I stop breathing and strain to listen to the house, but all I can hear are the hum of the crickets outside.

Did the kids come home with the neighbors? We didn't do our bedtime routine! Should I see if they're okay? No, it's got to be almost morning. I should head back to Studio City and get four pills from the stash before they wake up. Then I'll be all straightened out, I'll be a more fun mom today. Maybe I'll take them to Coogie's for pancakes when they wake up . . .

Suddenly I feel sick to my stomach. The fabric of my sweatpants feels cold and heavy.

What the . . . ?

I peel the duvet away from my legs and the harsh smell of ammonia wafts up and smacks me in the nose.

I peed the fucking bed.

As if on cue, the air-conditioning clicks on, and icy air blows cold over my wet thighs. Knitting needles pierce the tender area behind my eyes, and I place my right hand flat against the mattress beneath me. It makes a squishing sound as I press it.

Oh my God.

I look over at the clock.

Fuck me. I've only been asleep for an hour??

Just then a cannon booms and rocks the windows, lighting up the walls. I shriek and hunch forward, instinctively shielding my head from whatever is about to fly through the glass. Suddenly the sky is resplendent with blue and white streaks of light.

Fireworks.

Oh my God. July fucking fourth. Those last for what, twenty minutes? They'll probably be home soon.

I fly out of bed and peel off my wet sweatpants and underwear, leaving them in a heap next to the bed. I wash myself quickly with some hand soap and cold water and then slip on clean underwear and pajama bottoms over my damp skin. The dark floorboards are freezing under my bare feet as I pace around the bedroom. Shaking my head to clear some of the Ambien-vodka-Benadryl fog, I try to think of what to do next.

Sheets!

Sheets, sheets, sheets.

I run to the linen closet and pull a pile of sweet-smelling, freshly ironed bedsheets from the shelf. Another boom causes me to drop the pile beside the bed. I leave it where it is and start pulling the wet sheets off with trembling hands.

Shit! Shit. Shit.

I never felt more like crying in my life but now the numb is back. After what feels like hours, I have clumsily remade the bed and stuffed the wet sheets and mattress pad into the bottom of the kids' hamper. I pace again while trying to figure out how to get high again before the boys get back.

I can't let them see me like this.

I should drive back to Studio City right now. It would only take about half an hour at this time of night. I'll just call the neighbors and ask them to keep the boys for a while. I'll tell them I'm just running to the store.

Where are my keys?

I miss twice while trying to slip an Ugg boot over my icy foot. I'm shaking uncontrollably now, both from the cold and fear of the pain of withdrawal.

Where are my keys?!

A clicking sound from the front porch startles me. I freeze, one hand on my purse, the other clutching my BlackBerry.

"Mommy!" A voice floats in from outside.

I hear a key in the lock and my heart sinks.

That's right, I gave them my keys, so they wouldn't have to ring the doorbell when they came back.

The front door swings open, and I hear two pairs of boys' sneakered feet come bursting into the hallway.

"Mommy!"

"Laura, we're home," the neighbor calls.

I put my purse down and let my BlackBerry fall onto the bed.

"I'm here." My voice sounds like I'm five years old. I clear my throat and take a step toward the bedroom door, fixing what I hope is a smile on my face.

"I'm here."

CHAPTER NINE

Confession

July 5

"Hey Mom, it's me, Laura."

I've been quietly crying ever since we got back from Malibu this morning.

Late last night after the kids finally fell asleep in my bed, I knelt at the foot of it and pressed my forehead into my clasped hands. I could see the boys breathing, and hear their soft sleep noises, feel the air moist with their sweat.

"Laura?" I can hear her trying to quiet the alarm in her voice. "What's wrong?"

"Um, Mom. I'm not doing too well."

"What's going on?"

"I think, I . . ." I stop, unable to finish the sentence.

"Confessing" to Nancy that I need the Ambien for sleep is one thing. Telling my mom that I can't stop taking it is another. I'll be admitting OUT LOUD for the first time that I'm an addict. That I've failed as a mother.

"Laura?"

The phone is hurting the skin on the side of my face, like the metal contains some type of corrosive. I pull a corner of the sheet up and place it between my face and the phone. Turning away from Jacob, who has now fallen asleep. Earlier, from inside the toilet closet, I'd called a place in Arizona, whose website said they offered private rooms. My tears kept steaming up my reading glasses as I pored over their site, checking for any sign that they would try to keep me there against my will, or refuse me drugs while I detoxed. But everything I read seemed very gentle and reassuring. Also, it was far enough away so that I wouldn't run into anyone I knew. No one could ever know I'd gone to treatment. I would make up necessary excuses for my absence. But right now I needed my mommy.

Am I really going to do this?

"I think I need help," I blurt. My whisper sounds like the hiss a deflating balloon makes.

"Talk to me . . ."

I swallow hard and grit my teeth.

Say it.

"I need to go somewhere to get off this Ambien. And before you ask any questions, I just need to know that you'll be around to help with the boys when I'm gone."

"Gone?"

"Poor choice of words, Mom." I feel a smile forming and marvel that I'm able to find the humor in anything. "I meant away."

"Oh, I see. I mean, yes, of course, Laura, whatever you need, but . . ."

My jaw relaxes and a fresh flood of tears soaks my pillow.

"When are you going? Where are you going? Are you okay?"

"I don't know. It's July fourth weekend so no one's answering. I've decided on this place called The Meadows in Arizona. I'll call again first thing Monday. But I just needed to know that you'll be here."

"Do you need me to help with the calls?"

I start to sob now so I muffle the sounds by stuffing my face in the pillow. My mom is a great respecter of privacy, I knew she wouldn't ask me a ton of questions. She listens quietly until I catch my breath.

"I don't think so, Mommy. I think I need to do this myself. But I'm ready. I need to put some distance between me and these pills."

"Oh sweetheart," she says. I can hear the tears in her voice. "So, this is a rehab then, not a hospital?"

"Yup."

"I'll be here," she says. "I've been waiting for this call, Laura. I'm ready."

She's been waiting.

Oh God. My poor mom, watching me slowly kill myself, wobbling around, passing out, shutting her out. I never even thought about what this must be doing to her. I fucking hate addiction.

I'll call them again on Monday, and thank God I get one of my refills the next day. I'll need just enough to get myself to treatment. One last spectacular run, in the vein of a last meal. This needs to be as painless as possible because I'm absolutely terrified of the pain. Maybe more scared of it than I've ever been of anything before. So just as soon as they can take me, I'll go. I've got to make it happen while I have the nerve.

The clock is ticking.

—

"Hey, thanks for seeing me on such short notice, I have something I need to talk to you about."

"And baby, I have something to tell *you*!" Nancy is beaming as she jumps up and grabs my shoulders, steering me toward the small sofa in her office.

"The forensic accountant just sent over his report, and they did good. Really good. Look!"

Nancy winks at me as she springs over to her desk and grabs a tome in a clear binder, at least three hundred pages. I know she's moving at her typical high-speed pace, but through my Ambien haze it looks like she's teleporting from place to place. One minute she's behind her desk, and nanoseconds later, she's sitting next to me on the sofa, like one of those baby-doll creatures from a horror film.

I fiddle with the loose threads at the bottom of my denim miniskirt. I'm seven days away from heading to treatment and in full catastrophic withdrawal. But "Talk to Nancy" is the next item on the pretreatment checklist I've made for myself, and I need to cross it off.

"Nancy," I can hear the hysteria in my voice, and I close my eyes to try and settle down a bit.

I just fuckin' need to get this out.

"Nancy, I really need to go first."

I watch for a second as Nancy works to compose herself. She reminds me of a little kid, impatient to play with a new toy, who has been told she has to wait her turn. Having her full attention is almost worse though, as her eyes are scanning back and forth over my face like a klieg light.

"What's going on?" she says finally. I can almost see the chess match going on in her head, trying to predict what category of bomb I'm about to drop on her and exactly how much collateral damage she'll need to repair.

"Remember the sleeping pills we talked about a couple of months ago?"

"Yes." Her voice scales up to a falsetto.

"I need help getting off them. And I'm going to get it one week from today. I leave next Monday."

"Wait, what? What do you mean you need help getting off sleeping pills? What kind of help?"

"I don't know if I can explain it right, but over these last few months, I've become addicted. Pretty bad. And I'm afraid to stop on my own."

"Is he threatening you in some way? Is he making you do this?"

What?

"No, he, he doesn't know yet."

"So what are you telling me? That you're voluntarily going to rehab in the middle of your divorce?!"

I look down and allow a few tears to fall on my bare thighs.

I'm in hell.

"Yes."

"Rehab, Laura? You realize that the timing could not be worse. You know this is going to kill us. Now you'll look more like an addict than a doting wife and mother.

Does one necessarily have to exclude the other?

"He'll go for everything, Laura. And he'll win."

She's up now and whirling around the room like a dervish. I keep my eyes downcast while she rants.

"We had him, Laura. Look at me! We had him."

She's staring me down while holding the forensics binder above her head like Charlton Heston in *The Ten Commandments*. I wait for lightning to strike and part her office in half like the Red Sea.

"You go to rehab and we don't have him anymore."

"Yeah, I'm sorry. But, uh, also there's something else."

"What?!" She's yelling at me. I feel my head disappearing into my shoulders.

"I, uh, he took pictures of the pills, my medicine cabinet, and some instructions from the doctors."

"*What???* When?"

Right before I hired you.

"A couple of months ago."

"And you're just telling me now?"

"Sorry, I was scared."

"Of telling me?"

"I think of saying it out loud."

I'm crying now.

"I'm sorry, Nancy. I wasn't ready. I wasn't ready to stop yet."

Nancy goes to her desk and grabs her notepad and a pen.

"How many pictures? What exactly were they of?"

I shake my head. "I don't know, ten or twelve. I was sneaking a look at his camera, so it was really fast. But he took pictures of all my meds, even the ones like birth control and Advil."

"And he never said anything about them?"

"No."

"And as far as you know, he doesn't know that you've seen them?"

"As far as I know."

"Well, that does it," she says, shaking her head dramatically. "You're really going to need to wait. If he thinks you're an addict, then he could just be waiting for you to go away before he takes action against you."

"Wait? For how long?"

"Just let me get you divorced, and then you can go take an extended vacation at some medical spa or something. I can find you the best place, very discreet, no one will know."

Molten shame rises through my core like lava, and I wish that it would render me dead like the victims of Pompeii—or maybe just unconscious. Then I could be removed from her office in the fetal position, and we'd never have to speak of this again.

"I'm sorry," I whisper. "But I can't wait, I have a reservation. I have to go next week."

She's sitting on her haunches now in front of me like a raccoon. I take a moment to marvel at how agile she is.

"Laura, real talk? Forget the forensics."

She dramatically tosses the report on the floor next to her desk. The thud sounds like a gunshot and I flinch, stifling a shriek.

"You can't fight for your kids from rehab, you need to be here. I'm telling you this for your own good. You go to rehab and you will lose."

I look up at her and see that her eyes have softened.

The shark is trying to summon its humanity.

"Real talk? Nancy, if I don't go, I think I might actually die. And that's worse than losing custody of my kids. That means they'd have to bury their mother."

Our eyes are locked in a staring contest. I know that I can't break first or she will have won. Her office, normally buzzing like a beehive, is suddenly dead silent. I roll and unroll a used tissue between my fingers and hold her gaze, not bothering to wipe away the tears that are streaming down my face.

Finally, I see her shoulders drop.

"Okay," she says, standing and throwing her arms up in defeat and walking back to her desk.

"Let's get to work and come up with a plan. Maybe if you do well there and get out early this could still work in our favor. Noel! Get in here, I need you."

She turns her attention back to me.

"Where did you say you were going and how long will you be there?"

I hadn't said.

"Thirty days I guess," I say. They really won't commit to a discharge date. And I'm going to The Meadows," I say, sitting down in the chair opposite her.

She's staring blankly back at me, a hand on her phone.

"It's in Arizona," I say. "Someplace called Wickenburg. I wanted to go somewhere I'd be sure not to run into anyone I know, and they promised to give me a private room."

"Surely they don't keep mothers the whole time when they have young kids to take care of," she mumbles, making a note on her legal pad. Noel hustles in then, and Nancy starts rattling off instructions.

"Call Margie and ask her about her client who went to treatment for gambling. I want to know what she was up against."

Noel glances up at me, like *Guuurrrlll, what did YOU do???* then looks quickly back at Nancy.

Nancy's talking to me now.

"Her husband was a real prick. He did everything but brand her with a scarlet G when he found out where their money was going."

In less than a minute the beehive was buzzing again, and it seems like they've both forgotten that I'm there. And even though I feel as if a slight weight has been lifted, I can't shake feeling like a bad kid who's being sent to the principal's office.

―

He's stopping home to see the boys before he heads out to a dinner with the star of his next movie. No one knows I'm going to The Meadows in six days except Nancy and my parents. It's hard to describe what it's like to be this fucked up and yet have something this important to do. He and I haven't had an actual conversation in months, and I really hate that I need him now. I'd love to just disappear to one of those rapid detox places for a weekend and come back all cured without ever admitting I'm an addict. I am loath to give him the satisfaction of confirming his suspicions about me. I'm afraid that if we talk I won't come off as sincere. I think he'll know intuitively that I'm not really done. He'll see right through me and know that I'm harboring this fantasy that after rehab I'll be able to get high again without all those pesky consequences.

A hope that I am determined to keep alive.

But the alarm in my head is ringing louder every day—"You're going to lose your kids," it says. "Get your ass to rehab before this gets any worse."

Jesus take the wheel.

He's been around more than usual the last few days, and I've had plenty of opportunities to tell him, but I keep coming up with excuses. I gathered myself up to do it twice this week but chickened out each time we were in the same room.

But this time I'd locked myself in by making an appointment with him. When I called him at work to ask if we could talk, he told me he had some time before his dinner. I asked him to meet me in our bedroom at six.

It's five forty-five. I have fifteen minutes to prepare.

"I need to talk to you," I say to my image in the closet mirror. "I'm taking too many sleeping pills, and I've decided to go to treatment."

"I need to let you know that I'm going to treatment next week. I'm sorry, I know it's bad timing, but it has to be now."

"I need to talk to you. I think I've become physically dependent on Ambien. I figure I'd better go to treatment to wean off—just to be safe."

Better.

"I need to talk to you . . ."

"What's going on?"

He's early.

He's behind me in the closet. The blood drains from my head so fast that I have to reach for something to hold on to. Last time we said more than two words to each other it was in this closet. He was asking me about the pharmacy receipt he'd found in my car, and I was trying to buy time, hoping I could come up with something clever. But I could feel that my words were coming out slower than they should have. Ambien brain fog strikes again. Finally, he just looked at me like I'd stolen something and then walked away. I sank to the floor and tried to cry but couldn't. The Ambien had dried me up inside.

No saliva, no mucus, no tears.

"You all right?"

His eyes don't look as accusing as they did last time; in fact, he looks almost concerned. I try to focus on trying to look confident, but my knees start to give out.

"Yes," I lie, plopping down hard on the bench in my closet.

He raises his eyebrows and moves toward me.

"Really?"

"Um, no, actually, I'm not all right. Can you sit? I need to talk to you."

"What's going on?"

I'm confused by the energy he's giving me.

For the first time in a long time, I don't see my mortal enemy next to me. Instead, I see the man I married almost twelve years ago. The man who proposed to me on one knee in the middle of a crowded restaurant and gave me the wedding of my dreams. Suddenly, instead of the husband I could never please, he is that wicked-smart, ambitious B-boy I fell in love with. All at once, this conversation feels so surreal and unnecessary.

Maybe things aren't so bad. Maybe I don't need to tell him. Maybe I don't have to go to treatment. Maybe I can stop on my own. Maybe we don't even have to get divorced.

This wasn't the way this was supposed to go.

Tears are streaming down my face, and I'm terrified to speak, but somehow, something else takes over.

"I'm sorry it's terrible timing," I hear myself say. "I've decided to go to treatment for the Ambien."

He holds my gaze and covers my icy, trembling hands with his warm one.

"Hey, hey," he says gently. "Don't worry about the timing. I think it's a really good idea."

I search his face now for some sign of vindication or surprise but there is only compassion.

That was too easy.

Has he been waiting for this moment? Why is he being so kind? He's totally going to use this against me, right? I should have asked Nancy precisely how to tell him I was going. What if I say the wrong thing and he takes the kids like in that CSI *episode? What if he smiles in my face now and then once I've left, he changes the locks, files for sole custody, and secures our bank accounts? She'll be so mad at me. I'll be so mad at me.*

"I'll take care of everything, okay?" he says. "You just get better; our boys need you."

I'll bet you'll take care of everything. Oh my God, this was a huge mistake.

"It's going to be okay," he says.

But I'm already almost out of pills, and I'm fucking out of excuses.

I'm out of options.

I don't remember much else after that. He left for a moment to grab tissues for me. I sobbed and sobbed into my hands, until he came back a few seconds later. He put his arm around my shoulders and leaned his head against mine while I cried. I showed him what I printed out from The Meadows' website. He used the wall phone in my closet to make the arrangements to take me there on a private jet.

"Monday, right? The fourteenth, right?" he said, covering the phone. "What time do you need to check in?"

In a snap, it feels all kinds of wrong to be discussing this with him. I'm mortified to hear my check-in date coming out of his mouth.

I look around my closet, the rows of color-coded coats and jackets, my purse cabinet, my hat shelves, my custom-built shoe racks, and my heart starts to race. My eyes land on my green and black Gucci fur coat. Suddenly I'm swept back to the moment he gave it to me. My thirty-fifth birthday, we were on our way out to Chateau Marmont, where ten of us would be celebrating at dinner. I was wearing a slinky black dress with a thigh-high slit, and he asked me if I thought I was going to be cold. I laughed and said that the champagne would keep me warm and then he told me to close my eyes and hold out my arms. It was the most beautiful thing I'd ever seen. I screamed and hopped around while he held it out for me to try on. I had never felt anything as soft as that coat. I felt like a million bucks in it and wondered vaguely if that was close to what it cost. If he really knew who I was he would never have given me that coat, or married me, never trusted me to be the mother of his children.

I glance over to my right and realize that my Filofax is sitting beside me, and I slyly tuck it behind me, leaning back so it's out of sight.

Why did I do that? It's over. He already knows.

Jordan runs in then, shooting me back to the present, a furious Jacob close at his heels, swinging an old rubber Bob the Builder hammer toward his head.

Jordan stops short and searches my face.

"What's wrong, Mommy?" he asks, looking from me to his dad.

This can't be happening.

"Nothing, sweetie, I'm fine," I say quickly, exhaling and wiping my face.

"See?" I smile weakly and attempt to make a silly face.

He removes his arm from around me and stands up, grabbing the hammer out of Jacob's hand.

"Mommy's fine," he echoes.

"We were just talking about a sad story, that's all. Now, Jordan, how about you tell me what you did to your brother to make him so mad?"

"What's the sad story?" says Jordan stubbornly, shaking his dad's hand off his shoulder and starting back toward me.

My heart.

As their voices disappear down the hallway, I turn back to my mirror.

It's official. I'm a Black drug addict mother going to treatment.

I'm a cliché like a motherfucker.

CHAPTER TEN

Bar Rescue

Now that he knows, I really have to get down to business. I want us to stay the way we were in the closet that night. Me, his pitiful but not horrible soon-to-be ex-wife and him, the compassionate, sympathetic soon-to-be ex-husband. But if I'm to remain worthy of his sympathy, I need to do my best to hide the wreckage of my present. If I'd been thinking straight, perhaps I would have made things whole before I told him, because now once again the clock is ticking.

In other words, I've got some cleaning up to do.

Over the last few months or so, I've run through all the booze in my closet faster than I can restock it. A fact that forces me to sneak downstairs after everyone is asleep, squat behind the wet bar, and guzzle as much as I can from a bottle that I hope he won't miss too much. For optimum effectiveness, I have to time it just right so that I'm chugging the bottle just as the Ambien hits my system. Then I have just under a minute to get back upstairs before I'm too loaded to navigate the upstairs hallway without slamming into the walls or passing out on the floor. And if I drink too much from any one bottle, I have to make sure I have enough time to fill it with water from the bar sink tap (and sometimes a little food coloring). The other fucked-up thing is that I've found that the combination of the drugs, booze, and fear power-washes my consciousness clean, so I have to keep a cheat sheet of the diluted bottles in my trusty Filofax. My notes have become my most precious possession, my notes are an answer key. My notes are my memory.

> GG 1 up L = Grey Goose, one inch above the label
> 2 fing Pat = Patrón Tequila, two fingers up from the bottom
> RF = refilled

It's important to keep track of the refilled bottles as well, so HE doesn't pour himself a vodka martini one day and realize it's just water and vermouth. I try to keep the key simple, because sometimes thanks to the Ambien brain fog, I can't break the code.

I need to make the bar whole again before I even think about going to rehab. If he were to ever find out that I've basically drained the whole thing over these last few months, he'll go for sole custody for sure. It's one thing for your wife to have a legitimate pill problem, but totally another for her to be a boozer too. I mean, I could try explaining to him that I hate alcohol. That I only drink it because my tolerance is so off the charts, the Ambien won't work without it. I never drink when I'm out of Ambien, even when I'm desperate. I don't particularly care for the taste, it's messy, people can smell it, and on its own, it just serves to make me feel dull, headachy, and sick to my stomach.

I think that pills are much more civilized. No odor, and easy to conceal.

But there's no way he'd let me come back to the boys if he finds the bar empty.

The front gate rings, and I jump up quickly and turn down *Zoey 101*. The boys are lying on their stomachs on the carpet in my bedroom watching and eating grilled cheese sandwiches. I stub my toe in my rush to pick up the wall phone by the security monitor.

"Yes?"

"Vendome Liquors."

"Yes, yes, come in." I force my shoulders down and exhale.

Be cool, Laura.

I intercept Maria as she is striding toward the front door.

"Hey, I got this. Can you go and sit with the boys till I'm done, please?"

She stands there for a moment eyeing the door warily, like she's torn. I suspect my husband has asked her to report back to him on the goings-on in the house. Every time I turn around these last few weeks, she's right there, and it's starting to piss me off.

After I see her disappear into my bedroom, I crack the front door open and watch Archer pulling up in the van. Besides Jerry, my beloved pharmacy delivery guy, Archer is my main man. Jerry is a kid, maybe nineteen or twenty. Always eager to please me, he even broke company policy and gave me his cell number a couple of months ago so I could check in with him directly about my refills.

But Archer is different. He's older, tall, and wiry, with ebony skin. I usually have a whole silly teasing thing going on with both of them, but I know I have to up my flirt game today, because I need to ensure Archer's discretion in order to pull this off.

I'm not wearing a bra (intentionally) and I've chosen a T-shirt that accentuates my boobs nicely. My jeans are good too, tight and high-waisted.

"Hey there," I call out seductively.

The very idea of physical contact with anyone other than my kids makes my stomach wrench up sharply and yet, I need to make this man think he has a chance. Fighting the impulse to push his Snoop Dogg–looking ass back in the truck and run back upstairs, I stand in the doorway grinning, all teeth and tits.

Archer smiles widely when he sees me, exposing his gold grill. I brace myself for what's in front of me.

Stick to the plan.

The large cardboard box he's holding is heavy. I can tell by the way he keeps using his knee to push it up toward his chest. He motions behind him toward a short white guy with a long blond ponytail exiting the Vendome van.

"Hey there, Mrs. R, Ryan's got the rest of it."

"Great, great. Come on in."

I take a deep breath and coach myself to stay put, just beside the doorjamb, so that Archer's left arm has to brush across my breasts when he passes me.

Ugh.

Ryan has used too much cologne, and I'm forced to switch to mouth breathing as I follow them in. I worry that he's going to stink up the family room, which could raise some questions about who's been in the house. I motion the guys over to the bar and walk across the room to open a window before settling into the work at hand.

"We need to be done by five, so we don't have too much time," I say, sitting down cross-legged on the floor behind the bar.

"We're at your service." Archer's voice is syrup on pancakes as he sits down beside me.

"Here's how we'll do it, okay?" I say, clearing my throat.

"I'll call out the brand I need, you pass me the bottle, then I'll pass you the empty."

"Sounds good."

My self-loathing mixes with the grit of the Ambien half I took upstairs and makes me gag. I swallow hard and go to work, wishing I had something to drink.

Archer and I then begin something of a call-and-response.

"Bombay Sapphire, liter," I say.

"Yo!"

"Johnnie Walker, Black and Red Labels, two each please."

"Two Johnnies!" he stage-whispers.

"Baileys Irish Cream . . ."

Baileys is one of the few drinks I like, because it tastes like coffee ice cream (which I love). My mouth waters a little as I think about pouring it over ice, I can practically taste its creaminess on the sides of my tongue.

I clench my teeth.

Ten minutes in, I start to feel my throat relax a little. There's a certain satisfaction in watching the bar filling back up. But I know that I can't leave a full bar of unopened bottles, that's as much of a giveaway as if I left all the bottles empty. I'm going to have to do some extra bottle doctoring after the guys leave.

"Hey, this one's full," says Archer. "Are you sure you want us to take it?" He's holding a stupidly large bottle of Grey Goose out toward me, and I feel my face flush.

"Yes," I say. "It's only water."

Archer doesn't move.

"It's um, ahem, it's just a decoy bottle. We used it for a scene or something. They filmed something here a few weeks ago."

Lie.

Archer knits his brows as though he's multiplying fractions and then a look of understanding spreads over his face. He smiles and nods to Ryan like it's a totally normal thing to have a magnum decoy bottle of vodka in one's bar.

Fifteen minutes later the entire bar has been replenished, and the empties and decoys are boxed up and on their way out the door. Outside, I stuff three one-hundred-dollar bills into Archer's front pants pocket, then remove my hand slowly while maintaining eye contact with him. His breath starts to come heavier and smells of clove cigarettes.

"Thank you, Archer," I say, smiling. "You know I appreciate you and your discretion."

"I got you, Laura," he says, his voice throaty. I'm startled by him using my first name and concentrate on not looking like my skin is crawling. I raise my eyebrows slightly as I step away from the van and chew lightly on my lower lip alluringly.

"They'll send an invoice later on."

What a rookie mistake that would have been: an invoice for $1,100 worth of booze showing up. Of course, I'd already paid for it with my secret debit card.

"It's been taken care of," I grin. "See you soon, okay?"

"Absolutely."

Archer's eyes are fastened on mine now. I giggle like a twelve-year-old as I step back onto my stoop. I'm afraid if I look down I might see a bulge in his pants, so I look up at the sky like I'm trying to tell the time by the sun.

"Well, better get back in," I say after a moment, holding up my hand to block out the brightness. He licks his lips at me before slamming his van door.

This connection is officially burnt.

I watch the gate close behind the van and feel like a fire alarm has just been pulled in my head. I shut my eyes against the twin screeches of shame and withdrawal tearing through my body.

That half an Ambien is all I've had since this morning. I have the other half in my jeans pocket, but I'll need something to wash it down with. My mind goes to the Baileys, but my Filofax note said that the bottle was basically full, so I can't really mess with it.

I close the front door with quivering hands and look upstairs to make sure Maria's not peeking her Cabbage Patch doll–looking head out the bedroom doors, but the coast is clear. I know I have about fifteen minutes to siphon the right amounts off certain bottles, so they look the way they did before I started my midnight bar raids, but I'll need something to steady my nerves first.

Before I start, I grab a coffee cup and a punch bowl from the kitchen and sit down cross-legged behind the bar again.

I take the Ambien out of my jeans pocket and pop it in my mouth. Then I fill the coffee cup with Amaretto and suck down its sweet, sticky goodness as fast as I can. The heat of the liqueur hits my stomach and acts like a disinfectant, dispelling some of the shame that has been festering there.

I crack the gin and pour half into the punch bowl. The Christmassy/mouthwashy smell hits me in the face like a smack.

I hate gin; it's so annoying to have to drink it when I run out of vodka.

The Johnnie Walker Red Label is next. My punch bowl looks like a science experiment as the cloudy brown fluid cuts through the clear gin and settles to the bottom. Next up is a 375 mL bottle of Belvedere. I trace my fingers lovingly over the frosted branches before pouring half into the punch bowl. I finish the last one just as I hear the rumble of feet on the back staircase. As quick as I can, I jump up and dump the bowl of booze down the bar sink, pushing my coffee cup out of sight behind the bar.

"Mommy, we're going on the trampoline," says Jacob.

"What's that smell?" asks Jordan, crinkling his nose. "Are you wearing perfume, Mom?"

Since I've made the decision to go to treatment, I shouldn't want to get high anymore, right? If anyone were watching me, they'd be all, "What the hell is she doing? Didn't she say she was ready to stop?"

But that's the nifty thing about addiction, want has nothing to do with it. There is no such thing as having willpower or being "strong." Being an addict is like being strapped into a roller coaster. Maybe you didn't realize how scary it was and you've decided "No thanks, I'd like to get off before the big drop, please."

But it's too late.

You can try and pry the bar up on your own, you can scream at the top of your lungs, but you're locked in, and you can't get off until the ride is over.

The reason I have to go to treatment is that I have a body that can no longer process Ambien and a brain that thinks it can't live without it. If I could stop on my own, I wouldn't go.

So I have to go to treatment.

But this also means that I will be in for the most painful and agonizing withdrawal of my life. Oh, I'm sure they'll medicate me enough to keep me from having more seizures, but fuck that. Take away my Ambien and all the blood vessels in my head will explode, my anxiety will go through the roof, and I'll never EVER be able to sleep.

I'm going to need to sneak in some drugs.

While watching my new favorite show, *Celebrity Rehab*, I'd taken notes when Dr. Drew Pinsky listed shocking ways drugs are smuggled into rehab. Today I ransacked my office, rummaging through stuff until I found them.

1. In the bodies of dead birds (thrown over fences)
2. Under postage stamps (on postcards sent to patients)
3. Vaginally

Hmm . . .

Dead bird? Disgusting.

Stamps? Not even sure how that works. Grind them into a paste and then coat the back of the stamp with it? And then what? Send it to myself?

Vaginally?

I'd have to insert some kind of waterproof pill holder inside me. Something smooth enough to fit without being uncomfortable, but roomy enough to fold all the pills I'm planning to bring.

I check on the boys, who are watching *SpongeBob* in the family room, and scurry upstairs to open a box of tampons.

Okay, plastic applicator, that's good. But it's not sealed. If I put pills in here they'll absorb all my coochie moisture and melt.

I pick the cotton out of the tampon and consider how I'd stuff the pills inside the applicator and then insert it into me without plunging the cotton.

But it's still not sealed, the moisture can still get to the pills.

Shit.

There's got to be a way.

I head over to my office and double-check the list of approved items you can bring to The Meadows on my computer:

Undergarments

Jeans

Comfortable shirts and pants and knee-length pants (no shorts)

Comfortable shoes

Robe

Motivational books

One-piece bathing suits

Empty notebook or journal, personal stationery, stamps, pens,
    $200 in cash

Personal hygiene items (toothpaste, tampons, soap, shampoo,
    deodorant)

Pillow

Pillow? That could be something.

But I'm sure they uncase the pillow and inspect it for tampering, plus the pages of any book you bring. I'm sure pockets are gone through and socks unfolded.

It's gotta be the tampons.

I'm still holding an unwrapped tampon, so I inspect it from different angles.

Let's see, I'd have to have it inside me on the flight and I won't be able to remove it until I'm alone in rehab, which could be hours later, maybe four or five.

Fuck.

I need to be able to put the pills inside the tampon, and then I need to put the tampon inside me without them melting.

Or do I?

I rush back upstairs and grab the tampon box again.

What happens if I just bring this whole thing?

They might look over the box, but surely they won't inspect each individual tampon, right?

Invigorated by the possibilities, I quietly jog over to the art closet and grab an X-ACTO knife and a glue stick.

What if I cut a small slit in the bottom of each individual wrapper, put pills inside, and then reseal it, ever so neatly with the glue? Who would think that anyone would go that far to smuggle in pills? I mean who would do something like that?

I lay the tampon down on my desk and slit the bottom carefully with the knife on the seam.

Okay.

I take three small-head pushpins from my desk and place them carefully inside the wrapper, then seal it back with the glue stick.

My fingers are sticky from the glue as I fan it back and forth, blowing on it to hurry the drying process.

"Mom!"

That's Jordan.

I freeze, listening for his steps on the stairs.

"Mom, can we watch *Avatar?*"

"Go ahead," I call. "I'll be right down."

His footsteps disappear back down the stairs. Holding my breath, I pull another tampon out of the box and lay it next to the altered one.

They're so close, I have to squeeze one to be sure and get stuck with one of the pins. Oh my God, it's going to work. I'm going to be okay.

Excitement barrels its way from my toes to my head, setting my scalp on fire.

"Fuck yeah," I whisper.

Now for the booze.

I need the booze because without it the Ambien is practically useless. But how am I going to smuggle booze into rehab?

By the time I put the kids to bed, I was losing my mind trying to figure out this last piece of the puzzle. After they fell asleep I jumped out of bed and paced around the dark bedroom, my bare heels chafing against the carpet as I walked.

In less than thirty hours we're getting on that plane. Pills in tampons were one thing, but I can't very well waltz into rehab with a flask or a vodka-filled travel cup.

I sneak down the hall to my office to look at the list of approved items again.

Here! Mouthwash and bottled water are allowed if they are sealed in their original packaging.

But a regular mouthwash bottle won't give me enough booze for more than a day or two. Maybe jumbo size? But I'd still have to get it the right color with food coloring or something.

Bottled water?

I do love my Evian. I never go anywhere without it. What if I arrived with a six-pack of 330 mL bottles in my bag? Water is the right color, but if they check the seal I'm screwed.

What to do?

I scurry downstairs to the pantry and pick up a small bottle. I try to open it gently, but it doesn't budge. I crack the seal and open it, reclose it, and try to open it again.

Too easy. FUCK. They'll know.

Back in my room I grab a vodka bottle from one of my rain boots and bring it into the bathroom, dumping the Evian in the sink and refilling it with the vodka.

So far so good.

I twist the cap on as tight as I can, but it still comes off too easily when I twist it. Once more, I can see the separation of the cap from the bottle.

Shit.

It would be great if I could glue-stick it shut like the tampons.

Glue-stick it shut like the tampons . . .

WAIT A MINUTE!

I set the bottle down and sneak down the dimly lit hallway past the guest room, where he's sleeping, back to the art closet. I use a flashlight to search quietly through the stacks of clear organizer containers until I find one with the glue gun.

"Yeah, baby!" I whisper.

I wrap the long, loose cord around the device so that it doesn't dangle while I run, and quickly head back to the bathroom, plugging it in next to the sink. The two minutes I have to wait for it to heat are agonizing. I keep checking the gun for warmth, listening for the boys, and listening for him, but the house is still.

Ready.

One simple squeeze of the trigger and a perfect, clear line of glue enters the space between the cap and threads of blue plastic on the neck. I hold my breath as I slowly turn the bottle in a circle, sealing it all the way around.

The glue can take hours to dry, so I hide the vodka and Evian bottle behind the towels under the sink, and tiptoe back to bed with my heart beating out of my chest.

This has to work.

As soon as it's light out the next morning I dash to the bathroom and pull out the bottle. I look at it first and momentarily experience the same wave of confusion I did with the tampons the previous day.

Is this the doctored bottle or did I put an unopened bottle back here by mistake?

It looked factory sealed . . . almost.

On closer inspection, I can see a small drip of glue below the line and the seal on one side is slightly more evenly distributed.

I can do better.

But when I grab the top and turn, it won't budge until I give it a really firm tug—and then it snaps open, filling my nose with the smell of rubbing alcohol.

Done.

PART TWO

———

The Meadows

CHAPTER ELEVEN

Checking In

've completely blocked out saying goodbye to my kids.

I do remember agonizing over whether to bring a bathing suit before we left. I remember Jordan rushing into my closet and asking me why I was taking my pillow with me to "mommy school" (that's what we'd decided to call rehab), and why I had to go for so long. I remember telling him with a weak smile that I would be back before he knew it.

I distinctly recall placing my toiletries in a separate bag along with the Ambien-laced tampons. I know that I put my six-pack of Evian in a duffel bag underneath my shoes and my green terry-cloth Juicy Couture sundress.

I have flashes of being driven to the airport in a black SUV while sobbing into a T-shirt I'd pulled out of my luggage. I remember seeing the Raytheon sign at Van Nuys Airport and avoiding the eyes of the pilot and flight attendant while getting on the G5 he'd chartered. I have a vague watery memory of a tissue-strewn cabin floor and a bumpy landing at the Wickenburg airport. But stepping off that plane into stifling 112-degree heat and then getting in a startlingly cool Lincoln town car may be etched in my memory forever.

That's when I knew it was real.

The next thing I remember is standing in the lobby of The Meadows, soaking the admission papers with tears. I can recall him looking grim while we said goodbye and being handed a copy of the paperwork I'd signed. I remember catching the amount at the bottom of the last page he signed and being stunned to see my thirty-day stay would cost him forty thousand dollars. I remember looking over at him then with a mixture of guilt and gratitude as an older Black man came out to collect me and my bags and told me to follow him. I remember watching him until we rounded the corner and then bursting into fresh sobs.

"When they bring you over to orientation, a lady tech will give you your name tag and check out your person and make sure you didn't 'accidentally' put something in your pockets that you're not allowed to have."

His name is Clarence, and he walks with a slight limp. He explains he's usually a night tech but today he's working a double.

"But while we're waiting, let's take a look at what you brung."

He stops walking and sets my bags on a table, unzipping the suitcase right away. I see that we've entered some type of intake area.

I watch him and hold my breath as he goes through my toiletry bag. He picks up my Colgate and throws it in a small bin beside him.

"Sorry, items have to be unopened. You can get some toothpaste at the commissary here."

Damn.

"Really?" I say as though I'm astounded. "People sneak stuff in their toothpaste?"

"Oh, you'd be surprised," he says, chuckling. "People come up with all kinds of ways to bring their dope in here. You would not believe some of the ways."

I nod, wanting to continue to engage him, but am now paralyzed with fear.

He has the tampon box in his hand.

He flips through the tampons one at a time with wizened mocha fingers and then places his open hand over the top of them and turns the box upside down, shaking it hard over a cloth-covered table.

I feel myself start to get light-headed, so I will myself to breathe.

"Yeah, you wouldn't believe," he says, shaking his head. "But I understand. I was one of them once." He winks at me. "So I knows all the tricks."

Hopefully you don't know this one.

I try not to look relieved as he sets the tampon box to the side and moves on to my unopened Jam hair gel. He raises his head again though when he opens the duffel and moves my green dress aside.

"You can't bring outside drinks in here now."

He picks up my Evian six-pack and places it next to the bin with the toothpaste.

"They shoulda told you that. You can't bring this in."

Gulp.

I cover my throat with one hand as I'm positive he'll be able to see the arteries pounding in my neck.

"Oh, I thought the website said you could bring water, but only if it's in the original packaging." I try to look as innocently confused as possible. "And I know there's no sugar allowed here," I add quickly. "That's why I didn't bring soda or anything."

Don't push it, girl.

"I'll check," he says, pulling his walkie up to his face with his free hand. "Maybe you know something I don't."

He radios to someone who doesn't answer, waits for a moment, then decides to move on.

"I'll put 'em in your room with the rest of your stuff if they give me the okay. But you'd best be going to orientation now. That's the lady tech waiting over there, it's starting in a few minutes."

———

Heroin addict, drunk, sex addict, heroin addict.

A twentyish guy named Willy is sitting at the front of the room. He has asked us all to introduce ourselves by saying our first names, where we're from, and why we're here. I'm instantly resentful that we have to do any talking at all; I thought they were supposed to be orientating us. There are about eight of us here in the cool, dimly lit room. It's a stand-alone building that looks as though it might double as some sort of chapel. I'm the only Black one, there's one other girl.

"I lost custody of my kids."

"Four DUIs."

"I'm here for sex addiction."

"Eleventh time in rehab."

Oh my God.

I'm just a housewife with a pill problem. These folks are hard-core. This is a huge mistake.

"I'm from Los Angeles," I say when it's my turn. "I'm getting a divorce, and I came here because I don't want to lose my kids, but I think there's been a misunderstanding."

I say it like it's all one word.

"And your drug of choice?"

"Um, I get why everyone else is here, but I'm only here for a dependence on sleeping pills."

"Okay," he says, looking smug. "We try to encourage people to look for the similarities and not the differences."

Okay, guy in charge. You don't want to come for me today. You really don't.

"When I asked why you were here," he continues, "I meant what are you addicted to?"

Suddenly I feel a swelling rising in my chest. I close my mouth against it.

I've got to get out of here.

Standing up quickly, I look for the exit and bolt for the door. I hear a male voice calling after me, but I make a sharp left down the path and keep running. My heels are kicking up sand and gravel behind me, but suddenly I can't breathe. The air is a solid wall of heat, I've never felt anything like it. Each inhale is like sucking on the business end of a blow dryer. Tears blur my vision and suddenly I'm all disoriented, and I don't know which direction I'm supposed to go.

I can't stay here. I've got to get to the office. I've got to catch him before he leaves me in this place.

I stop at a fork in the path. There are actual tumbleweeds blowing across a field to my left. The dry air tastes like charcoal in my mouth. I head left.

My heart is beating erratically now. I wonder if this is it, how I'm going to die. Not of an overdose in bed, not choked out on vomit on my bathroom floor. But right here in the middle of this desert.

I look up and see that I am finally in front of the admin building. I gasp audibly when I enter as the cool air inside causes my lungs to contract. The office air-conditioning is ice-cold lemonade. I stand there and drink it in for a moment.

I approach the woman behind the desk. My anxiety is building at an alarming rate, and I know I'm about to explode. I want to appear calm and rational, but I can already feel rashy withdrawal toxins bubbling underneath my skin. I need to get my words out quickly before the mania sets in and I burst into flames.

"I need to speak to someone about leaving, please," I tell her.

Please. That's a good touch. Be polite. She'll see you don't belong here.

She takes a glance at my name tag without any sign of alarm.

"Okay sweetie, uh—Laura. Have a seat, and I'll git someone for ya."

I am sobbing again.

I cover my eyes with my hands. They feel like ice against my hot face. My skin feels as though it's disintegrating.

"You can go right in, honey," says the nurse.

The facility director stands up when I enter his office and motions to the seat in front of his desk. He's thirtyish and white, with brown hair parted on the side and wearing a navy button-down shirt.

I glance up at his wall clock and sit down.

Four fifteen. Shit! He's probably just getting to the airport now.

"Hi Laura, I'm Martin. I understand you've just checked in? Welcome to The Meadows."

"Yes, and sorry to waste your time, but this is a big mistake. I need to go home. I might lose my kids. You see, I'm at the end of this huge divorce. I really shouldn't have come. And I really don't even drink. I only take doctor-prescribed sleeping pills. I didn't really understand how bad off the people are who come here. I'm just not there, you understand?"

"I see."

You do?

"Oh good. So can you call my husband and tell him to hold the plane? Or better yet, if I could please have my phone, I can do it myself."

"You're detoxing," he says matter-of-factly, leaning toward me.

Shit, he's going to try and keep me here.

"I just have a little sleeping pill dependency, that's all. This is nothing, it's not so bad. I'll be okay when I get home."

"Yes, except that when you checked in earlier, you signed some documents that put you under our care. You flew here all the way from Los Angeles to get better, and you just got here. Leaving now would be very risky."

"I'm willing to take the risk," I say, biting the edge of my tongue, hoping the pain will keep me steady. I look him right in the eyes. "I know you can release me AMA."

Martin looks at me as though he doesn't understand.

"Against medical advice." I say this in the most condescendingly patient tone I can muster. Still, my voice is louder than I had hoped, so I swallow hard before speaking again. "And I'm asking you to do so now, please."

He gets up and extends his hand to me.

Oh, thank you God.

I put my hand in his to shake it, but instead, he turns my arm over and places his index finger on the inside of my wrist.

"Your heart is racing dangerously," he says. "I'd like to give you some medication to calm you down and get you comfortable."

Sneaky fucker.

"And then what?"

"Stay, just for a few days."

"Nuh-uh, no way. I can't. My kids need me."

"Look." His voice has become more urgent.

I step away and pull my arm back.

"You could have another seizure."

He knows about the seizures???

"I just can't allow you to get on a plane and possibly have a medical emergency midflight. Stay, Laura. If you still want to leave on Monday, I'll make sure someone helps you with the arrangements."

Monday? That's eons from now. I can't stay here that long.

"That's all the way next week."

"Then split the difference. Saturday. How about just staying until Saturday?"

Fuck.

I recognize the bitter, metallic taste filling my mouth. It's not just blood from the small gash I've made in my tongue, it's defeat.

"Just till Saturday," I say finally.

I'm embarrassed to be crying in front of him, but I can't help it.

"Saturday," he says, walking back behind his desk. His shoulders relax, and I notice the crucifix around his neck for the first time.

"Can I call my kids, please?"

I'm crying so hard I know it's difficult to understand me. The tissues he hands me from the box on his desk make a sound each time he pulls one out.

One, two, three. *Whoosh, whoosh, whoosh.*

"Yes, of course. After dinner, okay? You can use my office."

He walks me back out into the waiting area and has a hushed conversation with the nurse. "Hold My Hand" by Hootie & the Blowfish is playing softly on a mini boombox sitting on the nurse's desk. I catch a glimpse of myself in the mirror. My eyes are puffy and red from crying, and I have mascara circles under my eyes. Self-consciously, I try to wipe them and re-tuck my curls into the bun I'd fashioned on the plane, but I give up the moment I see that the nurse is ready for me. She motions me over and hands me a short white paper cup with three pills inside.

The blue one with an etched V in the center is a valium, but I don't recognize the other two. I check out her name tag, Eliza, the same as my best friend when I was five.

Her dark eyes are searching mine as I take the cup from her.

"Lift your tongue, please, dear."

Don't worry, lady, I'm a pill addict. I'm definitely swallowing everything you give me.

"Good girl," she says, and tells me to return at seven for another dose.

"Can I go to my room now?"

I want to see if my vodka made it there. I want to empty out my tampons and inventory my pills.

"Not just yet. Dinner's in forty minutes in the dining hall, right outside. Your room should be ready after dinner. Just come back here then, and someone will take you there."

There's a guy in a Hawaiian shirt and shorts sitting on the reception-area sofa flipping through a pamphlet on opiate addiction. His blond bangs are too long and obscure his eyes completely. Brushing them aside with an absentminded motion, he looks both strangely familiar and irritatingly at ease.

Oh, it's four DUIs.

"Hey," he says when he catches me looking at him. He smiles slowly, his eyes lighting up with recognition as he stands and holds out something red toward me.

"You forgot this."

My sweatshirt. I must have left it at orientation.

"Thanks," I say, taking it from him. I turn in the other direction quickly, keeping my head down because I don't want him to see me crying.

Four DUIs jumps up and somehow beats me to the door. We both walk outside into the blazing sunlight.

We're walking shoulder to shoulder now. He smells of cigarettes and clean laundry, and my mind fastens on that contradiction as I read his name tag:

Scott S. 412.

"Yeah, I'm Scott," he says, following my eyes to his shirt. "These are our patient numbers. You must have checked in right before me." He snaps his fingers, "Hey, you're information, right?"

"Huh?" I stop walking for a second to catch my breath. Being near him feels strange, and I'm not sure what that's all about. But my meds are also starting to kick in nicely and suddenly I don't really care.

"Your name tag, Laura R. Four-one-one? Like Mary J. Blige, what's the four-one-one, hon." He smiles, revealing two rows of slightly uneven white teeth. I'm pretty sure he can tell I'm high now.

"The dining hall is this way," he says, pointing to the path ahead of us. "I hear they have a pretty decent chef here."

CHAPTER TWELVE

Three Hots and a Scott

My three-day detox was a blur of me sleeping alone in a dark, musty room, waking at med time, peeing, then heading back to sleep. I have no memory of showering or eating, but apparently I did both because there were empty dishes on the tray and twice there were wet towels on the bathroom floor. The nurse who did my arrival exam explained that they would be weaning me off Ambien very carefully because of my seizures.

"This is going to be what is called a medical detox," she said, while fastening the Velcro of the blood pressure cuff.

"We're going to continue your Ambien. You'll be starting with six per day: two in the morning, two midday, and two at bedtime. You'll also have some phenobarb for these first few days and then at night we'll add Ativan to help you sleep. We'll step you down a little each week, so you'll be off your meds except for a mild antidepressant the doctor prescribed for you by the end of week three."

All I heard was "We're going to continue your Ambien."

Hallelujah.

I was in a brownout for my entire detox, which is a less intense form of a blackout. In a brownout, you can have vague memories of events, or maybe you don't remember something until someone else brings it up later. While in this sunken, delusional state, I could have sworn that both my tampons and vodka were in my room when I arrived. I have a memory of waiting for Clarence to leave, and then inhaling the three pills and six gulps of hot vodka as fast as I could.

I think.

I realize now that while still at home, I'd chipped away at the Ambien, opening tampon after tampon, fishing out a piece here and a piece there. When I was shown to my "private room" four days ago, I thought I was smuggling in thirty, but it may have only been eight or nine. All I know is that by the time a new tech came to collect me to move me to out of the detox room to a real room with roommates (apparently the promise of a private room was just a bait and switch) it was just me and my luggage. No Ambien, no vodka.

I had no idea how custodial rehab would feel.

The smell of Lysol wafting from rock-hard plastic mattresses, four women to a room, prisonesque-flashlight evening bed checks. We have breakfast at seven in the dining hall and then we're herded into a lecture, then to "group," and then it's lunch. Like they said in orientation, women sit with women and men sit with men. Women walk with women, men walk with men.

One of my roommates was born the same year as me, in the same city, and is also named Laura. (What are the odds?) She's a flirtatious blonde with ever-present red lipstick and long tan legs, which she shows off as often as possible. She says she's getting off cocaine and Jack Daniel's, but I secretly suspect she is here for love addiction (a new term I've learned). I'm jealous of her dope YSL resort wear and the ease with which she conducts herself in this hateful place. I find her to be the most tolerable of my three roommates, so I sit with her at lectures and meals, listening as she drones on about how much this guy wants her and that guy wants her. And wherever I am, Scott S. 412 finds me with his eyes and stares at me from a distance with that intense, familiar smile. Laura spots this instantly and presses me on it.

"What's with you and Scott S.? I think he likes you. I mean *likes* you, likes you."

"I don't know about that," I say with a shrug. "We checked in at the same time is all. Also, in case you forgot, I'm not checking for anyone right now. I'm in the middle of a divorce."

Also, I could just picture Nancy saying, "What???? Someone likes you??? You stay far away from him, Laura. You never know who might be watching!"

There's this mindset that people adopt to get through periods of incarceration or confinement. To do "easy time," one has to forget about the outside world. As soon as I checked in to The Meadows, my divorce, my PA presidency, even the contractor who was still working on my kitchen at home, all faded all the way to the background and one thing zoomed into focus—my kids. My kids are my daily mantra. They're the only reason I am here, the only thing I care about. We're not allowed to access our phones, and we're allowed to watch only sports on the communal TV set, so I feel completely insulated here. I've only been at The Meadows for a week, and already anything that doesn't directly have to do with my children feels extremely inconsequential. My divorce doesn't feel real in here. I can't seem to summon any sense of urgency when I think about my husband and what I'll return to in twenty-three days. Additionally, when I do allow myself to think about my failed marriage, it rockets me down into a thick, murky depression. Better, I think, to avoid that sludge.

So I'm resenting Laura right now. I'm sitting here minding my business, trying to do easy time and not think about my divorce and there she goes, bringing up the way Scott S. 412 looks at me.

I mean could there be a private investigator camped out in the cow pasture next door snapping pictures of me and everyone I talk to? Should I mention Scott S. 412 to Nancy on our next weekly call?

We all have counseling sessions during the week. During mine, I do my best to gauge how I should act. Ever since Laura's observation, I'm terrified that other people are noticing too. What if my husband has paid one of the techs to keep tabs on me and report my movements to him? Or worse yet, what if his attorney planted a spy in here pretending to be a patient? Yes, that's a hefty $40K fee for a little intel, but chicken feed compared to what his client will save if he can get some dirt on me. Either way, I am definitely too paranoid now to stay here for an entire month. Today I've decided that I need to find a way to convince my counselor Deborah that I don't need to be here for as long as the other patients do.

Should I be PA president Laura? Laura whose kids desperately need her? Laura who might actually be here by mistake?

But I've stopped asking about going home, because every time I do, someone makes a note in my fuckin' chart. Deborah had all kinds of notes about me in there; I spotted at least three different people's handwriting. One tallied how many days I spent in detox (three), another wrote how often I'd participated in group (zero). My pleas for extra nighttime meds had been noted, along with who I sat with at meals and what I ate, everything.

Now, not only do I feel sentenced to this time, I feel doubly suspicious about the big-brotherism of it all. To stay under the radar, I try to blend in (as best as I can being the only Black one and all). I try not to make faces when the others hold hands and "pray out" after meetings, or not to roll my eyes when one of these kids bitch about their privileged life in group. I can't believe that anyone would take this cowboy-ass, forty-grand-a-pop kumbaya shit seriously. No one here is getting any better. And anyone that buys into this crunchy, higher-power, turn-your-life-over-to-God nonsense is wasting their money, or more likely, their parents' money.

Also, I'm still fucking detoxing.

Detoxing from the Ambien, detoxing from my kids, my bed, from TV, from busyness, detoxing from sugar and caffeine and from privacy.

The body aches and pains of this withdrawal are excruciating. Nighttime is agony, as I can't sleep without the vodka and the extra Ambien. I lie awake writhing in pain on my hard, disgusting bed, listening to the noises of the other three women. I cover my face with my pillow against the smells of their flatulence and bad breath, counting the hours until sunrise.

At five thirty I get dressed and head to the office. The desert morning is cool and, even though I'm loath to admit it, exquisite. The dawn sky is painted with layers of pink and orange shining brilliant against cottony cumulus clouds. The office itself is a vantage point on top of a hill. There's a wide porch, complete with rocking chairs, overlooking the entire campus and miles of desert and mountains. A faint, earthy smell drifts up in the morning breeze from the surrounding cow pastures. Every morning the outgoing night tech puts out a fresh copy of that day's *New York Times* for us patients. By seven the paper will be haggled over, separated into pieces, and the crossword puzzle will have been smuggled into someone's room. But at six I have the porch and the paper all to myself. The added bonus being that I get to be first in line for meds when they open at seven. My skin hurts just a little less while I wait, knowing that I'll have something in my system within the hour. Today they're stepping me down off my crucial lunchtime dose, but I still get my full morning and evening doses. Next, they'll cut out my lunchtime dose altogether and start stepping down my morning dose. They'll do the evening dose the following week. And then the week after that it's thirty days. And if I've been a good girl, I'll get to go home.

Thirty days away from my kids.

Every time I think about my kids I have to stop myself from collapsing where I stand. But since that check-in day, I purposely haven't cried in front of anyone. My counselor, Deb, keeps trying to break me, trying to get me to crack, but it's clear she's used to dealing with these little rah-rah white girls. I doubt she's ever even had a conversation with a sister, especially one in my position.

"I think you may be separating yourself by identifying as an addict. Here, everyone who has a substance abuse problem uses the word 'alcoholic,' meaning we abstain from alcohol in any form, whether that be pills, powder, or liquid."

Okay, that's fuckin' weird, and drastically inaccurate, but whatever.

I shrug and look out the window.

"Okay." My voice is dripping with hostility.

"Also," she says, ignoring my posturing, "I really think you'd have an easier time if you'd just try to connect with some of the other patients. I want to help you look for the similarities while you're here, okay?"

Similarities, Deb? How about at forty-three, I'm one of the oldest people here? How about the fact that not only am I the ONLY Black patient here, I'm the only nonwhite person in the whole friggin' place besides Clarence?! I'm the only one who didn't start fucking, boozing, and drugging while I was still in middle school. And as far as I can tell, I'm the only one here who isn't blaming everyone else for their problems. I can't look for the similarities, bruh, because we are NOT the same!

One of my roommates went home yesterday, and a young mom named Shauna moved into our room. She arrived at noon. Two of the techs helped her with her Louis Vuitton trunk and three matching monogrammed suitcases. I was in group when she arrived, but apparently Laura greeted her by pulling rank and relegating her to the bed with the least amount of privacy. By the time I got back to the dorm, Laura had moved all my stuff to the bed across from hers and strung up a sheet like a curtain separating us from the others. After lights out that night, Laura was telling me about some guy who got kicked out for licking toads (apparently it gets you high) when the sound of a jackhammer broke the quiet. Laura jumped out of bed first and threw open the sheet/curtain. I followed closely behind her, smacking into her after she stopped short in front of Shauna's bed. Grabbing Laura's narrow shoulders from behind, I peeked around to see what type of alien machine had invaded our room. And there was Shauna, sitting up in bed with the biggest vibrator I'd ever seen, sticking up between her legs.

"You've got to be kidding me!" Laura shouted above the noise. "Shauna! What the fuck is that??"

"It's for migraines," Shauna said, cutting it off like a lawn mower. "I get them at night, and I can't sleep. This is the only thing that helps," she said pitifully.

"This one hasn't slept one night since she checked in," Laura said, pointing to me. "You don't see her waking the whole room up. How'd you even get in here with that thing? Also, what the fuck? You get migraines in your pussy?"

There was a split second of silence, and then Laura and I looked at each other and fell out laughing, on the floor, on each other, rolling around, clutching our sides, gasping for breath. Shauna kept talking but we couldn't hear her over our howling. It was the first time I'd laughed, because something was actually funny, in a long, long time.

—

A skinny kid named Matt plays his acoustic guitar on the porch before lights out every night. Picture a kind of pathetic rehab coffeehouse vibe. After he finished last night, a few people were stalling going back to their rooms, smoking and shooting the shit, when the talk turned to how fucked-up it was to get up so early in the morning.

"Got to wait for James and Jeff to shave every morning before I can even get in there to pee."

"Try having four girls sharing one bathroom!"

"Seven a.m. breakfast is cruel and unusual punishment. They should let sleeping alcoholics lie . . ."

I joined in then, and I joked that getting up is easy for me since I never actually go to sleep.

"I'm literally up all night," I said. "I don't know how I'm even functioning. I'm here on the porch, watching the sunrise every morning."

I understand completely now why people use sleep deprivation as torture. The days were terrible, unbearably long and tedious. But the nights. It was then that all the bad thoughts came pouring into my head like waste from a burst sewage pipe.

You weren't there again to put your kids to bed. Can you imagine what this is doing to them? What happens when they wake up during the night now and ask for you?

To block out the thoughts I would read my only "rehab approved" book, *Traveling Mercies* by Anne Lamott (all my others were confiscated on arrival), and turn my iPod up full blast (the only device we were allowed to bring). It was filled with oldies, my parent's music.

Carole King's *Tapestry*, Marvin Gaye's *What's Going On*, Sly and the Family Stone's *Stand!*, Earth, Wind & Fire's *September*.

As we were all walking down the stairs, Scott S. 412 sidled up next to me.

"So that's about, what? Five thirty?"

"Huh?"

"When you get here in the morning."

"Yeah," I said slowly. "Like, five thirty or six."

"Maybe I'll join you tomorrow."

"I dare you," I laughed. "Believe me, I wouldn't be up that early if I had a choice."

———

It's five forty-five, and I'm sitting on the porch again when I make out someone's silhouette walking toward me. It takes a minute before I can tell that it's a man, and then a few more seconds for me to recognize his walk.

Oh my God, he actually came.

Immediately my heart starts racing, and I look to see if anyone's around.

One of those spies is going to tell my husband about Scott S. 412 showing up early to sit with me! I should have told him not to come instead of daring him. What the fuck was I thinking?

He looks casual as he climbs the porch steps, like he could be making a morning Starbucks run with his shower-wet hair, T-shirt, and surf shorts. Jenn, one of the younger girls here, was rating the "men of The Meadows" yesterday and declared that if Brad Pitt and George Clooney had a baby, it would be Scott S. 412. I laughed with the others even though I felt this whole protective vibe stealing over me.

Other women are noticing Scott S. 412?

He asks permission with his eyes before taking the chair next to me. He smells of Dial soap and mint toothpaste, and I'm caught off guard by a sudden swelling of gratitude in my throat. I find myself fighting to keep from smiling, and I'm terrified that whoever is watching is going to snap a picture like that, me smiling and sitting alone with him at sunrise like we're on vacation or something.

I'm also embarrassed by this crushy reaction I'm having, and I don't want him to think I'm happy to see him. As soon as he sits down, I feel my heartbeat regulating itself. I mean my whole system slows down, just like it does when I take a pill. Out of the corner of my eye I can see that he is looking straight ahead at the sunrise, and I am mortified by the goose bumps that appear on my left arm, the arm that's closest to him. He makes this super-intimate noise then, a soft, satisfied-sounding "hmm," and I turn red. We sit there in silence until six forty-five when a tech unlocks the door. Scott S. 412 winks at me when I go in for my meds. He waits for me, then walks me in silence to the dining hall where he and I separate for breakfast. I know it was risky, and I also know that there'll be a big fat note on my chart for walking with a man, but I don't care. I can't sleep, I'm fucking detoxing, and for whatever the fuck reason, being next to him made me feel better. Walking with him made me feel better. Hearing him breathe made me feel better. After breakfast, I watch him disappear with a bunch of other men around the bend of the dining hall path. I wonder if he's going to look back.

———

"How's it going there?"

"It's hell."

I can tell Nancy has me on speakerphone, which I hate. I hear her tapping that signature silver Uni-ball pen against a notepad while waiting for me to expound. I'm sitting in the cool—on the floor of the dimly lit admin office hallway, talking on the patient phone. It's a dingy, yellow, old-fashioned wall phone with a long cord that I keep curling and uncurling around my index finger.

"It's hot enough to be hell," I say finally, laughing a little. "But seriously, it's really hard. And it's going fucking slowly. And I miss my kids so much it feels like it's going to kill me."

"Still calling them every day though, like we talked about?"

"Of course."

"I know it's hard, but this will all look good to a judge, or mediator," she says quickly.

"It's not hard to call my kids," I say, bristling. "It's being away from them that's hard."

"No. Of course, that's what I meant."

Silence.

"Do they keep records of your calls? Something that someone could subpoena? It might be useful to have a record of your regularity."

"I, I don't know. I guess I can find out."

"Good. They won't tell me anything when I call. All they ever say is 'I can neither confirm nor deny' when I ask for you."

"Yeah, they're not allowed to, that's kinda the law."

I need to ask her what happens if I leave early.

I've been sitting up all these nights thinking about it. I mean since The Meadows can't confirm or deny whether I'm here, that means they can't legally reveal to anyone what level of treatment I received. I could say that they'd decided I was well enough to leave in fourteen days instead of thirty days and then my husband and his attorney would have to take my word for it.

"I was thinking maybe I could possibly leave a little earlier than they're recommending."

"What? Why? How much earlier?"

"I don't know, just earlier."

Nancy's tone becomes more confidential as she picks up the phone and talks directly into it. "I'd love to get you back here now; we're going to have a hell of time winning your case while you're in rehab. But before you come back you need to be off all your drugs, and we need some documentation to that effect . . ."

She's thinking about it!

"Wait, no," she says, interrupting herself. "No way, it's too risky. If they were able to subpoena anything that contradicts what we tell them then we're done. Your only shot at custody is getting a full endorsement from The Meadows, certificates and everything. You'll have to wait until they discharge you."

I don't ever actually remember feeling my heart sink before this moment. My body releases a shudder as it thuds onto the roof of my abdomen.

"And I'd like to start putting some things in place for your return," she continues. "I talked to a colleague about your case. Don't worry, I used a pseudonym. He's represented two or three mid-divorce rehab returnees, Charlie Sheen, a couple of Real Housewives, I think. He's giving me a list of suggestions for us to address once you're home again."

Really? The Housewives? Charlie Sheen?

"What kind of things?"

"Things that will provide evidence of your rehabilitation."

Ugh.

"Okay, so we can talk about all that when I get back, right?"

"Right. Anything else?"

"Um, he's bringing the kids to visit next week. He didn't know if it was a good idea, but I begged him. I told him I didn't think I could make it the whole time if I didn't see them at least once. I know it's gonna be fucking weird, all four of us together, but I don't care, it'll be worth it."

"He's bringing them!" Nancy sounds giddy. "Well then you're definitely not leaving early. This is a great opportunity for you to look like the doting mother, the model patient."

God, she spins absolutely everything. I doubt she even knows when she's doing it.

I get nauseous when I think about the fact that he's going to fly our kids out to visit their mother while she's incarcerated in a treatment facility. At the same time, I'm hyperaware of the fact that talking to my divorce attorney from the rehab hallway feels like bad fiction, or some schmaltzy Lifetime movie.

"Anything else?"

I open my mouth to tell her about Scott S. 412 but then shut it again.

My mind flashes to the porch yesterday, the fear that we were being observed, that crushy feeling that enveloped me when he sat down.

Stop it. It's not like we're hooking up or anything. If anyone saw us, all they would see would be two people waiting for their morning meds. It would be silly to bring that up.

"No, that's it."

"Okay. Well get back to me on the call records when you can. Hang in there, kid, do good. Get home soon."

———

"Can I show you something outside?"

It's Sunday, and there is literally nothing to do. My skin is sore from being crisped daily in the 114-degree heat. Everyone who wasn't lucky enough to have a day pass is crammed into the TV room watching a golf tournament. I'm bored as shit, but we're not allowed in our rooms during the day, and now I have an armchair all to myself (something for which I would have happily paid good money). We patients are basically on our own on the weekends; there are very few scheduled activities, and the weekend techs expect us to organize our own recovery meetings in the evening (sex and love addicts in the rec room, drug addicts in the covered area, alcoholics down at the tables by the swimming pool).

Yesterday I kept busy doing my laundry and getting my nails done until dinner. They bring a couple of manicurists into the girls' dorms for a few hours; you have to make an appointment. But Sundays there's nothing to do but watch TV and smoke, and I don't smoke. The ache of being away from my kids is constant and debilitating, like I'm walking around with a butcher knife sticking out of my chest. And while that doesn't distinguish it from any other day, it does feel especially acute when things are slow and there's no one here to boss us around. And now Scott S. 412 is standing next to me asking if he could show me something.

"Sure," I say.

Laura is sitting on the floor in front of me between Shauna and Matt. I get up, keeping one hand on my chair to "save it," and tap her on the shoulder, signaling with my eyes that she can take my seat. Scott holds the door for me, and we both shield our eyes as we step out into the sun. We walk in silence over to the counseling building, him looking straight ahead with a funny smile on his face and me glancing at him between steps. I want to ask him what's up but it's too hot to speak. He motions for me to head up the stairs, and I'm self-conscious as I step ahead of him, knowing that his face will be level with my ass the whole climb. It's so hot that my rubber flip-flops stick slightly to each step as I walk. When we get to the top, all I see on the other side of the railing is the neighboring pasture, a dry field with a single tree, under which about fifty or one hundred black and brown cows are attempting to huddle.

I look up at him for an explanation, and he puts his fingers to his lips and points straight ahead.

"Wait," he says.

As if on cue, a single cow starts to low, then suddenly the air is filled with mooing. It reminds me of the howling of wolves, each cow starting a new moo just as the last one ends. Finally, it all crescendos to a long, single note with all the cows adjusting their moos to the same pitch. Then it ends—just as abruptly as it started.

"What was that???" I say with a laugh after a moment.

"Sundown." He smiles.

"That's so wild," I say, still laughing. I'm pushing on the railing with my hands and standing on my tiptoes.

"Do they do that every day? The cows?"

When he doesn't respond I look over at him and see that he's not looking at the cows, he's looking at me.

Before I know what's going on, his hands are on my shoulders and he's leaning in.

My eyes are wide-open when he kisses me, and my arms are limp by my sides. I don't kiss him back, but I don't pull away.

Oh my God.

The kiss is chaste but tender. Just his soft lips pressing against mine for a moment or two and then the slight flavor of a lime Spree candy after he pulls away.

Faaaaaaaacckkk!

It's been so long since I've been looked at like that, held like that, kissed like that. My sexuality has been shut down for so long that I think I've gone blind. I mean, I didn't even see this coming. I was totally unprepared.

What did I do to make him think that kissing me was an option?

He looks at me and his eyes grow wide with fear.

"Hey, oh hey, did I fuck up?" he asks. He sounds scared, his eyes searching mine. "Was that okay?"

Oh shit, oh shit, oh shit, oh shit.

Scott is still staring at me, waiting for me to say something.

Say something.

"Sorry, I, I wasn't expecting you to . . ."

"Yeah, I could tell," he says. "I really hope I didn't fuck it up."

"I think I just need a minute."

Oh my God, what have I done? I'm in a restricted area alone with a BOY. What was I thinking? What if someone saw him kiss me and reported us to a tech? What if there really is a private investigator in the cow pasture and they got pictures?

FUCK.

"I think we should head back," I say, starting toward the stairs. Then all of a sudden I feel jittery, like I've smoked a bowl of cocaine. I think I really fucked this up, and I can't get down the stairs fast enough.

He reaches for my hand, but I shrug him off and keep walking.

"Are we okay?"

"Sure, don't worry about it."

He grabs my arm and turns me around on the top step, looking down into my eyes.

"Hey, I don't want to blow our friendship, okay? It's important to me, so if we're just friends, that's okay."

"Okay."

I really have to get out of here.

As I'm heading down the stairs with my back to him, the corners of my mouth force my face into a smile.

He kissed me.

CHAPTER THIRTEEN

Breach

Shauna and I are sitting alone in the dining hall. It's seven fifteen, just after dinner, and everyone else has gone outside to the smoking pit.

"Hey," she says, after I throw my napkin on top of my plate. "Did you really fly here private?"

I'm caught off guard by her question.

Even though we're roommates, she and I rarely talk about anything outside of bathroom logistics. I inspect her face for motive. Her wide brown eyes look curious, not shady. I know that she herself arrived with all that Louis luggage, so I figure she's not trying to take my financial inventory.

"Yeah, my husband chartered it. It's not ours or anything," I add quickly.

"About your husband," she says, casually wiping her fingers on her napkin. "I've been meaning to tell you that I've met him."

I gasp for breath like I've just been dunked into a vat of frigid water. Carefully and quietly, I place the pads of my feet on the floor beneath me, so I don't lose my balance.

This can't be happening.

As far as I'm concerned, confidentiality is the one thing rehab has going for it.

The Meadows is its own ecosystem, a bubble, totally siloed from the outside world. And while we patients do know incredibly intimate things about each other—the horrific stories of our respective bottoms, childhood traumas, romantic relationships—we don't know the things that might allow us to identify each other out in the real world, like last names and career specifics. I chose The Meadows because I knew there'd be twenty to thirty degrees of separation between my family and any of these patients. Going all the way to Wickenburg meant being far away from anyone who might be interested in who I am on a tabloid level.

Wickenburg was supposed to be safe.

What an idiot I am.

With only a sheet/curtain separating us, I've been pillow-talking to Laura about everything. About my husband, about wanting to leave early, about Scott S. kissing me.

SHIT.

She's met my husband. She knows who he is. She'll tell him about Scott S.

I remind myself to breathe and try to read her face.

What's her angle here?

"My husband?" I stammer. "How? I mean when? Why?"

Shauna smiles, and my mind races faster.

Oh my God, I have to get out of here. I have to call Nancy and tell her that there's been a breach. That we have a spy in our midst.

"I auditioned for him once, a couple of years ago."

I'm trying to keep my face as cool as hers, but I feel like the time I went snorkeling and a wave sent a gush of cold, salty water down my breathing tube into my lungs.

Panicked.

Auditioned?

"Wait! You? You're an actress?"

Even though that's completely beside the point.

The point is we don't have access to phones or computers so there's no googling anyone. And even though I've talked to Laura in a general way about him and my kids, I'm positive I've never given any specific details. Details that might allow anyone to identify me as THAT Laura Robbins from Hollywood.

So how does she know who I am? How does she know who he is?

"I was a model before," says Shauna.

She's talking faster now, probably picking up on my frantic energy.

"But I just started acting a few years ago. Your husband was casting this new series, the *Batman* spin-off? I was auditioning for the role of the science girl. You know, the one who had chemistry as her superpower? They were looking for a sexy librarian type . . ."

Arkham Angels. *Oh God, what was that? Two years ago?*

"But Shauna, we've been living together for almost two weeks and you never said anything?"

"Well, I thought it might be you, but I wasn't sure. I mean your last name starts with R, and it's no secret in the industry that your husband is married to a pretty Black woman. But I didn't really put it together until that day you were talking about *The Runaway Cat*.* My kids love that movie, and I know he directed it. So when you mentioned that you'd been on the set, then everything just clicked."

The fucking Runaway Cat!

I force the corners of my mouth into a smile.

I have no idea how to handle this. Should I downplay it and act like this isn't a big deal? Like I have nothing to hide? Or should I throw myself on her mercy and ask her to treat our time here like Vegas?

What happens at The Meadows stays at The Meadows.

I wonder how long it's going to take her to figure out how much she's fucked me up.

How often have I hung back to talk to Scott S. in front of her? How often has she seen us sitting next to each other? All this time I thought she was just a spoiled housewife, when I bothered to think of her at all.

---

*Fictitious.

How did I not know she was an actress?

My head and neck are starting to heat up, and I feel my throat tightening with fear and . . . anger.

This is juicy fucking gossip. If she's not his spy, she's definitely telling someone. And hold up! Yesterday when she was on the phone in the admin building, she kept looking at me. Is this why she kept looking at me?

Shauna leans forward and puts her hand on my wrist. I pull it away from her instinctively.

"I only brought it up because when we get out of here, I'm looking at my own divorce. Gerald is threatening me, saying he's going to move all my things to my mother's house while I'm here."

Huh?

"And then last night my agent told me she's trying to line up an audition for your husband's new project, *Dr. Sleuth* or something like that, and I thought, maybe it's a sign. I told her that I thought I knew someone who could put in a good word for me."

Wait? She's angling for a part?

"I didn't give her your name or anything," she says quickly. "I know you're getting a divorce too, but I figure you and he can't be on too bad of terms since he flew you here private straight to Wickenburg instead of making you go commercial through Phoenix like the rest of us."

Shauna giggles then and it reminds me of Janice's laugh on *Friends*. That, plus the absurdity of her logic almost makes me want to laugh with her. And even though my heart is still pounding like I just finished a sprint, I feel like there's a chance she's telling the truth. She's either shifty as fuck or clueless as fuck.

"Shauna," I hear myself say.

I'm not on my heels anymore. I can tell she's trying to read my expression. And while I had thought I only had two options before, acting like this is no big deal or throwing myself on her mercy, suddenly I've thought of a third.

A carrot to dangle in front of her to keep her loyal.

"Sure, I'll see what I can do, okay?"

CHAPTER FOURTEEN

Halfway

"Mommy!!"

Jordan and Jacob have broken free from his hands and are running toward me full speed. I just have time to wipe my eyes before they come barreling into me, rolling me backward onto sharp, thick blades of grass as they tackle me. Burying my nose in their curly heads, I inhale deeply as I rock them back and forth, squeezing them with all my might. A barrage of smells hit me like a spray of bullets—bubblegum, soap, french fries, sweat, fruit punch.

My heart sizzles in my chest, threatening to burst.

"I missed you, I miss you so, so much."

"Hi," he says, finally catching up. He's wearing new Adidas, with a white T-shirt and jeans, and holding a large lidded coffee cup from the Prickly Perk Coffee Shop.

"Hey," I say, smiling. "Thank you. Thank you for bringing them."

He shrugs and smiles a little. "I couldn't keep them away."

The boys are both talking at once now. Jacob has a gash near the knuckle of his thumb that he wants to show me, Jordan says that he watched the movie *Bird* with Daddy and now he wants to be a saxophone player.

"Is there someplace I should go and wait?" he says flatly. "How does this work?"

His tone momentarily makes me forget that this is a rehab visitation. Something old in me remembers that once upon a time it felt as though my whole purpose was to make him feel more comfortable, to smooth out the edges of whatever it was that might be sticking him. Whenever we traveled and anything went wrong, I would take over and fix everything, finding an alternate flight that wouldn't delay us too long or getting an appointment or reservation that we needed. Whenever it was something with the household help or something with the kids' school, I would do my best to run interference so he wouldn't have to be inconvenienced.

Now, I want to jump up and soothe him and take care of things for him like I used to. At the same time, I realize I'm probably the last person in the world from whom he'd want any soothing. I gave standing in his life away when I chose drugs over our family, again and again and again.

"Mommy, what's there to do here?"

I try to keep a smile on my face even though I'm starting to panic. As much as I was dying to see my kids, I realize I have absolutely no idea what to do with them. The dewy grass around us is steaming, as it's quickly pushing 113 degrees. There's the TV room, but as it's Saturday, all the other patients will be in there trying to escape boredom and the heat. Plus, last time I checked, they were watching the bowling channel.

"Hey! How about I show you guys around?" I say getting up and brushing off my capris. I pick Jacob up and stumble under his weight.

Oh my God, they're so gigantic. How did they get so big in just two weeks?

He's watching me intently with a difficult-to-read expression, and I can practically hear him thinking, *Is she slurring? Is she high? Is she safe for the kids to be around?*

Making sure to enunciate while speaking as cleverly as possible, I walk the three of them into the dining hall, stopping abruptly when I see Scott S. sitting at one of the tables, reading a book.

Oh my God, he knew they were visiting today, he was probably trying to stay out of our way.

I try to fix my face quickly, so my husband doesn't see how terrified I am, but I'm too late. He's followed my eyes and is now watching Scott stare at me. Flustered, I hear myself jabbering about the five-star chef they have here. But when Jordan asks if we can check out the kitchen, I say that I've just remembered "the perfect" place for us to go. Even without turning around, I can feel Scott's eyes following me out the door.

Next, I take them to the art room; large, air-conditioned, and filled with paints and large rolls of paper. But there are six or seven women in there quietly finishing their "graduation" recovery circles, and I decide against it. We end up in the orientation room/chapel, where we're allowed to watch movies on Saturday nights. But as soon as we walk in, I see it through their eyes and am embarrassed by how empty and dingy it looks. He sits on a dusty black office chair and pulls out his phone, while the boys and I flop down on a beanbag chair in the corner. First, they want me to act out the "Best Day Ever" *SpongeBob* episode like I used to when they were younger, but then Jacob has the idea that we should go to my room.

"We want to see your bed, Mommy. Can we go to your room?"

My room?

Only patients are allowed in the dorms; in fact, only female patients are allowed anywhere near our building. Add to that, I'm not even allowed in my room during the day.

"Please, Mom?"

A surge of tears swells up in my throat, and my heart aches so badly that I fear they'll be able to see the anguish in my eyes. I just can't look at him and say no.

"Just for a second, okay? We can't stay long."

Leaving him there with a promise to be back in fifteen minutes, the three of us hold hands and run over to my dorm. For a moment, it feels like it could be one of our epic secret adventures in the backyard or the playroom. The ones for which we'd wear spelunking helmets and pack sandwiches and juice boxes. We're all giggling as we climb the stairs, and I open the door to my room with the key pass. Jacob, out of breath, flops onto Shauna's bed with his arms sprawled out and says, "Ahhhh! Cool air!"

Jordan spies my red satin pillowcase immediately and runs over to my bed with a whoop. I grab Jacob off Shauna's bed and we head over to join him, pulling the sheet curtain closed behind us. We all squish together on my little half-twin bed, Jacob lying fully on top of me and Jordan in the crook of my left arm, his head on my shoulder. Time seems to stand still as we all just lay there, studying the colorful wall collages of paintings that Laura has made during her time here. My heart is beating wildly and I'm trying so hard to focus, but I can't make myself stay present. I'm so afraid of a tech walking in on us. At the same time, I'm terrified of leaving our little sanctuary and having to go back to the rec room. I'm afraid that when I see him he's going to say, "Who was that guy staring at you in the cafeteria?" I'm afraid of them getting bored and saying, "What should we do next?" I'm afraid they're going to grow up and say, "Remember when we went to visit Mom in rehab?"

"Do SpongeBob now, Mommy," Jordan says, interrupting my thoughts.

As I'm doing my best Sandy the Squirrel imitation, Jacob nuzzles my neck with his nose.

"Mommy, you smell different here. I think you'd better come home with us."

His little face and nose and eyes are all so innocent, so perfect. It's then that I realize the magnitude of the grave, short-sighted mistake I'd made. A mistake I'd made because I just knew I would die if I didn't see my kids for thirty whole days. The thing that I didn't consider when I begged him on the phone last week to bring them for a visit. Then, I could only see that it felt as though I were being suffocated or boiled alive without my kids, and I wanted to be free of the pain. I could see nothing beyond that. I hadn't anticipated that there was indeed one thing that would be more painful than not seeing my kids for a month.

Saying goodbye to them and then staying behind in this place for two more torturous weeks.

In twenty minutes I'll have to walk them to the lobby and watch them head out those glass double doors and then back to LA without me. I'll have to smile and tell them that I'll be home soon. I'll have to lie through my teeth and tell them that the days will fly by.

I won't survive it.

Instantly I become a ghost, leaving my body and watching from above while I cheerfully gather the boys up and take them back down the stairs. I see us all giggling and holding hands while bolting across the lawn back to the rec room. I hold my breath as he checks his watch and puts his hand protectively on Jacob's shoulder when he says it's time to go. I'm impressed by the casual way I tousle Jordan's hair as we all stroll into the lobby. I feel my legs giving way when I give them little kisses all over their faces at the door, but I steady myself on a nearby cabinet, making the excuse that I've just stubbed my toe. The woman at the front desk has turned her head discreetly to give us privacy, but I feel extremely observed, and become acutely aware of the nature of my captivity. Legally, of course, I'm free to go, but then I risk losing them, so there doesn't really seem to be a choice. I'm to stay in this institution while they get back on the G5 he rented and go home to LA. In an instant I am overcome with a jealousy so violent that it makes me want to punch him in the face.

How dare he waltz in here like this and flaunt his phone and his store-bought coffee? Why is he free to get on a plane with our boys right now, sleep in our big comfortable bed, while I'm to remain incarcerated here in that disgusting communal room? Why am I the addict and he the normal one?

I'm so envious of him and his freedom right now that my teeth are throbbing. My pulse races, and I fight the urge to snatch them both up and run back to the sanctity of my dorm room.

Actually, it's been two whole weeks. Maybe that's enough treatment. Do I really need to stay for two more weeks of this bullshit? What's the point? I should just leave with them.

But something in me knows I can't do anything that might cause a scene. I'm three days away from being completely detoxed from all my meds, and I know that if I bail now, he'll fight me for custody. Staying is my only shot at getting to stay in their lives without a court battle. I've got to convince him that I'm serious about being sober.

I keep my face together at the window until I can no longer read the license plate of the black Chevy Tahoe they've driven away in. The woman behind the desk is watching me openly now, and even though the look on her face is more of concern, I take it as pity and begin to fume with shame and humiliation. As I race past her toward campus, I can feel myself starting to come unhinged. By the time I get outside I am literally choking on my tears, inhaling a stream of them each time I take a breath. Instinctively, I start to run toward the office, but when I see the crowd gathered in front, I cut right so quickly that I fall and skin my bare knee on the gravel. I manage to get up and keep going, ignoring the sound of a far-away female voice calling my name. Pain is a tsunami hanging over my head threatening to overtake me the moment I slow down. I find myself in front of the girls' dorms and collapse on a bench in front of my building, panting and gasping.

Breathe, breathe, breathe.

I know I need to get up quickly and run again before the great wave breaks and puts an end to me. I try to push myself off the bench with my arms, but they are as useless as noodles and I fall again. I hug my knees to my chest and rock back and forth with my eyes closed.

And just like that, I'm engulfed.

Pain sears up and down my spine, piercing through my stomach and lungs, forcing tears, saliva, and snot to fountain from my eyes, mouth, and nose. Covering my face with my hands I succumb to the ferocity of it and hear myself wail out loud. I'm drowning in the cold undertow of grief. It pulls me under, again and again, until I am over-come and too exhausted to resist. I no longer care who sees me cry. I am unaware of the fact that my body is on the ground. I am helpless and don't understand how it is that I'm still alive.

Laura runs up then, out of breath. The smell of her sage shampoo envelops me as she hugs me around the shoulders with both arms and timidly whispers platitudes like "It's okay" and "You'll be home before you know it."

But I am inconsolable and entirely unfit to receive her attempts at compassion. I shake her off gently between sobs and beg her to leave me alone.

She doesn't matter, The Meadows doesn't matter, none of this matters. I have to get out of here and get to my kids. I cannot spend another two weeks in this place. Nothing has ever felt more wrong than watching them go and staying behind. Nancy was right—I can't fight for them from here. I've got to go home.

Finally, Laura removes her arms, and with a kiss on my forehead, I feel her withdraw. I listen to the crunch of gravel under her Gucci flip-flops growing fainter as she walks back down the path toward the office. When I am sure she's gone, I open my eyes and again try to regulate my breathing, but I can't take in a full breath. Minutes tick by, and I'm surprised to find that I feel slightly forsaken by Laura and the ease with which she left me. It's then that I hear footsteps again and decide to forgive her for leaving me.

I hope she brought some tissues with her.

I look up toward the sound and through the blur of my tears make out that it's someone else, a man. And he's peeking around the corner of my dorm building at me.

Scott S.

What's he doing over here by the girls' dorms? He could be kicked out for less! How did he even know which dorm was mine?

In a few short, hunched-over strides he's snuck over and sits next to me on the ground. His blond hair is hanging in his eyes, and he's wearing another one of those horrific Hawaiian shirts. He looks a little terrified, and I imagine that he's scared I might go even more ticky-boom and call unwanted attention to us.

"How did you find me?" I sob quietly.

"I took a guess," he whispers. "I waited, just in case you needed someone. I knew it would be hard to, you know . . ."

The dam breaks again and I collapse into him, sobbing and clutching him as though he were a life preserver. I grab fistfuls of that awful shirt and soak his shoulder and chest with my tears. He holds me and strokes my back in silence, offering no platitudes, no words of encouragement. Close to thirty minutes later, I'm listening to his heartbeat and find that my breathing is slowing to match his. I look up at him after a while and use the bottom of my T-shirt to mop my nose and face. His blue eyes are liquid, filled with tears as he looks down at me.

"Hey, you'd better get back to the other side," I say, pulling away from him suddenly. "Before someone catches you over here."

The magnitude of the risk he's taken by coming to comfort me is beginning to seep through my self-centered sorrow. True, I might have a custody court battle in front of me if I leave early, but Scott . . .

Scott has those four DUIs and an upcoming court date with a Utah judge who has grown weary of seeing him in his courtroom. If he gets kicked out of treatment, not only is he possibly looking at some serious jail time but he could also be looking at spending some time in prison. And then his daughters would grow up like that—separated from their jailed, alcoholic father. All at once I feel guilty, selfish, and spoiled. I'll be home with my kids in two weeks and divorced soon after. I'll be in my beautiful home with all my access and resources and no threat of legal trouble. Scott S. must not go to jail because he came to comfort me.

"Thank you. I mean really, I don't know how to thank you," I whisper. "But I'm okay and you'd better go back."

Laura has reappeared. She's standing a few yards away, over by our dorm, with a box of tissues in her right hand and something I can't quite make out in her left.

"I'll see you at dinner, okay?" he says, starting to get up.

I sigh and quickly consider what's in front of me. I don't know if I'll make it for two more weeks, but I guess I'm not leaving tonight.

"I'll see you at dinner."

———

"So." Deborah sets her mug down and leans toward me.

She's wearing a long denim smock dress and orange rubber clogs. Her thin red hair is scrunchied in a half ponytail on top of her head. As always, I'm instantly irritated by her whole therapeutic "let's unpack this" vibe.

"We've never really talked about your stepfather. I mean you've indicated that he was a tremendous source of pain and fear for you while you were growing up, but not much else. What's his name again?"

I hold my breath like I'm about to dive underwater.

"Kenny, his name was Kenny."

Deb was looking for a pen in the mug on her desk, but now she looks up.

"Was? I'm sorry, has he passed?"

"Yes, he died. He died the year Jacob was born."

"Oh? How, how was that for you?"

"I don't know. I thought it would be kind of a relief, but it wasn't. Honestly, it was like nothing had happened. I never really talked about it."

"Would you like to talk about it?"

"Not really."

"Then we'll table that for now!" she says, bursting into a toothy smile and picking up my chart. "So! I know you had your visit with your kids on Saturday. How did that go?"

Every time she speaks I want to reach out and turn the volume down on her screechy voice. I am also salty about the fact that her office smells of fresh brewed coffee, which seems especially insensitive since all we patients have is that decaf swill they serve out of that shit-brown coffee dispenser in the dining hall. And now I am deeply resentful that she seems excited to discuss my children. A subject that is none of her fucking business and that up until now I've handily evaded.

Give her nothing.

"The visit was amazing," I say finally, picking at a chip in my French manicure.

She leans back in her seat and wraps her hands around her mug. Her face has turned stoic, no more toothy smile. So I look up and try again.

"Well, equal parts amazing and excruciating."

"What was hard about it, Laura?"

"It was hard to say goodbye to them, to not leave with them."

I hear the break in my voice and tense up, lowering my eyes, hoping she didn't catch it.

"Your, um, husband brought them, right?"

"My soon-to-be ex, yes."

"How was that?"

"Fine," I say. "We got along well, considering . . ."

"Considering . . . ?" She's circling her right hand around like she's guiding me into a parking space.

"Considering that his wife is a drug addict in rehab—a rehab that he's paying for. Considering that I'm the mother of his children, children he's now got to take care of full-time, and considering that we're in the middle of a divorce."

I'm looking her in the eyes now.

Yeah bitch, that part.

"Actually, about the fee," she says, picking up my chart again. "You have very good insurance. I'm pretty certain it covers your entire stay."

"He has very good insurance, you mean." I can taste the hostility on the back of my tongue. "I don't think I'll be able to afford to go to rehab again after the divorce, so I'd better make sure this sobriety sticks, right?"

"I wonder, are you aware of it when you're doing that?"

"Doing what?"

"Using humor to deflect. It seems to happen when you're feeling vulnerable."

I stare at her again, not sure what to say next.

Definitely nothing funny.

Deborah leans toward me again, elbows resting on her knees.

139

"Actually, that leads me to one of the things I wanted to discuss with you today."

"My imminent lack of insurance?"

Fuck.

Deborah smiles slightly at me and grabs my chart from her desk.

"Your insurance covers the standard thirty-day stay, but it also covers extended care in some cases."

Okay . . . ?

"As it stands right now, you'd be leaving us in, um"—she looks at my chart again—"in twelve days, on . . ."

I mouth the words with her:

"August fourteenth."

"Yes," I say, clenching my teeth to keep my face together.

"Well, I and the other members of your team . . ."

I have a team?

". . . We've been reviewing your progress, and the consensus is, Laura, that we think you might benefit from some additional time away from your home environment."

Huh??

"We have a ninety-day transitional program for women. Some mothers have gone there after they've completed their thirty-day stay here to . . ."

A siren sounds in my head as her words begin to evaporate into the air.

"Listen, I know you've been counting on going home, but a lot of women just aren't ready after a thirty-day stay . . ."

Now her words are falling out of the sky like bricks. I squirm in my seat to avoid the blows.

Transitional. Ninety days. Transitional. Ninety days.

Transitional.

"You mean a halfway house? Here in Wickenburg?"

I'm trying to force myself back into my body.

"Transitional living," she says emphatically. "It's less than a mile from here, and never any more than eight women at a time. And it's a

140

house, not inpatient treatment. You could come and go. A few of the residents even get jobs while they're there . . ."

As she reaches for a brochure, panic jolts through my nervous system, and I feel my shoulders starting to tremble. I look back at the door as though I'm going to make a run for it.

A job? Where? The Horseshoe Cafe? The Prickly Perk Coffee Shop?

"We'd just like for you to consider it, okay?" she says softly, handing me the brochure. "We can talk more about it next time."

I take the brochure and pretend to read it.

Fuckin' cactus and fuckin' adobe and fuckin' nothing for miles around.

And sixty-five thousand in bills too? Oh, you really got the wrong bitch.

"Well," she says, opening my chart again. Her tone is brighter now, like she's happy to have that out of the way.

"It says here that you've been doing well stepping down on your meds and you're taking your last evening dose . . . Oh! Tomorrow night—is that right?"

"Uh, yeah."

"That's a huge accomplishment."

I know I need to respond, but the alarm is still roaring in my ears.

I can't. Can NOT stay past the fourteenth. My kids have been marking the days off on the calendar. I've got my first board meeting on the twenty-ninth. I'm turning forty-four on the twenty-seventh.

I CAN'T spend my birthday in rehab.

I have to get home to my kids.

Plus, Nancy would kill me.

"Yes, right," I manage. "Last dose—is a big deal."

"You're giving up something you've depended on for a long time," she continues. "This can be a very real kind of grief. Some people find it helpful to write a goodbye letter to their drug of choice. A few of our patients . . ."

I want to jump up and scream at her until I'm hoarse. I want to pound on her desk and snatch that scrunchie off her head and knock that fuckin' coffee mug out of her hand.

Why are you trying to keep me here? Why are you punishing me? I'm giving up the only thing that lets me sleep, the only thing besides my kids that makes me feel good. I've done everything you muthafuckahs have asked me to do!

Every day that I'm gone, my kids are bonding with someone else. Every neighborhood party I miss, I'm that mom in rehab. Every day that I'm gone, he's the hero, the one whose junkie wife is failing him. Every day that I'm gone, someone else controls the narrative.

And suddenly I realize how stupid I've been.

I've been doing this all wrong.

I've been giving them self-sufficient Laura. Independent Laura. Laura who isn't sick enough to need to be here with these low-down drunks and sex addicts.

But to get home I'm going to need to be someone else entirely.

Reformed Laura. Vulnerable Laura. The Laura that has had an epiphany and realizes that her recovery is more important than getting back to her kids quickly. I've been serving them compliant Laura, but they need to see surrendered Laura.

The Zen archer never aims at the bull's-eye.

"Actually," I say, putting on what I hope is an earnest-looking face. "I think I was a little thrown off by the idea of a longer stay. Okay if I take a little time to process everything?"

"Of course," Deborah says. Relief softens her expression a bit.

"It's a lot to take in at once, but you have your whole life in front of you when you return home. Our whole goal is to get you back with your family. We just really want to make sure you're as prepared for it as possible."

Oh, is that really what you want, Deb? Or could it be that you and "my team" really want those sixty-five Gs?

I give her my most believable melancholy smile then and move closer to her, taking my journal out of my bag.

"And also, you're right—about taking this last dose tomorrow. It is kind of like saying goodbye to a friend. In my case, a best friend. Do I just start the letter like, 'Dear Ambien . . ??'"

CHAPTER FIFTEEN

The Ice Woman Melteth

At seven o'clock, I wait for Shauna and Laura to leave for the Love Addicts meeting and then take the long way down to the pool patio. I feel like I'm sick or dying or crazy—my head is pounding, and my chest and throat are hot and shaky. I stop in my tracks when I get near the meeting and hear the others going around the circle, identifying themselves one at a time. Holding my breath, I'm stuck around the corner peering at them through the bushes. A celebrity checked in today, and he's sitting at the end of the table. His name tag says Tommy T. 423, which I find to be kind of hilarious because we all know his real name (his show's been running in syndication for years). "Tommy" is sitting next to Scott S.'s roommate James, and James is sitting next to Scott, who is casually leaning back in his chair and looking around. To an onlooker, it might look like Scott's making an aimless survey of his surroundings, but I know he's looking for me, worried about where I am. I also know that I'm acting a little Looney Tunes, standing in the shadows, looking through the bushes, but I think I'd do anything to stall the inevitable. As soon as this meeting ends, we have the eight o'clock med call, and I'll be getting my last dose of Ambien.

I close my eyes and take in a five-count breath through my nose like they taught us in group meditation, but my heartbeat is so erratic that I'm scared I'm having an anxiety attack. If I could only sit next to Scott, I know my heart would slow down some, and maybe my discomfort wouldn't be so obvious. But that thirsty blond Jill has parked her little ass right on the other side of him.

As soon as they get a chance, all these bitches are always right up under him.

The only empty chair is on the far end next to a crazy old man named Guy who reeks of patchouli.

Fuck.

I inhale as though I'm about to dive under a wave and then emerge from the bushes, walking toward the table with my shoulders shrugged and an apologetic look on my face. Scott S. spots me first and smiles and then the whole group turns around to look at me. I start to skulk around to the left side of the table toward the empty chair, but then James stands up and motions me toward him.

What's he doing?

Mortified to have everyone's eyes on me, I freeze, unsure what he wants. But then he pulls out the wrought iron patio chair, which makes a wretched squeaking noise against the concrete, and motions for me to take his seat instead.

Flustered by all the attention, I switch directions and speed-walk around to James, mouthing "thank you" before sliding into the seat and slinking down as far as I can.

Scott's grinning and looking right at me. "You okay?" he whispers.

He leans toward me and puts his hand next to mine on the armrest. Even though we're not touching, I know that the others see this gesture of intimacy and I'm horrified. I glance at my watch and see that it's just past seven fifteen and my mind starts racing again.

The only thing that has gotten me through the day for these last few years is the promise of an Ambien at the end of it. And now, not only will I not have that anymore, but because I'm supposed to be all "sober" now, I won't even be able to take a fucking drink. I mean, I should at least be able to have a glass of wine, right? EVERY MOM I know has a glass of wine after a day with their kids.

I deserve at least that.

That's what I'll do. I'll take this last pill tonight, but I'll insist on a nightly glass of wine once I'm home. I don't think anyone can argue with that, after all . . .

Scott S. elbows me gently and tips his chin toward the group leader.

"Hey, it's your turn," he says.

Huh?

"To identify."

"Oh, sorry," I say quickly. "Yeah, my name is Laura and I'm an alcoholic."

———

It's only been two nights since my last Ambien, and I feel like my skin doesn't fit anymore. I keep tripping over my feet while walking, like the ground is made alternately of Velcro or motor oil. I also seem to have developed some sort of speech impediment. All my words fall from my mouth in a jumble instead of coming out one at a time. The rub is that I still have to go to eight o'clock med call every night to get my birth control and the antidepressant they've prescribed me (to help relieve some of the anxiety and the withdrawal brain zaps, which feel like someone intermittently snapping a rubber band at your temples). I'm both edgy and forlorn as I wait in that line. It is a line that once held so much promise for me, for I knew that the instant I tossed my empty med cup in the wastebasket, I'd already be feeling the glorious buzz of that Ambien. Sometimes, while waiting, it was just the idea— the knowledge that I was about to get loaded that sent me into that euphoric stratosphere.

But apparently my body doesn't know that I won't be getting the good drugs anymore, because waiting in this line is still like ringing the dinner bell for my addiction. Now every night at eight, no matter how hard I try to suppress it, fresh hope begins to course through my veins, and one thought pulses through my head, pushing out all the others.

They might give you one by mistake.

I have to shake myself like a crazy woman as we inch along one at a time, casting that cruel hope from my head like an evil spell.

So once again, when it's my turn at the window tonight, the nurse gives me the white Solo cup. I look inside hopefully, but of course it's just the two pills. The disappointing ones. The ones I want to pulverize and then hurl against the wall.

The Solo cup is mocking me.

But I force myself to try and look as grateful as possible. I have to appear to be better now, more humble, more normal. Because there can be no question as to whether I'm going home in eight days.

As I am moving over to one side like we've been instructed, the nurse suddenly yelps a little and leans forward, putting her arms through the window and grabbing me by the shoulders—all in one motion.

"Wait!" she shrieks.

The passion in her voice startles me, and I immediately look down at my cup.

Hey—maybe they did give me the wrong one by mistake!

"Laura," she says, her eyes misty.

Twenty-two days here and I don't think I've ever actually really seen her until just now. I mean, I've looked at her because she's the one who doles out the drugs, so of course I looked at her. But I don't think I could have picked her out of a lineup. She looks like so many of the locals here, severe ponytail, sun-worn skin, and coffee-stained teeth. But now I see for the first time that her eyes are deep brown, almost black, and surrounded by a spiderwebbing of deep, craggly lines.

What could she want?

"The lights have come on," she says, smiling and leaning closer, her irises darting back and forth quickly from one of my eyes to the other. "The lights have come on in your eyes."

Huh?

"We've all been a little worried about you, but oh . . ." She clasps her hands together in front of her chest. "This gives me hope, Laura. This is good. Really, really good. I see you now."

We've all?

I feel annoyance rising in my chest about the idea of a group of these yeehaw fuckers sitting around discussing my odds of making it. My inner cynic wants to shut her down with extreme prejudice and let her know that no matter what she thinks she sees, her ass is mistaken— she does not see me.

But instead, and very much against my will, my whole body warms, I feel my eyes getting moist, and a tightness in my throat.

"It's really good, Laura," she repeats. She's still staring right into my eyes.

I can feel the new girl behind me shifting around and getting impatient.

Suddenly I'm back to day one, clawing my jawbones with my fingertips to keep my teeth from chattering and praying that no one tries to talk to me until after I've had my nightly dose. I couldn't imagine then that one day I'd be the one off all my meds getting ready to go home and that there would be some new girl crawling out of her skin. I didn't know then that the light in my eyes had been extinguished, so I couldn't imagine it coming back on.

"Um, wow—thank you."

I don't know if my smile looks forced or not. I look down at her name tag and realize that she's that same nurse, the one who was in the office the day I checked in.

Eliza.

I feel tears escape my eyes and run down my cheeks and am suddenly flush with shame, afraid that the squirmy girl behind me will see me crying.

"Thank you, Eliza."

―――

Do you startle easily?

Laura and I are taking a computerized psych evaluation in a tiny building on a part of the campus I've never seen before. As I understand it, this assessment is just one item in a series of *i*s to be dotted and *t*s to be crossed before we can be sent home. Deborah hasn't brought up the halfway house since that last session, so I'm hopeful that the fact that they're giving me this eval means they've changed their minds about keeping me here.

Ever since this new girl named Dawn referred to me as "Black Laura" last week, Laura and I have been calling each other Barbie and Christie, like the dolls. I, of course, am Christie, Barbie's Black friend.

We are sitting opposite each other, separated by two dingy, oversize computers that could be right out of *You've Got Mail*.

"You have thirty minutes to complete it," says our monitor, Sarah. She's pear-shaped with round glasses and Birkenstocks. I think she might be Scott S.'s counselor.

"Don't worry if you haven't finished when time's up. Just get as far as you can."

As soon as she leaves, Laura bounces over to my side of the table. She pops a stick of contraband bubblegum in her mouth as she reads the questions out loud.

1) Please check the following words that describe yourself:
   1. Considerate
   2. Confused
   3. Suicidal
   4. Crazy

"Should we check 'Crazy'?" she laughs. "Just to see what they say?"

2) Have you ever belonged to a gang?
   If yes, please state your position and rank.

"That's racist," she says with a deadpan face. "They didn't give me that question."

"What!? Really?"

I get up to look at her screen and she pushes me back down with a belly laugh.

"I'm just fucking with you, Christie!"

3) Do you startle easily?

"Yes," we both say at once and then burst into giggles.

Once she goes back to her side, I take a deep breath and wiggle my fingers. Laura has no kids, no one at home depending on her to get well, so she can fuck with them all she wants. But I need to give them the answers that will graduate me the hell out of here with an honorable discharge. I've decided that I'm going home by August 14 regardless, but I know I stand a better chance against what's waiting for me if I leave with the blessing of "Team Laura." I check both "Confused" and "Considerate" and then continue down the page. Thirty minutes later when Sarah taps me on the shoulder to let me know time is up, I jump and stifle a yelp.

I go back and reopen the third question, "Do you startle easily?," and check "Yes."

Once we're back outside, the sun is starting to go down. Laura heads over to the smokers' pit, and I wander down toward the pool where Scott S. can usually be found eviscerating folks at the ping-pong table. I want to tell him about the psych eval and see if he was given one as well. I want to know if we're on track to go home at the same time.

Before I see him, I hear him happily talking shit to whoever he's playing with. A few steps later, I see that a couple of guys are standing around watching as he's playing his roommate Jeff. Jeff reminds me of an elf with his short legs, round face, and red hair and beard. Just as I hit the bottom step, Scott slams the ball past Jeff and raises his arms in triumph.

"Hell yeah!!!"

Jeff tucks his ball under his paddle on the table and puts his hands up.

"Yo dude, I surrender. Um, also? Your girl is here."

Scott is still smiling from his victory when he turns to look for me. He strolls casually over to me then, putting his arm around my shoulder and guiding me toward the table.

"Hey," he says so only I can hear. "Where've you been?"

I tell him about the psych eval and am both relieved and irritated when he tells me he did his a couple days ago.

And you didn't tell me?

"Trippy questions, right?"

He's facing me with his back to the setting sun and taking a drag on a cigarette. Normally I find smoking to be disgusting, but with Scott for some reason I don't hate it as much. Sometimes, when he's in silhouette, like now, I even find it to be slightly sexy—like Brad Pitt.

"How'd you do?" he asks.

His blond hair is tousled from ping-pong and his bare arms are glistening with sunscreen and sweat. I move closer to him without answering and he starts to back up, tossing his cigarette in a butt can without looking.

"I guess I startle easily," I laugh.

"I figured," he says, smiling.

"But I think I did okay. We're so close to going home now, can you believe it? I'm so fucking ready to be out of here, and at the same time, I don't know if I'm ready."

"You're ready," he says. "You've done the work. You stayed the whole time. You're clean and sober, and now your kids need you back home."

"Yeah, I stayed, that's true. But do you understand that I would never have stayed if it hadn't been for you? If you hadn't been there from the beginning, if you hadn't snuck over to comfort me after my kids left that day, I definitely would have bailed."

"Yeah, but you didn't."

"Again, because of you, Scott S. four-one-two."

Scott's smile creates a fireball inside me that barrels its way from my toes to my skull. I fully understand at that moment that inhaling his breath is the only way to extinguish the burning. I feel like if I don't get his mouth next to mine in a matter of seconds, I might combust.

"What's up?" He grins widely, holding his hands up in the surrender pose, still moving backward.

"Nothing," I say, walking closer.

Something.

I've backed him to the edge of the stairs. If he takes another step, he's going to fall back. I reach out for him and put my arms around his shoulders, pressing my breasts against his chest and pushing my thigh against his fly.

Now he's looking around, but Jeff took the other two guys with him when he walked off. This area is quite literally off the beaten path, and the sun has just disappeared from the sky.

We're all alone.

I hover in front of his face then and gently capture his lower lip with my teeth, pulling it into my mouth, sucking on it for a second before I find his tongue with mine. His right arm is still around my shoulders, but now he cradles my head with his free hand and kisses me back.

I taste his cigarette and an undertone of something yummy, like cinnamon. His tongue is practiced, smooth, and full.

Promising.

I lose myself for a moment and enjoy the rush of this, whatever this is. We had a lecture three days ago about transference. Trading one addiction for another.

Have I traded pills for Scott S.?

I feel parts of my body pulsing and coming alive one at a time like lights on a Christmas tree—my nipples, my thighs, my fingertips, my ears. I'm breathing in his breath and he's breathing in mine. When I start to reach down to his pants he freezes up but I don't move my hand.

"What's wrong?"

"Um." He looks anguished.

"No one can see us," I say, giggling.

"I know, it's not that—it's just that I can't do this. I'm sorry, I want to . . ." He looks into my eyes. "You know I want to, but I can't. I can't risk getting caught."

Say what?

"Look," he says. "When we get out of here, if you still want to do this"—he motions back and forth between us—"I'm right here for it."

I'm staring at him like I've never seen him before.

Are you kidding me with this?? I'm finally giving in and you're out?? You fucking kissed me first!

"Laura, you're married."

I open my mouth to protest, and he puts his finger up.

"Okay, but you're not divorced yet. Both of us have to be really careful because our actions affect more than just us."

Oh, I see what's going on—he doesn't want me anymore.

I pull away from him petulantly, wiping my mouth dramatically and turning toward the stairs.

"Fine."

Fuck you.

"No, not fine," he says, spinning me around. "I don't think you're hearing me. I *really* want to be with you. You're the only thing I'm thinking about—all the time. You know that, from the very moment I first saw you. But I can't. Not here."

I'm glaring at him now, trying to hurt him like he's hurt me.

"And just think about this," he continues. "We haven't even been sober a month. Do you really want to take a chance and maybe lose that? After everything you've just gone through to get here. Do you think some make-out session with me is worth it when there's so much at stake?"

Yes.

"Look, we're both getting out of here in a few days, and then I have a court date."

He cups my chin and raises my face until my eyes are level with his.

"I go to jail if I get kicked out, right?"

I nod slowly.

"I need to see my kids. And I really don't want to be the reason you don't get to be with yours."

Shit the fucking bed.

I lower my eyes again and sit on the stairs with a defeated motion.

"Hey," he says, sitting down next to me. "We still have a few more days. Let's enjoy hanging out before we get back to reality. We've both got hella shit to face out there."

He's right.

What is this impulse that blocks me from seeing the impact of my actions on other people? Am I a bad person? Is it self-preservation? Is it fear?

Let it go, Laura.

I feel something uncoil in my chest and my lungs expand, drawing in a stream of air. I close my eyes and exhale before looking over at him.

"Sho nuff shit," I say, smiling a little.

"Sho nuff shit," he says, smiling back.

———

Laura went back to Chicago today.

The sun was just coming up when her car arrived. I walked her down to the front of our dorm, carrying one of her heavier bags. She kissed me full on the lips, pressing her forehead gently against mine and held me to her. To me, she bequeathed all the artwork she'd completed during her stay, her super-soft blanket that no one was ever allowed to touch, and a tremendous stash of contraband candy and chocolate.

"Look," she said, stroking my cheek. "I'm coming to see you in Cali soon, so this is *not* goodbye, all right? Three more days, Christie. Three more days until you hold them in your arms, sleep with them in your bed. You got this."

Now I totally get how people get so bonded on all those "strangers-living-together-for-a-month" reality TV series.

I used to scoff at those shows, dismissing them as overproduced, scripted nonsense. But here I am, a forty-three-year-old mom, twenty-seven days into a rehab stint, and I am tearfully saying goodbye to a self-consumed, love–addicted white girl from Chicago—aka, my new "best friend."

It feels real. Just like the electricity that runs through my system whenever Scott S. is near feels real.

After she leaves, I trudge over to the main office. Today, they're allowing four of us to make our arrangements to go home. We get to use the computers and our cell phones for this special occasion.

My fingers tingle with excitement when I hold my BlackBerry in my hand for the first time in twenty-seven days.

"Hello old friend," I whisper, cradling it gently.

Deb has approved my call list, which includes Southwest Airlines to book my ticket home, Marguerita Doukas, an LA-area therapist specializing in addiction, and a woman named Morgan who apparently "graduated" from the program a little over two years ago and lives near me in Studio City.

"I think you'll like her," Deb said, smiling. "She's a mom and a pill head, and she hated it here too."

While the tech is busy with someone else, I add a number of my own. I have a secret.

For my first two weeks here, I savored the idea that I would get my Ambien refill the moment I got out. It was really the only thing that kept me going at times, the fantasy of being alone with a bottle of Ambien again. After the kids' visit, I tried to let the fantasy go, but it's resurfaced on its own now, and it's really compelling. During group and lectures, I daydream about hugging on my kids, watching *Friends*, and eating Ambien after they fall asleep. I can practically feel that golden oil coating my insides and sending me off into that silky smooth sleep.

Oh, how I miss sleep.

I get two, maybe three fitful hours a night here, during which I'm tortured by violent dreams filled with ghoulish chases down dark, endless hallways, bloody animals, and scenes from my own funeral. I wake every morning before dawn with a scream in my throat, drenched in sweat, and my heart beating out of my chest.

This can't be my life forever. No one could be expected to live like this. My mind never turns off.

The other truth is that I'm simply too much of a coward to go home without my pills. I can't possibly face what waits for me: the angry husband, the shameful post-incarceration period, Maria, the Ashley School moms, the doctors, and the pharmacists.

I can't make it without those pills.

So . . .

I need to transfer my final Linbaum Ambien refill, the one that came up last week to the CVS in Wickenburg. I can't wait until I go back to LA to get it. I've mapped out exactly how long it will take for me to get from The Meadows to the pharmacy.

Nineteen minutes.

Anticipating this opportunity before we left Studio City, I'd dialed both CVS numbers so they'd be at the top of "Recent Calls." That way I wouldn't have to risk anyone clocking me looking up pharmacy numbers and getting suspicious.

Speaking loud enough for everyone to hear, I book a one-way ticket from Phoenix to Burbank. Afterward, I reserve a town car from a local service to pick me up at The Meadows. I doodle around on my notepad then, waiting for the tech to use the restroom or something. The moment she steps out, I hit Send and call the Studio City CVS, praying they don't put me on hold. When a woman answers, I lower my head and speak in a hushed, hurried voice.

"Yes, R-O-B-B-I-N-S. I'm stuck in Arizona for a bit, can you please transfer this prescription to a local pharmacy for me? Yes, it's number six-zero-three-seven-six."

I feel that old familiar surge while I'm talking. The rush that confirms that I'm doing something dangerous, something for which there will be a tremendous penalty if I'm caught. But this time it's accompanied by a small nagging voice.

Really?

You're going to blow everything and get high? After a month away from your kids. After suffering through the medical detox? After enduring all that shame and humiliation?

I find a vacant room in my mind and shove the voice inside, slamming the door on it and then bolting it shut.

Shut the fuck up!

When I hang up, I type "San Fernando Valley recovery meetings" into the browser's search bar as quickly as possible and hit Return. These gatherings have mysterious, cringy titles like "Old Timers," "Came to Believe," and "Sundowners." I want to turn to the guy next to me and make fun of the meeting names, but he's crying quietly to someone on his phone.

Aw jeez.

I start to jot down a few of the places and dates as evidence to show Deb when I feel someone standing very still, directly behind me. Over the hum of the air conditioner, I hear someone swallow.

Someone's watching me.

I turn my head slowly and catch a glimpse of the tech behind my chair. I freeze, like maybe if I don't move, this isn't really happening.

Shit, shit, shit. I didn't see her come back in. Did she hear me on the phone? How long has she been there?

The tech, though, is either playing it real cool or is completely oblivious. She places her hand on my shoulder, bends down to peek at my screen, and then gives me a nod of approval, before moving on to crying guy.

She didn't hear nothing.

That payday feeling I get when I've fooled someone rushes through me, and suddenly I'm filled with a sense of fresh confidence.

When our time is up I head over to my session with Deb. As I'm approaching her office, I hear voices inside and I stop dead. Martin, the facility director who talked me into staying almost a month ago, is there with her—I'd recognize his voice anywhere. I heard him say my name, but I can't quite make out anything else. I'm scared to get caught listening in the hallway, so I peek around the corner and knock on the open door.

They might know that I called about the refill.

Shitfuckshit.

Keeping my expression as casual as possible I manage a smile and force a casual tone.

"Well, hello there!"

He stands up then and offers me his seat.

"Good to see you, Laura. I hear you're planning to leave us in a few days."

Fifty-two hours. And why did you say "planning"?

"Looks like it," I say as brightly as possible, sneaking a look at Deb to see if I can tell what's going on.

Deb keeps her head down though and is flipping through my chart.

"Laura's really been something these last couple of weeks," she says.

I'm feeling light-headed, so I grip the arms of my chair.

Why won't you look at me, Deb?

"So," says Martin, turning to me. "Something has come to our attention, and we wanted to discuss it with you."

Here it is.

"Um, forgive me, would you like some water?"

All at once, I'm aware that my mouth feels as though it's been glued shut.

"Yes, please," I manage.

It's the fucking refill for sure. They're going to try and send me to that fucking halfway house.

He clears his throat and waits until Deb hands me a water bottle.

"This isn't exactly about you, it's about Scott S."

Scott? What the fuuuuu?

"What about him?"

"Well, this is most unusual, but it seems he's requested permission to ride with you to the Phoenix airport when you leave on Thursday."

Wait wut??

"Normally we don't allow patients to leave with each other, regardless of gender, but Deborah tells me that the two of you have developed a, um, genuine friendship that she feels has been beneficial and she's okay with the idea."

I've heard a couple of stories about what happened to patients who tried to leave together. It's strictly forbidden, of course, because so many of the patients are here for sex and love addiction. Sending men and women home together from rehab is like sending a drunk home with a bottle of booze and saying "Good luck!"

Still . . .

Scott asked them if he could leave with me? And Deb said yes???

"So, if it's something you'd like to do, once your vehicle arrives, you have permission to pick up Scott S. at the male apartments on your way off campus on Thursday."

They don't know about the refill!

Hell yeah.

Two more nights in this place and then I get to get the fuck out of Dodge.

CHAPTER SIXTEEN

Checking Out

The two bronze-plated medallions in my right hand clink together noisily when I move my fingers. They are the trophies of my sobriety, surprisingly heavy Meadows trinkets I get to take home with me today. I'm standing at the meds window for the very last time, getting my departure instructions from Nurse Eliza. She's holding a ziplock bag with a birth control packet in it up near her ear. The now nearly empty birth control packet I came in with thirty days ago.

"Listen, love. I know you can't wait to get out of here, but did your counselor talk to you about what to do after you leave?"

"Um, yeah, ninety meetings in ninety days, get rid of all leftover booze and pills at home, avoid triggers . . ."

"Listen here, darlin'," she says, lowering her voice as she sets the bag on the counter between us. I have to restrain myself from grabbing it and running.

I'm so friggin' ready to raise the fuck up out of this bitch.

"I'm going to share something with you, okay?"

"Okay." I shift my weight from one foot to the other.

Shit, I still need to finish packing before I pick up Scott S. . . .

"You may have hated it here, but you were safe. Safe from the outside, but mostly safe from yourself. They say an alcoholic's mind is like a dangerous neighborhood, never go there alone. Once you get out there, it will be you and your mind. And all those things that were off the table in here will start to sound real good. Hell, I remember when I first got out . . ."

"Wait, you were in here too?"

"Oh heavens no. I couldn't afford a place like this. There's a good Salvation Army, right down in Phoenix. Listen, the price was different, but the feelings are the same. No one tells you how it's going to be once you leave these walls. When you do get triggered, and you want to use, whoo boy! You'd better have someone to hold you down, cause every part of you will be screaming at you to get something in your system. The obsession will be a monster, Laura, it will set your skin on fire. That's why ninety meetings in ninety days, that's why you avoid those triggers, that's why you empty the bar and the medicine cabinet. New sobriety is a balloon in a room with an open window. Eventually the balloon is going to blow right out of there unless somebody ties it down. When you leave here you're gonna need to fight like hell to tie yourself down, do you hear? Otherwise, when you get those cravings they're gonna win."

She thinks I'm like all those other addicts who go out and score from their dealer right after getting out of treatment. Yes, I'm going to pick up my refill at CVS, but I'm not obsessing about it all. These pills are just an insurance policy for me to carry with me to use only as needed. And unlike those junkies who overshoot the mark and OD, now that I've had this break, I know that I'll finally be able to take my pills as prescribed again—one per night.

An electric shock runs through me when I spot the CVS sign up the road.

Oh my God, here it is!

As we get closer, my heart pounds, and I concentrate on not twitching, sweating, or freaking out. Scott is talking to the driver, asking him annoyingly pointless questions like, "Where do you live?" and "How long have you been driving?"

I sit up straight as we get within a few hundred feet of the store and open my mouth, preparing to ask the driver to stop. I'd quietly practiced this over and over in my room at The Meadows.

"Oh wait, there's a CVS! Can you pull over please? I just need to pop in there for a couple of things."

I thought I'd whisper to Scott then that I needed tampons or something equally unappealing, then run in quickly without him before he could ask any questions. But I realize now that as carefully as I'd planned this little caper, I'd forgotten to factor in one major variable: Scott likes to go everywhere I go.

What if he comes in with me anyway?

I can't just say "No! Stay!" and leave him in the car like a puppy. But I also just can't waltz in there and get my Ambien refill with him standing next to me either.

Maybe I can throw him off the scent by sending him somewhere else. Hey! There's a post office right next door! *I could ask him to get me some stamps. Oh, wait! There's a Goodwill too. I could say that my clothes have bad juju and I need to donate them right away. There's also . . .*

And now it's gone.

I look out the back window of the town car until the CVS sign disappears behind us. A sharp ache pulses in my shoulders and I realize that I've been clutching my seat belt so hard that I've left ten little crescent-shaped nail marks in the stiff, shiny nylon.

I am numb.

"Hey, did you hear that?" Scott says excitedly. "He says there's a mall near the Phoenix airport with a movie theater. If we have time, we should see *Dark Knight* before your flight, I hear Heath Ledger is amazing . . ."

I can't believe that I'm not screaming at the driver to turn the car around. My heart and mind are both racing as the car turns onto Highway 60 and heads toward Phoenix.

Say something.

"Hey man," Scott leans forward and addresses the driver again. "Is there a Starbucks nearby? We've been dying for real coffee."

Faaaacccccccckkkkk.

I lean back against the seat, closing my eyes and leaving my arms limp by my sides.

Did I really just leave that refill there? What am I going to do? How am I going to go home?

The jonesy sensation in my hands reaches a fever pitch, and I become suddenly aware of different parts of my body feeling like they've burst into flames. I try to push Nurse Eliza's voice out of my head so I can concentrate on what words I need to say to get the driver to turn around without arousing any suspicions.

Oh, there go my feet, my legs, my hips, my stomach, my arms . . .

I should have said no, let Scott find his own ride to the airport.

Scott's grinning cheerfully at me now. His expression says, *I'm so happy. Isn't this great??*

"We're almost there," he says.

Even though his hand is warm, I jump when he puts it on my bare thigh.

"What's your coffee order?" he says. "I know all these crazy intimate things about you, but I don't know your coffee order."

Oh my God. He's killing me.

He thinks we're the same, he and I, that we both went to The Meadows to get sober. He has no idea that I've been plotting and scheming my relapse from day one. He doesn't know that the surety that I could have Ambien again was what kept me going during those thirty hellish, sleepless nights.

I envy how "done" he seems. How casual he is about going back to life, back to reality. I wish I felt the same.

And now my darling Ambien is miles behind us. I can practically taste the bitterness that bursts through the tablet's slick coating once you've held it in your mouth for too long. I can feel the weight that assures me that the bottle contains thirty perfect, tiny Tic Tac–shaped ovals. I can hear the rattle they make when I shake it, they sound like no other pill.

Oh, if only I could feel the relief that I know they'd provide.

But no. They'll stay there, unclaimed, waiting for me in some bum-fuck CVS in the middle of fuckin' nowhere forever. And I can think of no excuse to turn us around without coming clean.

A sunbeam is piercing through the front window and lighting up his face. I'm struck again by how kind his eyes are, but there is something else there now, way, way in the background. Behind the sunlight, behind the kindness, behind the joy of being with me, there's that thin corrosive thread of something I know all too well.

Fear.

He's scared to go home. This boy's been whistling in the dark.

"So, tell me, Laura Robbins. What is your coffee order?"

We've come to the turnoff. I can see the Starbucks. It's on a stand-alone island between the highway and another road. There's nothing else for miles.

I've been so in my head about getting these pills that I haven't really allowed myself to feel the magnitude of what he and I are both about to face. He goes back to a court date and his empty house in Kamas, Utah. I go back to my kids and who knows what? My husband could have told the whole city about my addiction, what a shitty wife and mother I am. He could have shown them all the pictures of my empty pill bottles. A lot could have happened in thirty days, I could be returning home to another ambush.

Scott's staring at me shyly now, coaxing my eyes to meet his.

If it weren't for my kids, I'd grab my pills and head to Utah with Scott in a heartbeat.

But my kids have been counting the days until I get home. I have disappointed them by leaving, by being away for so long and by sending them home without me when they came to visit. I can't disappoint them again. I can't run anymore. I can't hide from the pain that waits for me. For them, I have to try to be brave and woman up.

I meet Scott's eyes, not caring that he might catch the tears glistening in mine, and open my arms for him. He leans in and I bring his head to my chest, running my fingers through his hair. I hum a little as though I'm soothing a frightened child, feeling the warmth rising through the top of his head.

Crying heads get warm like that.

The urgency to go back to get my pills is draining out of me. Something defeated, remorseful, and sorrowful is replacing it, and there's also a mustard seed of some other feeling, way, way down—resolve. What if I go back home and actually stay sober? What if I become the mom my kids deserve, then what? I'm about to be forty-four years old and I still don't know what I want to be when I grow up. Could I go back to school? Is that me? Could I start writing again? All those journals, all those stories?

"Venti Americano, room for cream, is my coffee order," I say. "And like ten packets of sugar."

And just like that, I've tied myself down—this time.

PART THREE

Homecoming

CHAPTER SEVENTEEN

Out of the Frying Pan

My trembling is so bad that I feel ill-equipped to drive myself over to Nancy's office. Pacing the length of my closet over and over, I try to think of an excuse to cancel my eleven o'clock with her. I don't want to walk back into that office. I don't want to see all those people. I don't want to answer Nancy's questions about rehab. I don't want to pick up where we left off, strategizing, conniving, and scheming about how to "win" my case.

I just want this to be over. My anxiety is unbearable and my body aches like I've got Ebola or cholera. I just want to be divorced and detoxed enough so that I'm not so miserable. I want to not be so wounded and fragile.

My phone rings in my hand and it's a number I don't recognize, so I hold my breath until it stops, letting it go to voice mail. It's that woman Morgan, the one that Deb said graduated from The Meadows and lives in my area. She sounds older and very white. Her message says that there is a daily noontime meeting down the street from me and that she'd love to meet me there sometime.

Um, no thanks, sister.

Suddenly my thoughts turn to Scott, and every fiber of my being urges me to call him. He's the dopamine hit that my head needs now. He's also the only one who understands what I'm going through.

I start to cry when I get his voice mail.

"Hey, please call me back. I have to go see my lawyer and I'm scared. I need to talk to you."

Pulling up to Nancy's building, it takes everything in me not to gun the accelerator and flee, cars and pedestrians be damned. I refuse to make eye contact with anyone for fear they can see right through me, or worse, they've heard about my fall from grace. I avoid looking at the kind man with bushy eyebrows who always parks my car, barely nodding hello before walking briskly toward the parking garage elevator. I look away from the security guard at the desk as he prints out an ID badge for the twenty-seventh floor.

Can you see the shame pouring off me? Was there some type of building-wide memo circulated about me going to rehab?

It's unfathomable that anyone could be expected to behave normally after coming home from rehab. I imagine it's similar to the feeling one has when they are grieving the loss of someone they love, and then going out into the world to find that everything is business as usual: rush-hour traffic, a cruelly bright sun, oblivious and idiotically bubbly people. I'm mildly surprised to see that the office hasn't changed. Same receptionist, same sofa in the waiting room, same ridiculously extravagant lily and rose display on the entry table.

While waiting in Nancy's office, I spot my file on her desk.

Robbins v. Robbins.

Suddenly I'm flooded by the memories of the last time I was here. I had Ambien in my pockets then. I got to eat an Ambien on my way home. The last time I was here I was so scared, but now I think I am even more scared. I have never felt more alone in my life. My thoughts flash to Scott again. He is the only one who knows what this nightmare feels like, the only one who knows what this nightmare feels like. I also allow myself to fantasize about Ambien for the first time since getting home. I wonder how long it would take to get my refill transferred back from Wickenburg to Studio City.

I could do this if I had Ambien. If I could sleep, if I had some relief, then I could look people in the eyes again.

"Well, hello," says Nancy, her heels clicking on the marble floor. She's wearing crisp, wide-legged navy pants and a cream bowknot blouse. "Sorry to keep you waiting. Did Kelsey offer you something? Would you like some water or tea?"

Ambien?

"No, I'm okay."

"So, how are you? How do you feel?"

"I don't know. Scared, shaky, kind of like an alien."

"But how did it go there, though? I mean, were they able to get you, um, off it okay?"

"I'm sober as a judge," I say, giving her a two-finger salute. "Isn't that the saying?"

"Great," she says, shuffling through some papers. "Congratulations on that. Did they give you a certificate or something I can put in your file? Something that says you completed the program?"

"Uh, yeah, something like that. I forgot to bring it though."

"Make sure Noel gets a copy," she says, looking at her watch.

This wasn't the greeting I was expecting. It's like she's deliberately avoiding looking at me, like she's pissed or something. I was thinking about telling her about Scott, but now I'm not so sure.

"So, as we discussed before you left, your timing wasn't optimal. I'd like to try to use the fact that you sought help to our advantage. If he takes the stance that you're an unfit mother because of your problem, then we have proof that you've dealt with your dependence, real evidence to counter with."

I smile in her direction, giving her my best "straight A student" vibe.

"Okay, so what's next?" I say eagerly.

"Listen." She picks up her note pad. "I'm not usually this prescriptive, but I've decided to give you some clear-cut instructions. If you want to keep your kids, you need to do exactly as I tell you."

"Of course."

"You may want to write these down. I'll need you to follow them, all of them, until this divorce is final, understand?"

I nod and start to look for a pen in my purse.

"One: Starting this week, you're going to get drug tested twice a week for ninety days.

"Two: I need you to go to daily meetings, go to two or three a day if you can. Get documentation there too; I'll give you something to get signed. Collect chips, that sort of thing.

"Three: Get a sponsor. Someone who might be willing to testify about your sobriety if necessary.

"Four: No drugs. Nothing stronger than an aspirin and not a drop of alcohol can you consume. I'm talking about anything, champagne sauce, rum raisin ice cream, stay clear of all of it.

"Five: Get yourself into therapy right away. Twice per week at least.

"Six: Resume all your normal mom stuff—pickup, drop-off, lunches, bedtime, all of that.

"Seven: Get back to your parent association duties.

"Eight: Never, never negotiate with your husband outside of my presence. You two can talk about the kids, talk about the Lakers, talk about your housekeeper, I don't care. But you do not discuss the divorce.

"Nine: Reconnect with your friends ASAP. Lunches, tennis lessons, your life should look as normal as possible. I need your friends to stay on your side, testify on your behalf if necessary.

"Ten: And this may be the most important one, *never* bruise this man's ego. I've seen so many divorces that were just cruising along and then bam!, he suspects there might be someone else. He thinks there's someone else, that's like waving the red flag in front of a bull. Just the idea, the very suspicion of another man, and everything that we've worked so hard for will be derailed in a nanosecond. I'm talking custody to cars, everything."

Nancy puts her pad away and looks up.

"Make sure you document everything in that day planner of yours.

Committee meetings, snack mom and all that, okay? Sprinkle a few good details in there. I want a record of all those lovely 'upstanding citizen' activities. Also . . ."

But I was still back at number one.

"Wait," I interrupt her. "Drug testing? Is that necessary? Are they asking for that?"

"No one's asked for that. But it's a good idea to have it in case your sobriety is ever called into question."

Oh, she IS pissed. She's punishing me for going to rehab. Definitely NOT telling her about Scott S.

I fix my face before I open my mouth again.

"So do they just come at the same time every week or . . . ?"

"You'll call them to make the appointment. The address is right here," she says, handing me a green slip of paper.

Hold the fucking phone!

Everything is delivery now. Our doctor makes house calls for our yearly physicals. Hell, there's even a phlebotomist that comes over whenever the kids need a blood draw.

"Wait, I have to *go* somewhere and do this? Can't they come to me? I was picturing more of a mobile service, something more discreet."

"You would think they'd have something like that, wouldn't you? But no, and sorry it's not in a more convenient location. Noel could only find two places that do non-court-ordered drug testing. We've arranged for you to go twice a week for the next three months. Hopefully we'll have you divorced long before then."

Twice-a-week drug testing. For three whole months.

Up until now I thought I might be able to take the occasional Ambien. But now that she's talking drug testing, it's crystal clear that this option will be off the table completely. Suddenly—and probably because I know that I can't—I'm overcome by a craving so powerful that I feel a band of sweat forming across the bridge of my nose.

I'm so fucked.

In my head I'm frantically trying to recall the time I googled "how to pass a drug test."

You have to drink quarts of water, right? I think there was something about taking Advil. Also, lemon juice, right? And vinegar! Definitely vinegar . . .

I look at the slip and see the address.

"Hey, Nancy, this isn't just inconvenient, it's deep in the hood."

"Is it?" She's smiling now. "I'm not familiar with the Valley. But the only other place was in Lancaster."

"Where's that?"

"Exactly! It's so far away it might as well be the moon. In fact, it looks a little like the moon. Either way, this is our best bet."

FUCK! I can't do it. Even if I drown myself in lemon juice and vinegar, I won't be able to beat a drug test twice a week.

"So, are we all good?"

Not at all.

"Good." Nancy sets the pad down and leans in toward me, propping her small, pointy chin on top of her folded hands. I zone out on the stack of rose-gold bangles she's wearing on her left wrist.

"They also said you'll need a sobriety buddy, someone who you check in with on a regular basis. Do you have anyone like that?"

"I did meet someone in treatment . . ."

"Oh?" She peers over her hands. "Someone we can get on the record if need be? Who?"

Scott S.

"Um, her name is Laura. We were roommates . . . there. She's back in Chicago now, but we talk. I can make sure it's a regular thing."

"Make sure you make that urine analysis appointment before we lose any time."

"I will."

"Okay, and one last thing."

She takes a sip from a glass of water on her desk.

"Around this time, he might try to negotiate with you at home. He might say there's a way for the two of you to make a deal without lawyers. Don't you fall for it; it just means he's scared of losing. Always refer him to me. Say you'd rather let your attorney deal with it."

172

"Well, we haven't really talked about anything except the kids."

"And since you're still sharing the house, make sure you're the parent that people see at school, at games and playdates. Not that we'll need to, but I'd like to be able to call anyone in your life, other parents, teachers, coaches, as a possible character witness."

I nod and dig my fingers into my palms. My daily afternoon detox storm is starting to blow. My heart pounds and beads of sweat are forming on my temples. I make a show of looking at my BlackBerry.

"Are you okay?" She's inspecting me now, frowning as she looks over my face.

"Yeah."

"I didn't ask about what it was like coming home."

Oh my God, it was a nightmare.

"Did he change any codes, gate or alarm? Were your things as you left them? Did you check your bank account? Do you still have access to everything you did before?"

Oh, that's what she means.

"Um, gate and alarm codes are the same. Haven't been to the bank yet. I think he went through all my stuff, but it's too soon to know if anything is missing."

"Take pictures of anything that seems amiss. I should have had you take pictures before you left for comparison. Damn!"

Nancy starts flipping through a file on her desk. Signaling, I think, that our meeting is over.

"Well, I'd better get back over the hill," I say, standing up. "It's almost time for pickup."

"Yes, that's good. You go be the first mom in that line. Let everyone see how eager you are to pick up your kids. All of this is crucial to keeping custody, Laura. You'll thank me later."

Ohkayyyyy . . .

I get up and sling my purse over my shoulder.

"Thanks, Nancy."

———

I'm thinking about her on the drive back over the hill. She didn't really seem to care about the emotional toll of coming home from treatment. Her interest seemed to be much more targeted toward anything evidential that she needed to know, code changes, bank accounts, and riffled-through items. But I'll never forget the feelings of shame and fear that paralyzed me when I first walked into my house two days ago.

——

The flight from Phoenix to Burbank, which normally takes an hour and a half, seemed to last only seconds. It felt as though we were landing just moments after takeoff. I knew no one would be at the airport to greet me, as I hadn't given anyone my flight information. But I was still braced for some process server showing up at the gate with a document granting my husband full custody of the boys. Punishment for my shameful incarceration.

I asked the cab driver to pull all the way up to our gate box so I could punch in the code, and I was surprised to find that the code still worked. As the gates slowly open, down at the end of the driveway I could see Jordan escaping out the front door and Jacob right behind him. A sob caught in my throat as I fought to compose myself.

Jacob's little face and hands were pressed up against the window of the cab, and I smiled and motioned for him to step back so I could open the door. It's then that I noticed him standing in the doorway.

"How was the flight?"

"Oh, fine."

My voice was squeaky, like a guitar that's been strung too tight. I closed my eyes and cleared my throat. Jordan looked up at me sharply.

"What's wrong?"

"Nothing," we both said at the same time. I smiled weakly at him, and he held out his hand for my shoulder bag. I relinquished it, wondering if he was planning on going through it.

I lapsed into a dream state as the boys pulled me through the doorway. The house looked older to me, darker and slightly sinister. I wanted to tear all the drapes off their rods and flood the foyer with light.

Did he paint while I was gone? Weren't the walls a different shade of orange? The staircase runner looks so worn and stained . . .

My body stopped when I got to the double doors of the master. My legs wouldn't move, my breath stopped mid-inhale.

This is it.

I'd spent the last month dreaming of this moment, holding their hands, smelling their hair, being out of the fucking Meadows. I'd dreamed about my bed, my sheets, my TV, my remote control. But all of a sudden, I didn't know what to do. My throat felt obstructed when I looked down at the boys. I saw them talking, I heard them talking, but I didn't have the words to say back.

What if my Meadows team was right? What if it's too soon?

"Mommy?"

That nightstand drawer, those earring boxes, that space on the mantel behind the Buddha statue—I hid pills there, and there and there.

"Mommy?" said Jordan again. "Can we camp out here with you tonight?"

"Of course," I said. My voice sounded better, more like I remember it.

He'd joined us in the bedroom, dropping both my bags on the floor of the closet.

"Everything's covered in this dust," he says.

I should have wiped my luggage off at the airport, so as to call less attention to them. It looked like I was traveling through the red desert. My two journals from The Meadows are in that duffel, the ones they forced us to write, the ones Deb checked through, not to read, but to make sure I was keeping up. Journals where I wrote about Scott S.

"Yeah, sorry," I said. "Arizona has all this clay."

My hand movements felt awkward, flourishy. I balled them up and put them behind me.

What did I used to do with my hands when I talked? How do people just know what to do with their hands?

Dinner was quiet. I could hear everyone chewing their Jerry's Deli pastrami melts and french fries. I tried to eat, but my stomach wasn't cooperating. I steamed with guilt as I avoided his eyes, taking a few sips of the chocolate milkshake he'd ordered for me. I wish I could have said something to him, thanked him for the milkshake, for ordering dinner, for pulling double duty while I was in rehab, for not kicking me out of the house or poisoning the kids against me. But just like this sandwich, the words stuck in my throat.

Is he rooting for me? I wondered. *Does he hate me now? What did he dig up on me while I was there?*

I unpack my bags quickly before I shower. Everything looked to be in order. As fast as possible, I stashed both journals under a pile of sweaters in my closet. Afterward, I walked into the bedroom and stopped short when I saw that he was there saying goodnight to the boys. He looked up at me for a second with an anguished expression, and I stood in the doorway like a statue. I wondered if he saw me while I was stashing everything. I wonder if he's as frightened as I am, coaching himself through every moment too.

Smile now. Don't say that. Look pleased now. Don't let the kids see your (pain, hurt, sorrow, fear).

"Do you feel up to taking them to school tomorrow?"

So you can go through all my stuff while I'm gone?

His arms hung stiffly by his sides, and I forced myself to lower my shoulders.

Stop it.

"I'd like to," I said. I tried to smile but I could feel that it was more of a grimace.

"Okay."

Finally, he went to the guest room and shut the door. It made a hollow sound that I felt in my body. Its symbolism wasn't lost on me either.

The boys and I got in bed then and watched *Friends* for a while. First, the one where Ross gets double sprayed on his front at the tanning salon, and then the one where Phoebe's sister, Ursula, is a porn star. Jordan fell asleep first, with his long legs curved like a backward C on top of mine. Jacob pretended to watch but was mostly staring at me. Alternately kissing my cheek and burrowing his head into the front of my shoulder. He ran his fingers through my hair and traced my face until he finally let go and fell asleep too.

Sometime after eleven o'clock, I carefully extracted myself from between them, snuck into my closet, and took my BlackBerry out of my robe pocket with trembling hands. I scrolled until I found his name.

Scott S.

I felt like I was thirteen, sneaking a call to a boy in the middle of the night. Only back then, if I got caught, I might have been grounded. Now if I get caught I might lose my kids.

Holding my breath, I pushed the little green telephone symbol and chewed on my lower lip. The ringing sound sliced abruptly through the quiet and I panicked, diving on top of the phone like it was a live grenade.

"Hey," he said.

Instantly I was transported back to six hours earlier when he and I said goodbye. We'd been at the top of the Departures escalator. Wrapped in each other's arms, I stood there shaking and boo-hooing, soaking his shoulder with my tears and drool. Without breaking our embrace, he'd shuffled me gingerly to one side, getting me out of the way of all the folks who were rushing to catch their flights. I knew I should have been one of those folks, but I just couldn't bring myself to leave him.

"You're trembling," he had said, peeling off his dark orange fleece sweatshirt and wrapping it around my shoulders. "Take this, okay? You'd better go."

All at once I was enveloped by the smell of The Meadows: clean winds, sunscreen, and clay dust. There was also a faint under-smell of cigarettes, the pizza we'd had for lunch, and something masculine, like shaving cream. I held it tightly around me and then put it on, popping my head through the opening.

"Maybe we could meet here like once a month," I said. "Isn't Phoenix like halfway between LA and Utah? Even if we just met at the airport, it's such a short flight."

He kissed me.

"I don't want to say goodbye," I wept. "I'll call as soon as I get home."

"Enjoy your kids," he whispered, moving his hands to my shoulders. "Call me later on tonight, but only if you can."

"Hey," he says again. The sound of his voice spits me back out into my closet.

I'd been fantasizing about talking to him ever since we parted. Looking forward to calling him, thinking that would make everything feel better. But instead, hearing his voice for the first time was like a slap in the face. I was suddenly struck by the enormity of the risk I was taking. And ashamed to be acting like a lovesick teenager, sneaking away from my sleeping children to call a boy.

I went away for a month so that I could keep my kids. Why am I taking this chance?

I was also highly aware of the other things at stake: my home, financial support, my future. If my husband thinks for a minute that I'm having an affair (with someone I met in treatment of all places), there will be no more feigned civility. He'll fight me with everything he's got.

The Meadows is now officially in the past. Which means that my time with Scott should be in the past too.

So what the fuck am I doing then?

I glanced nervously toward the back hallway.

"Are you okay?" My voice was barely audible. I hoped he could hear me so that I didn't have to repeat myself. "How are you? How is it being back?"

Despite everything, I could hear the tenderness in my voice, and it scared me. It felt like something bigger than me. I haven't sounded this way toward my husband in a really long time.

"Fuckin' weird," said Scott. "Empty house, same as I left it. Garbage bags full of empty bottles. Nothing in the fridge but beer. Piles of unopened mail, bills."

"Jesus."

I couldn't think of anything else to say. I'd never thought about Scott's house before, and suddenly I could picture it all too clearly.

"Well," I say after an awkward silence. "I can't talk long. I just wanted to make sure you got home okay."

"I'm home," he said. "And I'll be okay."

Something rattled in the darkness, and I looked toward the bedroom. Cold sweat formed instant half-circles under my arms.

What was that?

"What are you doing this week?" he asked.

The hand holding the phone began to tremble uncontrollably, so I switched hands, putting the trembling one inside my robe, tucking it under my arm. A coolness started to settle over me like fog.

Self-preservation?

It's futile to share my plans with Scott. I am the reality-show contestant returning home, shaking her head in disbelief and wondering how she got so caught up in the game.

"I, I don't know. I gotta see my lawyer. I might go to a meeting."

"You should," he says. "That'll be good for . . ."

I hear the noise again and sit straight up.

"Hey, I'd better go."

"Oh, okay."

The sound of his disappointment split me in half. Part of me wanted to jump on a plane and hold him like I did in the back of the town car in Arizona, stroke his hair and kiss the top of his head. The other part was disdainful, cold, glad that he was so far away. Him being in another state means less chance of us getting caught. It's safer.

I stared at the red End button for what feels like a long time after I push it, rocking back and forth with one arm wrapped around my waist.

———

Daylight streams in harshly at 6:00 a.m. I've been awake all night, shifting and sweating between the two writhing sacks of snakes that are my sleeping sons. It is surreal being home again. I can hardly believe I'm actually in my bed, staring at the ceiling, between both of my kids. Three hundred and forty-nine miles away from that putrid communal room, the humiliating, mandatory schedule, and those thin, scratchy sheets.

But I'm in agony.

I want to shake myself and scream, "This is what you wanted! This is ALL you wanted. Why aren't you happy?"

Just because I completed my stay in treatment does not make me cured. I'm still an addict (and apparently an alcoholic) and I'm still detoxing. They told me at The Meadows that because of the level-one trauma I'd inflicted on myself with all those pills, this shit might last for weeks, maybe even months. The shakes, the wobbly knees, the lazy tongue, and sketchy eye contact. Not to mention the standard stuff: night sweats, diarrhea, loss of appetite, brain zaps, memory and attention lapses. It's the aftermath of having poisoned oneself to the brink, over and over on a daily basis. The payment due for my selfish recklessness.

And that's just the physical part.

Then there's the resentment—the fun house mirror that tricks me into feeling like the victim.

Why is this all happening to me? It isn't like he's always the perfect dad. At least I was there. The only time I ever left my kids was to go to treatment.

I'm still as scared, sad, and angry as before, only now I'm utterly without any method of soothing myself or buffering the pain. My self-pity is a mud puddle I am sitting in, reveling in, wallowing in. And the shame singes my skin like acid whenever I contemplate seeing anyone, talking to anyone. My mother, my kids, even our gardener. I want so desperately to find someone to blame for how things have ended up, but I only have myself. It is dawning on me that not only am I complicit in my own betrayal, I have also been the main perpetrator.

And even though I feel like shit, I need to figure out how to get the fuck up and fill the prescription my new doctor gave me, Dr. Nancy.

I pull the piece of paper out where I wrote down all the things she'd rattled off to me yesterday. Things she said I have to do if I want to keep my kids. All these things I don't want to do. All these things I'd rather die than do: Resume normal mom stuff, go to meetings every day, get pee tested twice a week, go to therapy twice a week, get a sponsor, get sobriety chips, get back to socializing with friends, resume all parent association duties, do not discuss the divorce outside of her presence. Obviously, not imbibing a drug or even a drop of alcohol, trust her guidance, and whatever I do—do not bruise his ego.

In the bathroom, I stare at myself in the mirror, willing my hands to stop shaking. My body feels hollow and weak. My ever-present headache requires three to four Advil every few hours, and I can feel them burning a hole in my stomach lining. But it's not just my head, everything hurts like I've been beaten with a bat—my legs, my ass, the hair follicles on my arms. I feel like I should be in a wheelchair. Surely I'm too ill to do any of the things she's suggesting.

But I need something.

I've opened the medicine cabinet ten or twelve times since I've been home. Both terrified and hopeful each time that there might be something, a piece of a pill or a whole one hidden in a bottle of one of my other meds. I know that as soon as I get even the tiniest bit of Ambien in my system, the aches and pains will ease, even if it's just momentarily. But the medicine cabinet has been wiped clean, and its stock carefully replaced with brand-new, factory-sealed bottles of OTC medicines like Tylenol, Advil, and Pepto-Bismol.

He did this.

An inferno of shame blasts through me whenever I think about what it must have been like while I was gone. Did he comb through all my stuff by himself? Did his family come and help him? Did he bring in an investigator? Who advised him? Who purchased these items from the drugstore? Was it he who went through my boots and purses and got rid of all the empty bottles? I tried to get ahead of this before I left, tried to make sure everything was in order, but I know I missed some things. I was so deeply impaired then, toxically high the entire time.

What did he find? How will he use it against me? Will he search through my closet when I take them to school?

I want to lie down on the cool floor near the shower like I used to, anything to get some relief. For the sixth or seventh time in a month,

I wish I smoked cigarettes. I feel like he's watching me though, like maybe he's installed cameras everywhere I used to hide. And he's waiting for me to start rooting through everything, looking for any pills I may have left behind. To be the addict of yore, to show my true self.

Then he'll have me.

I hear Nancy's words then, reminding me to get on prescription item number six: Resume all my normal mom stuff.

"Whatever you usually do with the kids, do those things the moment you get home," she had said. *"Take them to school, pick them up, do their homework with them, tutoring, dinner, bedtime, whatever."*

While Maria gives the boys their breakfast, I spend about twenty minutes trying on things to wear to drop them off. When Jordan runs upstairs to get me, I'm still in my robe, standing in the middle of the closet amid piles of inside-out jeans and T-shirts.

"Aren't you taking us, Mom? We're going to be late."

Defeated, I throw on one of the rejected T-shirts, a pair of jeans, and don the required uniform for any disgraced addict—a baseball cap and dark glasses—before grabbing the keys to the Rover.

"Okay, baby, let's go."

CHAPTER EIGHTEEN

Ninety Meetings in Ninety Days

I't's 10:30 a.m.

The kids are at school, and my husband is at work. Maria is downstairs ironing, and I'm in my closet again, pacing back and forth. Today at two I have my first drug test, and I'm talking to myself and rocking like a madwoman.

I've already moved my journals twice today because I thought maybe someone riffled through my sweaters. Maria got to the hamper before I could remove Scott S.'s fleece though, and I caught her just as she was about to put it away with my husband's stuff.

"Wait!!"

She looked startled so I tried to be all "tee-hee-hee" casual about it because I didn't want her mentioning it to him. I know I can't trust her, but I feel like I can't trust anybody except for Scott S., who I've already called twice today. The second time he sounded sleepy, which I thought was odd for ten in the morning, but Lord knows how I must sound—crazy, manic, demented. I'm afraid to go downstairs because I'm afraid to talk to Maria. I'm scared to be in the vicinity of my bed because it calls to me, draws me in like a black hole.

Lie down in me, Laura, and turn off your phone, pull the drapes, curl up, and watch TV.

And as much as I want to lock the door and watch Meryl Streep movies for the rest of the day, I can't risk Maria thinking I'm getting loaded. She'll tell my husband that I must be getting high again and then it will be game over.

I clasp and unclasp my hands and walk over to my closet bench.

What can I do until two?

I already made my daily call to Laura and left her a message. I think about calling my mother, or Shelly, or my friend Nicole, but I don't want to talk about myself, and I can't imagine a conversation that wouldn't start with them asking, "So, how are you?" Major emphasis on the ARE.

I'm not ready for that.

All at once I remember that Morgan woman left me that message about the meetings on Moorpark and Whitsett.

Prescription item number two: Daily meetings.

I've seen those people milling around outside the Unitarian church, smoking and talking while huddled in groups. I always drive by quickly, eyes forward, not wanting to stare and make them feel more uncomfortable than they already must be. I would be mortified if, say, Trisha from tennis or Kerry from school happened to drive by as I was walking in. What possible explanation could I give them for being at that church during the day in the middle of the week?

I observe myself putting on my sandals and sundress. In the mirror I check my hair and my teeth and then put on some lip gloss.

I'll just park around back so no one sees me. If I leave now, I can go get a coffee and then head over. I'll just make an appearance and then when it's finished, I'll drive over for the drug test and then it'll be time for pickup. Jordan has tutoring with Ms. Darlene right after school, and then I'll swing back and pick up Jacob after flag football.

I can do this.

Coffee, meeting, drug test, tutoring, football, and then the day is over.

"Then the day is over," I chant to myself, closing my eyes. "Seven hours and then the day is over."

The large, bright meeting room is on the ground floor. Not the dark, smoky basement that I'd pictured. It's filled with rows of plastic armless chairs. Every seat is filled and everyone, and I mean everyone, there is white. I am deliberately late and have entered through the merciful side entrance off the alley. I'm hanging in the doorway looking around at the backs of fifty or so heads.

Aw hell no. Fuck this.

I think I can probably get out without anyone noticing me, and then I think about how I'm picking up Jordan and Jacob later. If I fuck this up and lose them, it might be Maria picking them up after school, or my mom or his mom—but not THEIR mom. They deserve to have their mom picking them up like the other kids. I need to gather myself here and get it the fuck together.

Suddenly, as if reading my mind, a tall, lanky man in a three-piece suit spots me and jumps up to offer me his seat.

"Here," he whispers, as he picks up his briefcase.

I shake my head no and smile politely.

"Please," he says, moving toward me.

People are starting to look, so I slink over, mouthing "thank you" as I sit down. I get a whiff of bad cologne and switch to mouth breathing. The seat is slightly sticky against my bare thighs; I can't bear to allow myself to wonder what might have possibly made it that way.

A cherubic-looking blonde is standing at the front of the room with what looks like a plastic tackle box. She's wearing jean shorts and a Led Zeppelin T-shirt.

"Hi, I'm Beth, and I'm your alcoholic chip chick," she says. She opens the box and takes out an orange plastic circle that looks like a key chain.

"Does anyone have twenty-nine days or less? Or is this anyone's first meeting?"

Murmurs ripple through the room as several young white kids stand and line up in front of her.

"Sandy, alcoholic, seven days; Rich, alcoholic, eleven days; Bastian, alcoholic, one day; Gloria, alcoholic . . ."

I watch in horror as they all get up one after the other and collect a disc from Beth.

Bastian gets the biggest round of applause.

How could they want to celebrate? Why aren't they embarrassed?

"How about thirty days," she calls.

Jesus, these people want to throw a party for everything. Look at me! I'm amazing. I should get a prize because I haven't gotten drunk for a month!

No one moves for a minute. Everyone is looking around with anticipation.

"Thirty days?" she says again. The hair on my arms stands at attention.

Oh my God—I have thirty-two days.

"Going once," she says. She picks up another disc and waves it in the air, as she turns slowly around in a circle.

Chips! Fuck. That's in item number two.

I feel my face getting hot as I rise from my seat, and I am very aware of my Blackness as I near the front of the room and try to make myself smaller. A few people start clapping even before I reach Beth, which causes me to turn red. When I get up to her, she grabs both my hands and pushes a white chip into the palm of my right.

"Hell yes," she whispers to me. "Thirty days is rad."

I simultaneously want to slap her and hug her.

"What's your name?" some man calls out.

"Laura," I mumble, keeping my head down.

I am humiliated.

"Are you an alcoholic?" cries out another voice.

Jesus, these muthafuckers right here.

"Laura, alcoholic," I say quickly, and scurry back to my seat.

"Woo-hoo!" The whole room bursts into applause and cheers as I walk. My arms get goose bumps as people reach out to high-five me on my way back to my chair.

So much for going unnoticed.

As I'm taking my seat, Briefcase Guy leans forward from my former perch and gives me a thumbs-up. An older woman with purplish hair turns around to face me and says, "Congratulations."

"To get sixty days," she whispers, her breath smelling like Listerine, "you just have to keep coming back and don't drink between meetings."

I nod, and turn my head away from her, hoping she'll be discouraged from dispensing any more unwanted breath and/or observations in my direction.

The speaker is a pretty brunette in her thirties. I pretend to listen to her until everyone claps. There seems to be a break now, people are getting up for coffee. I head toward the hallway with a bunch of folks headed for the bathroom and then duck out the back door.

I am curious about the odd combination of humiliation, relief, and exhilaration I feel as I start the engine, but not terribly surprised by it. My emotions have been nothing if not erratic for the past year or so. I call Scott as I exit the parking lot, twirling my chip between my middle finger and thumb, waiting for him to answer.

"Five hours and then the day is over," I whisper under my breath while it rings.

"You'll never guess what I just did," I say when he answers.

"Something good?" I can hear the smile in his voice.

"Something weird as fuck, the last thing you might expect me to do without someone holding a gun to my head."

"A meeting? Did you go to a meeting?"

"Yes, I did. And what did I get . . . ?"

"Not a chip?"

"Yes, sir! Got my thirty-day chip, bitch!"

"How was it? How were the people?"

"Big meeting, lots of white folks."

He laughs. "So you're doing this, huh? You're going to be one of those meeting people?"

"I don't know what I'm doing," I say. "Except right now I have to drive to the ghetto to get a drug test. If you don't hear from me in an hour, call the police."

I pull up to the entrance of a three-story apartment building sandwiched between a Circus Liquor and a Nix Check Cashing.

Prescription item number one: Pee test.

I triple-lock the Rover and fast-walk into the building. There is no elevator, so I begin to climb up three rickety flights of stairs, holding my breath as I pass a man with no shoes passed out on a sofa in the hallway. The air on the top floor is so heavy with BO and some kind of mediciney smell that I have trouble stifling my gag reflex. Signs and posters that read things like NEEDLE EXCHANGE HOURS and OPEN YOUR EYES BEFORE AIDS CLOSES THEM are Scotch-taped to the dilapidated walls. There's a large Latina woman behind bulletproof glass with full-sleeve tattoos. I walk timidly over to her, hold up my green slip, and say hello, giving her my best "I don't belong here, so please be nice to me" smile.

She doesn't smile back.

Instead, wordlessly, she taps the glass and points down, indicating that I should place my slip in the disgusting lazy Susan that sits between us. I set it there gingerly, holding it with my fingertips only, hoping not to touch any surfaces.

"You can have a seat," she says after a moment.

I walk over to a corner and stand near a window where I can see my car, careful not to let any part of me touch the wall. There are two kids throwing a baseball back and forth next to it. My heart skips when the ball narrowly misses my side-view mirror.

"Robbins," she calls.

I walk over and she steps out from behind the glass, handing me a cup.

"Down the hall, first door on the left."

As I'm walking I'm looking around in horror.

This must be a place for criminals and hard-core junkies, right? Shouldn't there be a safer, separate testing site somewhere for us law-abiding Ambien addicts?

The bathroom is predictably disgusting, and the lone toilet stall lock is broken.

Of course.

I do my best not to touch anything inside the stall while struggling to keep the door closed with my right elbow. Just as I'm pulling my jeans down, the door slams open and I scream. At first, I'm so startled and embarrassed that I don't even register that it's her, the woman who handed me the cup.

What the . . . ?

I'm expecting her to apologize and excuse herself, but she just stands there staring at me.

"Um, I'll be out in a minute," I say, using all my strength to close the door on her.

"Sorry," she says, but she doesn't look sorry at all. "I have to watch."

She tells me her name is Veronica and that she's responsible for making sure that the sample comes out of me and not from some Ziplock bag hidden in my purse.

Ziplock bag? Of pee??? In my Gucci hobo bag???

I want to laugh out loud at the absurd idea that I would carry pee around—let alone inside this two-thousand-dollar bag—but she's not playing with me, not even a little bit.

I cannot let this bitch interfere with me getting custody of my kids.

Crushed, I shift my purse to the back and pull my jeans back down.

"Do you mind running the water?" I ask. "I have what they call a shy bladder." I smile at her again. This time giving her my best "You know how it is, right?" grin, but she doesn't move.

I look at my feet, and we sit in silence for what feels like hours. Finally, a small stream comes trickling out. Mortified, I look away as I hand her the cup, but not before I see that she has double-gloved the hand she uses to take the cup from me.

Double gloves? Like she's scared of catching something from ME???

"It's probably not even enough to test," she says flatly, then turns and walks out.

CHAPTER NINETEEN

We Do Not Negotiate

"Do you have a minute?"

He appeared from behind me out of nowhere. My heart starts pounding as soon as I hear his voice.

It's nine thirty at night and the boys are asleep in their rooms (for once). I'm down in the dimly lit kitchen grabbing a fistful of chocolate chip cookies for the second time in an hour. Sugar, in any form, has become my new obsession. That, and Babybel cheeses, Lay's potato chips (Classic, of course), and Stouffer's Swedish meatballs.

"Sure," I say, releasing the cookies and sitting down at the kitchen table.

I study his face for a moment. His expression is hard to read, and my mind races. Careful to keep my face stoic, I turn my phone over because I haven't cleared my recent calls.

We sit in silence for what feels like a long time. Me looking for him to start, him looking at me like "Please say something."

"Well, I," we both say at the same time. I giggle nervously and motion toward him with my hand. "You go ahead."

"While you were gone," he begins, and my jaw gets stiff.

I don't want to talk about what happened while I was gone.

I don't want to relive the shame and agony of being there serving time while he stayed home with our kids. I don't want to face the fact that I am the cause of his pain. I'd rather talk about tutoring schedules or football cleats for Jacob or him moving out.

"Your mom was here a lot while you were gone."

I close my eyes as gratitude warms my throat. My mom did what I asked her to do. She was here in my place.

"And one day we got to talking and she told me some things I didn't know. Things I was pretty surprised to find out."

What the fuck! My mother talked to him about me????

"Why didn't you ever tell me you'd never graduated from high school?" he said.

He couldn't have shocked me more if he had pulled out a knife and jammed it into my shoulder. My mind begins frantically trying to come up with the response that will make him stop talking.

Everyone believes I have a diploma and a degree. Unless he has called Berkeley High, he can't prove otherwise, so I don't have to admit to anything.

"You know that's nothing to be ashamed of. You got your GED, right?"

I'm staring at my feet now, but my body is frozen with shock.

I can't discuss this with him. I can't discuss this with anyone because I haven't ever even allowed myself to think about it. Part of me knows that who I am and what I've been able to accomplish is nothing short of incredible. I mean how many welfare-poor, emotionally abused high school dropout, drug addict waitresses go on to create the only Black-owned entertainment PR firm in Los Angeles, marry one of the most successful men in Hollywood, and get invited to join the board of one of the most prestigious independent schools in the country?

But at the moment I can't think about all that. Right now, I feel like one of those cats who flatten their ears before dashing across the street, narrowly avoiding speeding cars. It makes no sense, but those cats would probably die if they stopped to look around.

I know he's being kind. I know he wants to have a real conversation, but I can't afford to stop and look around.

I have to keep going.

A pain forms around the edges of my heart like someone is squeezing it as hard as they can.

I nod yes, indicating that I got my GED, not caring that it's a lie and not trusting my voice.

"She told me about the guy too . . ."

What guy?

"When you were young, the drug dealer."

My eyes look up sharply without my permission. His face is contorted with discomfort.

Vegas! Oh, this just keeps getting better.

"Okay."

"I don't understand why you never told me. I had no idea you had a history with drugs."

My face is sizzling with shame. I look out the window so he can't see the humiliation in my eyes.

"Maybe I could have helped, faster or something, if I had known."

I hate him.

"And please don't get mad at your mother. We were just talking, and she just assumed I knew. She didn't know you'd kept it a secret."

"It wasn't a secret," I say with a scowl. "It just wasn't that big a deal. It wasn't like I was a drug addict." I can hear the venom in my voice.

"Crack cocaine is a pretty big deal," he says.

My gaze hardens as I lift my eyes toward his. "Maybe, but this was not."

"I just want to get all of this on the table," he says. "Can we just talk? You and me, no lawyers?"

Oh no, sucka Jones. I know what you're trying to do and I'm not falling for it.

I hear Nancy's voice in my head.

Give him nothing, Laura.

"I don't think that's a good idea." I stand up and cross my arms, signaling that I'm done.

He has a lot of nerve ambushing me like this.

Plus, he has no idea what I'm going through: the rehab, the detox, the not being able to sleep, being the scapegoat for everything that is wrong with us, failing as a mother, not knowing how to do anything without being loaded, the fucking meetings, the humiliation of someone watching me pee, nothing to buffer any of this with. Also, I fuckin' know he's having a drink every once in a while. I smelled wine on his breath last night when he got home. But me? No, because of my affliction, I am punished, and I get nothing.

"Anything else?"

"Yes," he says. "There is something else."

Oh my God, I knew it! Someone has been spying on me. He's been listening to my calls.

His voice is steely now.

"The bar."

Aw, shit. I forgot about the bar.

"You didn't really think you could replace the whole bar without me knowing, did you?"

Maria, that bitch! I'm fucking firing her the moment he moves out.

"And, Laura, it didn't take long to find the bottles hidden in your closet and under the sink. But it did take a long time for us to find all the pills, because you had pieces of Ambien hidden everywhere."

Us.

Holy fuck! There were other people going through my stuff! My purses, my pockets, my jewelry boxes? Who were they? What else did they find? I have to get those journals out of the house right away, give them to my mom or something . . .

My mouth fills with saliva like I'm going to throw up.

"Is this what you want to do?" I say through gritted teeth. "Shame me?"

I'm broiling now, alternating between fear, fury, and guilt.

"No, I'm not trying to shame you." He looks tired.

He rubs his forehead and I notice for the first time how red his eyes are.

Are those tears?

"I just want to know what's going on with my wife, with the

mother of my kids. I thought I knew you better than anyone, but it looks like no one really knows you."

"Well, it seems that you know everything now."

"Do I?"

Oh, I hope not.

My face goes rigid as I think about all the other things he doesn't know: the doctor-shopping, the cough syrup guzzling, the journals and back account, the CVS refill I wanted so desperately, the pee tests, and, of course, Scott.

"Look, Laura, you want this to be a fight? Do you really want me to come after you?"

His words hang there in the air for a moment.

"You know," he continues, "that's what they want, right? The lawyers? Not just yours, mine too. They want to pit us against each other and run up the bill. They don't want anyone to win, they just want a war."

Nancy's voice starts to wail in my head, and everything around me goes dark.

Do not negotiate with him outside of my presence.

Suddenly it's clear that he and I are in a siege state. I am surrounded by evidence that should compel me to surrender. And he is armed with the means to burn or starve me out. But as much as I would like for this to all be over, I can't capitulate, there's too much at stake. I can't risk talking to him about any of this because I can't risk losing my babies.

Give him nothing.

"I'm going to bed," I say, turning around, my whole body beginning to shake from the adrenaline coursing through it. "Unless you have something else to say."

He sits there staring at me with a crushed look on his face. He's just a matter of inches from me, but he might as well be thousands of miles away.

"This is Nancy."

"Hey, Noel called to confirm our ten a.m. tomorrow, but aren't we meeting on Friday?"

"Yes, but tomorrow I've set us up to meet with one of the private investigators I use."

I'm super confused.

"Why? I mean, why would we hire a PI?"

"We're not hiring him; we're consulting with him. If your husband has hired anyone, I want you to be aware of the kinds of things they might be looking for. The good ones are excellent at their jobs. They might show up at the kids' school one day or sit next to you at a coffee shop and see how you respond to a come-on. They might even show up at your house posing as a repairman or something."

"Oh shit."

"What?"

"Well, yesterday there was this guy, I'm sure it was just some kind of weird scam or something, but it creeped me out. He just showed up out of nowhere, claiming he was a location scout. But like I said, it was probably nothing. I'm sure I'm overreacting."

"Tell me everything."

———

"Missus, there's someone here for you."

I was upstairs in my office working on my speech for Monday's PA meeting. The boys were running up and down the hallway screaming at each other, and I felt like I could feel my nerves literally unraveling.

"Who is it?" I yelled back.

"He say he from the gas company."

The gas company?

My husband had been out of town for the last two days and wasn't due back until tomorrow. I didn't know the gas company ever showed up without notice, unless . . . I sniffed the air around me.

Oh my God. Is there a leak?

"How can I help you?" I asked him as I galloped down the front stairs.

Right away I could tell something wasn't right. He was a tall white guy with a beard and a blue construction vest. From a distance, he looked unhurried, casual, but up close, I could see there was a shiftiness about him, a kind of nervous energy. He had a camera slung over his shoulder and a phone-size strap-on video camera in his right hand.

"Hello, miss—is this your home?" He smiled widely at me and quickly put the video camera in his pocket as he stepped back behind the threshold.

"How can I help you?" I was standing on the bottom step now.

"Hi, I'm from Gas Company Locations. We do location scouting for movies and commercials. Do you ever allow filming here? You have a beautiful home."

Location scout?

"I thought she said you were from *the* gas company," I said, wishing I had my phone in my hand so I could call the police. I wondered how quickly I could get to the kitchen to grab a knife.

No, this muthafuckah is not trying to come inside my home.

"Oh yes, it's a bit of a tricky name. Definitely gets us in doors more often, but yes, it's Gas Company Locations. Now that I'm here, I'd sure love to get inside and take a look around. Like I said, you have a gorgeous home. I could get you probably at least ten grand a day for filming. We would of course relocate you for the night . . ."

I cut him off with a "we're not interested" (emphasis on WE so he knew that I wasn't some single woman on her own) and asked him to leave. I waited until he got into his navy Nissan Pathfinder and then ran over to the security monitor to download the video of him before he drove away. He sat in his car for seven nerve-racking minutes before heading down the driveway and out the front gates. Seven minutes during which he made a phone call and guzzled a bottle of water.

—

When I finish talking, Nancy asks me to send her the security video.

"It's pretty far away but you can make out his license plate."

"Good job. Listen, this is exactly the kind of thing I'm talking about. They may be getting desperate, trying to gather more evidence against you."

Fuck, really?

"My gut feeling is that that was no random thing. Location scouting is really the perfect cover for someone to get inside your house. Come to think of it, your husband may have even left town just so this guy could come by when you were alone. So he could catch you using again, or maybe even catch you with someone else."

Damn.

"Now, I know your drug tests are coming back clean, so hopefully we don't have any worries there. But does he have *any* reason to think there's anyone else? I'm not here to judge you, but I need to prepare."

She's saying he sent a spy to see if I'm high or if I'm fucking someone? Is this his lawyer telling him what to do? Has there been a plot all along to build a case against me? That's why he took those pictures of my meds way back then?

"Laura."

If I tell her about Scott S. she'll freak out and it'll be for nothing because he's all the way in Utah anyway. No way I could ever be caught with him.

"Yeah, sorry. I'm just processing what you said. No, there's no one you need to know about."

I hold my breath, hoping she'll be satisfied with that answer, that I won't have to lie to her outright.

"Okay," she says after a second. "Get me that tape. Maybe this gas man is someone I'll recognize. I'll see you tomorrow."

CHAPTER TWENTY

Marguerita Time

It's been a day, a night, and a morning since I last heard from Scott. I called him three or four times yesterday. But after waking up to find no missed call from him, I started hitting him up every hour on the hour. At first, I tried to keep my messages light and playful. But at around ten this morning, I could hear the panic in my voice betraying me, leaking out of my words.

"Please just let me know that you're okay. You can even just text me those words—'I'm okay.' I'll try to text back too, although I still don't quite know how to do that."

I hear my giggle at the end and know I sound pitiful, like some lovestruck teenager checking on her cheating boyfriend.

I call again thirty minutes later, and his voice mail is full.

This was not how I wanted to go into my first therapy session with Marguerita Doukas. I'd planned to walk in there so incredibly together that she would call The Meadows and tell them they'd made a mistake by sending me to her for treatment.

"This woman doesn't need therapy," she would say. "Next time send me someone who is truly disturbed."

As I step off the elevator, my head is buzzing with images of Scott, drunk somewhere, hurt somewhere, or worse, holed up with someone else and ignoring my calls.

She answers the door right away and shows me into her office.

"Hello, I'm Marguerita. It's good to meet you."

"Laura," I say, shaking her hand, which is large for a woman and crazy soft—like grabbing a piece of sponge cake.

She's tall, older, and white, with an old-fashioned hairdo and Coke-bottle glasses. I can't place her heavy accent until I see a framed map of the Greek Islands on her wall. She motions for me to sit on an overstuffed sofa opposite an equally overstuffed chair with a yellow lumbar pillow. It smells good in here, like bread baking and freshly ground coffee. My eyes fixate on the tissue box on the table between us.

She's going to be very disappointed if she's expecting me to cry.

"Would you care for coffee?" she says. "Or water?"

Suddenly my throat closes. I want to bolt for the door and make up some excuse about the kids being sick or something. But at the same time, I feel stuck because seeing her is prescription item number five. I also feel stuck because I'm having one of my time lapses and I can't remember driving here, where I parked my car, or how I got to her door from the elevator.

"So," she says, folding her hands in her lap. "You have completed a thirty-day treatment for a severe addiction to Ambien at The Meadows. And instead of going to transitional living, you are back in your home with your children and your husband . . ."

"Ex-husband," I say, inspecting my nails. "Or soon-to-be ex."

"Soon-to-be ex-husband," she says with a slight smile. "This must complicate things a bit."

I nod, trying to lighten my expression a little.

"So, instead of asking you to go back to where this all started, because I'm sure you must be tired by now of telling this part . . ."

You got that right.

"Tell me, Laura. Why are you here? What is going on in your life?"

"Do you want the short answer or the long?"

"I think I'd like the honest answer."

"Well, let's see. Why am I here? What's going on? I'm here because I've been sentenced to therapy, along with daily meetings. What's going on is I turned forty-four two weeks ago and no one cared. I'm the parent association president, which is a shit-ton of work, and I'm the new girl on the board of trustees, trying to look like I know what I'm doing. What's going on is that my husband hates me, and we still live together. Oh! And I can't sleep, but when I do I have such horrible nightmares that I'd rather be awake."

I realize now that she's just staring at me, not writing anything down.

"Well," she says, "that is all very interesting. May I ask again, why you are here?"

I open my mouth, but she raises her hand to silence me.

"Perhaps I was not clear. When I ask why you are here, I am more wondering what has motivated you to come here today."

"Sorry, you mean like, what? I just told you."

"Well, you said you've been sentenced to come here, let's start with that. Who is it that has sentenced you?"

My BlackBerry's bike-bell sound pings and I jump for my purse.

"Excuse me," I say, fishing around for it. "It might be my kids' school."

Marguerita waits patiently while I pull out my phone. I don't recognize the number, so I listen to the voice mail.

"This is Dr. J's Cleaners," says a man. "Can you call us back and let us know if we have permission to repair the zipper on the California king duvet . . ."

Not Scott.

I click off and tears fill my eyes.

"Sorry."

Silently, she hands me the tissue box. I take one and use it to wipe my nose, which is now running.

"I'm expecting a call."

"I see."

I sniff and wipe my nose again. Suddenly it feels as though her walls are closing in on me.

"Where were we again?" I say, looking at my watch.

"Who was it that is making you come here?"

"Oh, right. My divorce lawyer. She says I need to be in therapy for my custody case."

"So she believes therapy will be good for your case, or good for you?"

"I don't know. Both, I guess."

"So you are here today because your lawyer asked you to come?"

"Well, yes. I mean no. Not just because of her."

"Then who?"

Tears start to pool in my eyes.

"For my kids, okay? I'm here because I'm afraid if I don't do everything she suggests, I won't get to keep my kids."

I've been saying that for so long that I'm not even sure it's true anymore. Am I really only doing this for my kids? Is there any part of me that wants to do this for myself?

Marguerita picks up her pen and pad and leans back in her chair.

"Now we have somewhere to begin. Tell me about your children …"

———

On the drive home I'm crying so hard that I can't see, so I pull over on Santa Monica and try Scott again.

This time he answers on the first ring.

I want to jump through the phone and kiss him and then beat him senseless for leaving me hanging for so long.

"Hey," he says.

He sounds sleepy, like I woke him up, and all my relief evaporates.

"Where have you been? My voice is steaming with instant rage. "I've been calling for two days."

"Sorry, my phone was dead and I couldn't find the charger. You know I can't drive, so I had to wait until someone could drive me into town to buy a new one. I was just about to call you."

"And who was the someone that drove you?"

Too late, I snap my lips shut against my impulsivity.

I hate myself for asking. I have no right to be jealous. I am sharing a home with a man to whom I am still technically married. Scott and I have made no plans to be together, have never discussed a future, never declared ourselves a couple, so I know I am out of bounds. But the force of this feeling surprises me. It is like a noxious gas that has filled my car and is threatening to overpower me. I hate how weak I feel against it.

"A friend," he says. "Nothing to worry about."

Of course it's nothing to worry about. My kids are at stake! I can't be worried about some four-DUI-having, Utah-living, white-ass fly-fishing guide. What the fuck is wrong with me?

"Okay, I'm glad you're safe. I gotta go," I say.

"Wait, Laura."

"What?" I feel that familiar coolness descending on me now. I can't get off the phone fast enough.

"I didn't lose my phone charger."

"No?"

"No."

"What then?"

I flex my stomach so that I'll be braced for it when he says her name.

"The night I got back . . ."

"Yeah, the night you got back."

Is it the woman who drove him from Utah all the way to treatment, or his ex-girlfriend, what was her name, Jane, Jan . . . ?

"Remember I told you about all the empty bottles and the mail and everything all piled up?"

"Yes, yes." I look at the clock and see I only have twenty minutes before pickup.

"Well, all the bottles weren't empty.

What?

"What are you saying, Scottie?"

Silence.

"Are you saying that you drank?"

"Yeah."

I can hear him choking up, and all the jealousy instantly drains out of my body.

"You drank the night we got home?"

He's still quiet, but I can tell he hasn't hung up.

"Have you been drinking this whole time?"

"Yeah."

I'm trying to process his words.

My car is suddenly soundproof. I can no longer hear the sounds of the dog barking in the distance, the Catholic school kids walking next to me, or the cars passing by.

Those conversations in the closet, after my meetings, the times he didn't answer my calls . . .

"Have you been alone this whole time? I mean, are you . . . by your-self? No one's driving you around?"

"I'm by myself." And then as if anticipating my next question, "I walk to the store and get the booze."

Jesus, that's right. He told me about the mom-and-pop liquor store down the street from him. ABC stores I think they call them in Utah. Closed on Sundays so you have to stockpile all your booze on Saturday.

"Have you been to a meeting?"

I feel like such a hypocrite asking this. To me, these meetings are just boxes to check off to keep custody of my kids and a way to fill the unbearable hours between drop-off and pickup. I don't know if they keep you from drinking, and I certainly don't believe they're some magic panacea. But I don't know what else to say.

"There aren't any here where I live. The closest ones are in Park City, and I can't . . ."

"Drive," we both say at once. "You can't drive."

"Look, I don't want to live like this," he says. "And I don't know how long I can keep it up. I miss my kids, and their mom took them to Hawaii for I don't know how long. I'm lonely."

Suddenly I'm back at The Meadows and Scottie is convincing me to stay, reminding me about my kids and how much I have to live for. Risking his freedom by coming to comfort me after that devastating visiting day, keeping me from picking up that refill simply by being there in the car on the way home.

Where would I be now without him?

All at once, a version of the question Marguerita stumped me with pops into my head and out of my mouth.

"Why are you there?" I hear myself say. "I mean your kids aren't there, you're all alone, you're drinking, why are you there?"

"I don't know."

"Then maybe you should come out here."

I'm fully aware of how crazy the words are that are coming out of my mouth. I know Nancy would freak the fuck out. I know that if Scott comes to LA I'm giving up the one thing I had going for me, as far as not getting caught—proximity. I understand that if my husband were to discover that Scott S. moved to LA it would be catastrophic. Forget bruising, it would be like taking a baseball bat to his ego. I tried to reason with myself:

You're not yet divorced, you still live with your husband, you're only just rebuilding trust with your kids and your friends and at school. You have your own sobriety to worry about and pee tests to take. Do you understand how much you have at stake?

But this is Scott S. 412.

My first call in the morning and my last call at night. The man who saved my life by risking his freedom in treatment. And he's all alone in Kamas, Utah, with a disease that wants him dead.

"There are lots of meetings here, at all times of day." My words sound like they're coming from someone else. "Maybe you could get into a sober living and just do meetings for a while."

"To LA?" he says, as if I've just said, "Maybe you should come to Mars."

What the fuck are you doing???? This is crazy. Take it back! Tell him you made a mistake. Tell him you'll come up with another solution.

"Yes," I say, ignoring my thoughts and putting my car in drive. "Start looking for flights, okay? I'll try and figure out a place for you to go."

"Okay," he says. I wonder how drunk he is right now. *Will he even remember this call?*

"Good, I gotta go. I'll call you back tonight."

A car honks as I pull over again on Sunset and dial Marguerita's number.

"This is Marguerita."

"Hi, it's Laura, who just left. The one who didn't want to cry but then couldn't stop crying."

"Yes, Laura," she chuckles. "I know who you are."

"I need to book my next appointment, if that's okay with you? I just did something crazy."

———

It's close to a hundred degrees outside, and I'm struck by the fact that it's not much cooler inside as I'm following Veronica down to the toilet. Dozens of flies and an army of small, noisy electric fans line the hallway. Only for my children would I endure this special brand of humiliation. Maybe they'll appreciate it one day.

Hey, guess what Mommy did for you after she left rehab? Peed in a cup at a needle exchange while some strange lady watched.

We're standing toe-to-toe in the stall doorway, and she's passing the plastic-wrapped cup from one hand to the other. I look toward the exit, wondering if I have the strength to topple her if I need to make a run for it. It's then that I notice for the first time how gorgeous her nails are, long, glossy, and fire-engine red. Very much in contrast, I think, with the death tattoos all over her arms and neck.

"I get my coffee from the Sev," she says, noticing my Starbucks cup. "After I drop my kids at school."

The Sev: Translation, 7-Eleven. She has kids, plural, more than one, and she drops them at school every day. Single mom? And who doesn't have a Starbucks nearby? She either lives in the boonies or the hood.

I grab up the hem of my pink and black Ulla Johnson sundress to keep it from touching the urine-scarred toilet seat while I squat. A few seconds later when I hand her my almost overfull pee cup, I think I see the corners of her mouth turning up ever so slightly.

"Better," she says, as she writes my name on the cup.

Better is good. I'll take better.

Twenty minutes later I'm in Century City for an appointment with Nancy and the forensic accountant.

"What's your day been like so far?" says Nancy, as we walk from her office to the conference room.

"Typical recovering addict morning," I say wryly. "Two morning twelve-step meetings, dropped off lunch for the boys and"—I lower my voice to a whisper—"the pee test."

Nancy stops and faces me when we get to the conference room. I think we must look pretty comical together: me, Black with dark curly hair, almost five nine in flats, and her, white with straight blond hair and barely five two in heels.

"You've been doing well with the meetings," she says. "The drug testing, the therapy, and everything else. But that's all really been to get back the leverage we had before you went away. So we're going to pick up where we left off, with the forensic. Listen to me, what we're about to do is really important. Harry is the best in the business, and his whole job is to assess your husband's assets, so we have a complete picture of what you're entitled to."

I hear what she's saying, but her energy seems too intense for the occasion. She looks excited, no—exhilarated, yes. She reminds me of a lion with a gazelle in its sights . . . bloodthirsty.

"Look," she continues. "If they come after us, as I'm sure they will, we need as much ammo as possible, okay? This is the most important part of the case."

"Okay . . . ?"

She's eyeballing me so hard that I run my tongue around my teeth thinking maybe I've got something in them. She turns then and marches triumphantly into the room. I grit my teeth and follow her, trying to prevent the shutdown I feel descending on me.

Harry looks like central casting for an accountant, white and thin with short dark hair and glasses. There are four or five stacks of paper in front of him, along with a steaming mug of coffee.

Nancy motions toward the forensic and gives him a smile that reminds me of the red wax lips we used to get at the corner store when I was a kid.

"Harry, this is Laura."

"Hi, Laura," says Harry. "Well, I guess Nancy must have told you that we have pretty good news for you."

"We didn't get a chance to get into the details," says Nancy quickly. "I thought I'd leave that to you."

During the next few minutes, Harry lays out the last thirteen years of my life. Starting with how much money my husband had when we first met. Then going through deal after deal, film contract after film contract, detailing director's fees, benefits, and bonuses. I swallow hard when I spot copies of the Disney stock he bought Jordan three weeks before he was born.

———

It was February 1998. I woke up around six in the morning to get some water and stopped in the doorway of the nursery, absentmindedly rubbing my swollen basketball of a belly. When I went to bed the night before, the nursery walls had been white and all the furniture was still mainly in boxes. Now the whole room was sponge-painted a gorgeous deep azure blue, like a swirling Van Gogh night sky. Jordan's barn-red crib was assembled, and the nursery glider chair I had to have was out of its plastic and sitting in the corner. We hadn't been super concerned about the nursery being one hundred percent ready when Jordan got home because we knew he'd be sleeping with us at first.

"Did you do all this?" I ask him, looking around in wonder.

"I did." He's beaming, his face and arms slashed with blue streaks.

"I mean, you painted this all by yourself, while I was asleep?"

"I did."

Looking around some more, I realized he had placed five or six pictures of us on Jordan's dresser top, along with a framed picture of the Disney stock he'd just bought for him.

Baby's first stock.

"You're a good, good daddy," I said, settling into him, not caring that my belly and clothes were about to be covered in blue paint. "And I'm a very lucky mommy-to-be."

———

Now, back in Nancy's conference room, an alarm bell starts ringing in my head.

I'd never thought of financials as intimate, but it feels so vulture-like to be going over his life like this with a stranger. The instinct to protect my husband comes up suddenly, surprising me, as it's something I didn't know was still inside me.

"I don't know that I'm really comfortable going through all his personal finances like this," I hear myself say.

I interrupt Harry just as he's starting to go over the contract for his last blockbuster movie.

"Not his finances," Nancy corrects me. "Your collective finances."

"I mean, I know all this stuff," I say, ignoring her. "Can't someone just add it up and then we figure out what's what?"

"We need to make sure we have everything so that we can exclude the possibility of any hidden assets," Harry says. "My recommendation is that we hire a forensic investigator for that, although we may want to wait until we go to court to present that kind of evidence."

Harry is still talking but I'm not listening.

Hidden assets? Court?

"Wait, you guys think my husband has money hidden away?" I'm looking back and forth between them.

"They usually do."

Harry takes off his glasses. "Your husband is a smart man. I'm sure he, um, prepared for this."

"But wouldn't that be illegal?"

"Well, that will be for a judge to decide," says Nancy cheerily.

"But I don't want a judge to decide. I mean, I don't want a judge at all."

The sound of my voice speaking up so confidently startles me.

Who dat?

"I just want to sit down across from him like you said before and *we* decide who gets what, and then have this be over."

Nancy pulls down on my forearm, and I realize that I've stood up.

"Hey, hey, of course you want this to be over, but let's not get off track here, okay, Laura?"

She says this like I'm some zoo animal she's trying to lure back into a cage.

"I know we discussed mediation in the beginning, but that was before rehab and before we knew he had those pictures. We're asking for half of *all* the earnings for the past eleven years, half the acquired assets, both homes, Studio City and Malibu, child support, and alimony. So, we need to make damn sure we know what we're dealing with."

My head starts pounding, and I leap back from the table, catching my chair with my left hand before it falls over.

"Both houses? I don't want the Malibu house," I stammer. "I hate it out there. Plus, that's where he's been staying when he doesn't sleep at home."

"So sell it. Who cares?!" Nancy's eyes are as wide as saucers now. "It doesn't matter what you do with it once it's awarded to you. All that matters is that it is."

"No, all that matters are my kids, Nancy. I can't . . ." I'm starting to hyperventilate. "I can't do this."

"We're confident that a judge will see this as more than fair . . ."

"No, I mean I can't stay sober through a court battle, and if I can't stay sober, I don't get my kids. I don't care about the rest of this stuff."

Harry averts his eyes while Nancy and I look at each other. Her expression warns me to proceed with caution. Mine tells her that it's too late for that.

"Harry, will you excuse us?"

After closing the door behind Harry, Nancy approaches me cautiously, with a tissue box and a sympathetic smile.

"Look. Perhaps I mishandled this. I thought you understood what our strategy was, but maybe you just need a little more time . . ."

"No," I say, taking a tissue. "I don't think you understand. I don't need more time."

A champagne bottle has combusted inside me, filling me with jittery, fizzy adrenaline bubbles.

"I'm saying right now, Nancy, that I can't go to court. I can't have a judge deciding what we do. I've got to think about my kids and what's best for them."

"Yes," says Nancy, eyes flashing. "And don't you think what's best for them is seeing their mom get what she's worth?"

"But who says that I'm worth half of everything he's made ever since we got married. I mean, don't you think that's a little crazy?"

"No, it's not crazy, it's the law. The state of California says you're entitled to half."

"But Nancy, you and I both know he's not going to agree to give me half. I will have to fight him for it, Nancy. Do you understand what kind of toll that will take on him, on us, on my family? Court dates, my kids being compelled to testify? If dividing his money is going to further divide my family, it's not worth it. You know what I want. I just want to be comfortable. I want child support and to stay in my house."

Nancy is staring in my direction, but it's almost as if she doesn't see me. The walls of the conference room are glass, and I can see Harry out of the corner of my eye pacing back and forth on a phone call.

"Maybe we just need to break for today and pick this up again tomorrow . . ."

"No," I say. "I don't need a break. I want what we said in the beginning, no court, no judge."

"You realize you're tying my hands, then. I mean if court is off the table."

I nod, because I don't trust my voice.

"Yes? Do you?"

She's moved closer to me, practically in my face now. I take another glance at Harry, who is openly staring at us through the glass. Nancy glances at him when I do and adjusts her position so that he can't see her face.

"Well then know this." She starts counting on her fingers. "You've just come back from rehab. You know he has those pictures and God knows what other evidence he collected while you were away. Remember the 'location scout'? He may have even tapped your phone, found that bank account. You might think you're walking into a mediation next month, but I guarantee you'll be walking into a trap. As your attorney, I am strongly advising you to take twenty-four hours and just think about this. Continuing with Harry is your best move here. Your husband's team expects us to ask for more, they'll be prepared with a counter. And if we find that counter unacceptable, and we're not able to negotiate a favorable outcome, then we go to court."

"But going in and asking for half of everything? I mean, really? The stock certificates he bought for the boys when they were born? No, this whole thing feels wrong, vindictive even."

"Obviously we can remove those certificates from the inventory . . ."

As I'm shaking my head no, a jolt of electricity charges through my body, bringing me back to the summer of my twenty-first birthday.

I was out walking in Chicago when I got caught in one of those magnificent summer thunderstorms. While waiting for a light to change, the sky above me seemed to open up, and I heard the crack of the lightning bolt as it hit. Completely paralyzed for a hundredth of a nanosecond, light flashed in a circle around me and then everything turned white. Moments later, I fell to my knees, semiconscious and terrified. But at the moment of the strike, I wasn't scared. I felt strong, awed by the power I felt surging through me.

Standing here in front of Nancy, I feel that same force from years ago and am transformed from a fragile, intimidated detoxing disaster to a woman who finally understands what's important.

She doesn't get what's at stake. She thinks it's all about money and as-sets, but I know that none of that means anything if I start using again and lose my kids. She thinks that a "win" will be me getting half of everything in these documents. For me there is no "win" if my husband becomes my enemy.

"If we can't settle in mediation, we'll have to go to court anyway. But if you're set on this, I'll need to have you sign a document stating that you're refusing my counsel on this matter."

"Okay."

"I should ask for you to be examined by a psychiatrist. I'm serious. This is not something to play around with. Maybe because of your new sobriety you're not thinking right."

Is this bitch trying to say that I'm crazy?

"What are you saying, Nancy?"

"I'm saying you're not thinking clearly. And if you want your kids, maybe you should try taking the advice of your attorney. You agreed to trust my guidance."

I'm impressed by the calm, assured vibe I'm emoting as I look her in the eye.

"Nah, I'm good."

Of course, I'm far from good. I'm shaken to the core, but I can't let her see it. She doesn't get it. Maybe a shark was the wrong choice for me after all.

Nancy walks over to the intercom and calls for Noel before heading out to the hallway to speak to Harry. All at once, my lungs release the air they've been holding in, and I fall into my seat.

CHAPTER TWENTY-ONE

Four Women and a Mocktail

"The secret to sleep," Marguerita says, "is you can never chase it. If you do, it will always elude you. Sleep is a skittish cat you are trying to lure inside your home. You can't go running after it, or make any big, sudden movements. You do two things. First, you must ignore it, pretend that you are not interested in it. Then, you must place a saucer of milk on the back porch, each night moving it a little closer to the door."

"Soooo, okay. I like the cat analogy. What do I do to, um, lure, sleep in?"

"First, you must get your favorite books and a cup of tea, chamomile is good. And then sit down, ready for a nice, long cozy night of reading. Don't think about sleep. Nighttime can be a beautiful time to enjoy your own company. This time by yourself while the boys are in bed—this is a gift. Think of it this way. Do this tonight, do this tomorrow night. Do it every night until sleep finds you, but do not go looking for it."

I always feel like Marguerita is some fairy-tale sorceress casting a spell on me when she talks. I take notes in my new Filofax while she's speaking:

Favorite books

Chamomile tea
Don't chase sleep
"Okay, I'll try it."

As soon as I leave her office, my stomach starts fluttering and my jaw gets tight. I'm headed to lunch with my *Sex and the City* girls for the first time since I've been back, and I'm terrified, but this is pre-scription item number nine: Re-socialize with friends. I thought about seeing them one at a time, but seeing them all together was another of Marguerita's suggestions.

"Before, you hid with drugs and alcohol. Before that you hid behind your children. Now you have nothing to hide behind and it is scary. When your stepfather preyed on little Laura, you needed to hide. This hiding was a coping mechanism that saved your life. Thank God for it! But now you are grown, and he is dead. You don't need this survival skill all the time anymore, yes? Perhaps it is time to say goodbye to it, but gently. This hiding is an old imaginary friend who kept you safe ..."

Marguerita is still talking, but suddenly I am floating outside my body.

All I've ever done is hide. When someone gets too close to discov-ering the truth, any truth about me, I do one of two things: leave or lie. This whole time I've been so busy blaming others for why I have to hide. I blamed Kenny for my inability to trust anyone, I've blamed my marriage for my embarrassingly low self-esteem, I've even blamed my shameful addiction on the long line of alcoholics that I come from (on my father's side). Is it really time to leave hiding behind? Who would I be if I stopped? Will anyone care to know the real me, whoever that turns out to be?

"But these women you love are your friends," Marguerita continues, as though she's read my mind. "They are real friends, flesh and blood, and they love you. You will see. If seeing them one by one feels too intimate, too vulnerable, invite them out as a group. You pick the place, you set the time boundary so you feel safe. Perhaps two hours? No more. But you see your friends, and you let them see you."

Will I be able to step into the light and let them see who I am?

—

I'm ten minutes early when I arrive at the Polo Lounge in the Beverly Hills Hotel. I know being early is a mistake, more time to feel scared, more time to overthink. I don't know what these women know, what they've been told. I know that Tracey checked in from New York several times, filling my voice mail with messages of love and support while I was in rehab. I know that Nicole baked fresh banana bread every week and dropped it off at the house for Jacob. But instead of filling me with gratitude, these generous acts fill me with humiliation and self-loathing every time I think about them. I know that Shelly called my mother to ask her how she was doing with me in treatment, and my mom broke down and cried because no one had thought to ask her that. Another act of kindness that makes me want to crawl into a hole and die.

Look what you did. Look how devastated everyone is because of you.

I opt for the restroom instead of sitting alone. In the mirror I take note of how gaunt my face looks despite the fifteen pounds I've gained since going to treatment. While getting ready, I tried on dress after dress and then decided on Adidas Superstars, jeans, and a black sweater. The uniform of my twentysomething-year-old self. But I can't even hold eye contact with myself, and don't know how I'm going to face the girls. I know I'm going to do that weird thing I do with my voice. The warble that appears when I want to convince people that I'm okay. I hate concern almost as much as I hate pity and will do anything to avoid being the object of it. I'm guessing these women have probably discussed how they're going to handle me. Perhaps they've been coached by some expert on what they can and can't say to their fragile alcoholic friend.

At the table the waiter comes over and asks me what I'd like to drink.

Baileys on the rocks, a Black Russian. Ooh! A lemon drop martini . . .

"Cranberry and ginger ale, please—oh, and a pizza for the table."

I'm trying to look confident but am mortified that he'll know that my drink order is code for "I'm sober."

I hear the girls before I see them and feel my whole body go rigid.

Stay easy . . .

I fix a smile on my face and stand when I see them, fighting the brownout/time lapse that is threatening to overtake me, like a stage curtain coming down by mistake during a performance.

Fear. Fuck.

Fear is like a cat burglar, always robbing me of my ability to recall. Suddenly, I can't remember valet parking or how I got to the table from the bathroom. It's like the world splits in two, and I exit my body for another location entirely, like London or Lagos. Leaving behind a very functional Laura-shell in Los Angeles operating on autopilot. While this kind of dissociation is sometimes useful when I'm bored, when I am afraid, it blocks the memory of whatever event I am trying to escape.

After the girls all kiss me and settle at the table, the waiter comes over and offers to take their drink orders. Three pairs of eyes avoid mine while they look at each other.

I can almost hear them thinking, "Is it okay to drink in front of her?"

"Please," I say, as graciously as I can, "order whatever you like. I've already got mine."

Shelly looks over at me with a wink. "I'll have whatever she's having," she says, and hands him back the cocktail menu. Nicole and Tracey ask for sparkling water with lime and I feel my shoulders relax a little.

At first the girls make careful small talk, discussing safe things like jobs and kids, but I am on guard for those first questions that I know are coming. Not just about the Ambien and my time in treatment, but why I kept it from them. I feel like I can see the effects of my betrayal in their faces. I shut these beautiful friends of mine out of my life entirely. They had to hear about my addiction and subsequent rehab incarceration from my husband or each other. And for that reason, I can barely hold a smile while we speak. I want to run silently from the table and never look back. Every cell and nerve ending is screaming at me to hide, to conceal, to—give them nothing. But I hear Marguerita's words and check my watch. I promised myself I'd stay for two hours. I have ninety-three minutes left.

But these friends of mine don't pry. They don't let the conversation drop, and they don't regard me with wondering eyes.

When the pizza arrives, I get a flash of courage and seize it, knowing that it might be my only shot. I clear my throat then and announce that I have something to say.

The table instantly gets quiet.

"I know you must have a lot of questions," I say, looking at each of them for as long as I can manage.

"I hid a lot of what was going on, the drugs, I mean, behind the divorce. But going 'away' was the hardest thing I've ever done. I know I could have, I mean I know I should have, talked to you guys about it, but I couldn't, and I am so, so sorry for the pain that must have caused."

The girls are waiting, slices in hand, watching me with tears in their eyes. Finally, Shelly reaches over and grabs my hand.

"I'm sorry." She turns around and indicates the table. "We're all sorry that you felt like you had to go through all this alone. I can't imagine how hard it's been for you these past few months."

"We're with you, Laur," says Tracey. "We love you so much."

"How is it at home?" asks Nicole. "I saw him a couple of times when I went by the house and he seemed—quiet. How has he been since you've been back?"

"It's horrible. We barely speak."

"So why are you still living together?"

"Maybe he doesn't trust me yet? And truthfully, who could blame him?"

"Well," says Tracey, "the faster you finish getting divorced, the better."

"Yeah, about that. My divorce lawyer wants me to sign something that basically says I'm incompetent because I don't want to go to court. She thinks I'm crazy."

"What? Jesus, who is it? Laura Wasser? She did Angelina and Billy Bob, right?"

"No, this other woman, Nancy, in Century City."

"Is it too late to get someone else?"

"Yes. I mean no. I mean, I don't know, probably. We're almost done."

"Why don't you want to go to court, Laur?" asks Tracey.

Three pairs of eyes are fastened on my face.

"Because going to court will be war. I don't think I'm strong enough to go to war with him. I just want my kids."

"I hear what you're saying," says Shelly. "But you don't really *just* want your kids, right? I mean, you want your house, your house that you've raised these kids in, you want a nice settlement because like it or not, that's your money too. You want child support because kids are expensive, and you guys enjoy a really nice lifestyle. You want alimony because you gave up your PR company so you could raise your kids ..."

All three bob their heads in agreement.

"Yes, you went to treatment," she says, "which, by the way, was an incredibly brave thing to do and we're so proud of you. But does the fact that you asked for help negate everything you're entitled to?"

As I look from one beautiful, concerned face to the other, I feel a sense of defeat washing over me.

She's right. They're right. Of course they're right, but no one really understands where I'm coming from.

"Hey, I appreciate you all so much."

I cover my heart with both hands and look each of them in the eye.

"I'm so happy to see you all, and I missed you all, and I'm so grateful you still love me the way that you do. But you have to understand, I'm not saying that I'm willing to walk away with nothing but custody. Of course I want all those things."

Shelly furrows her brow and opens her mouth but I cut her off.

"Okay, I deserve all those things. But there are some things he and I can negotiate for with a mediator, and other things I'll have to go to court to get. The forensic accountant was talking about getting my half of things like future earnings from TV shows. Shows that may never exist, but concepts that were discussed during the course of our marriage, and all these film projects that I'd never even heard of. That's the kind of shit I'm talking about. Once we get into the weeds on that type of shit, I feel like I'm robbing him or something, taking stuff that doesn't belong to me. Lately I've been thinking about what my life would be like now if I'd never gotten married. Would I still have my PR company? Would I have written a book? Would I own a small candle store? I think whatever I'd have chosen I would be okay."

One by one they each nod in agreement.

"Yes, more money would be nice. More money is *always* nice. But even though no one else seems to be considering it, I have to think about how much the pursuit of that 'more' would cost me. And if there is even a chance that the price is my sobriety, is it worth it?"

I pick up Shelly's hand and hold it in both of mine.

"Feel how my hands are shaking just talking about it? I can't face him in court, Shell. I wanted a drink just because I was nervous about meeting y'all today. Can you imagine how good a drink will look if my husband becomes my enemy, and I have to face off with him in court over some shit that will probably never happen?"

CHAPTER TWENTY-TWO

Not a Drop

"Jordan is sick."

Maria says this to me as I'm walking in the door after my pee test. She's just standing there with an irritating look on her face. I open my mouth to curse her out for not calling to tell me and then shut it again. I find Jordan under the covers in my bed watching *Avatar: The Last Airbender*. He smiles when he sees me and immediately grabs my hand and puts his hand on his forehead.

"My throat hurts, Mommy. And I'm hot."

I feel his head and then slip into bed with him and hug him tightly. "Oh yeah, you're warm. I'm going to give you some Motrin, okay?"

"Don't leave, Mommy."

"I'm just going to get the Motrin. Where's your brother?"

"In his room, I think."

After checking on Jacob, I call our family ENT and ask him to call in an antibiotic for Jordan. We've been down this road before, and I want to nip this throat thing in the bud before it gets worse. This is the doctor that removed my tonsils eight years ago and removed Jacob's tonsils and adenoids when he was just three, so he's very familiar with our pharynx family history. I'm relieved when he answers and immediately agrees to call in Augmentin for Jordan. It's late Friday afternoon, and dragging a sick Jordan into Beverly Hills in rush-hour traffic sounds awful.

Jordan falls fast asleep as soon as I give him the Motrin. As I lower the volume on the TV, my husband walks in the house. I hear him calling out as he ascends the stairs.

"Are you guys ready to go to da BU?"

Shit. I forgot he was taking them to Malibu today.

"Hey," I whisper, rushing to the landing with my finger pressed against my lips. "Hey, Jordan's sick, sore throat, fever."

Instantly I feel his energy shift.

"Why didn't you call me?"

"Sorry, I just found out when I got home."

"You just got home now? From where?"

I can't tell him about the pee test.

I need to come up with a lie, but I don't do it fast enough and I can see it on his face. Now he's looking at me like I looked at Maria when I walked in, like I've betrayed him. Like "what the hell?!"

The feeling that I've fucked up smacks me in the back of the head. But that's the thing about being a recently "reformed" liar/drug addict. It still feels like I'm lying even when I'm telling the truth. And I always feel like I'm the biggest fuck-up even when I may not be one hundred percent at fault.

I should have called him.

I wonder if this is how it's going to be once we separate for real. If one of the kids is sick when it's the other parent's turn, then that parent doesn't get their time with them. I'm sure that's why some people keep the family home and leave the kids there, and then it's the parents who live somewhere else every other week.

Finally, he decides to go anyway and take Jacob with him. While walking them to the car, I try to apologize again for not calling to tell him, but my voice sounds weird and defensive. I can see that my excuses are agitating him, so I stop and give Jacob some kisses, promising to bring Jordan out the moment he feels better.

"Call me when he wakes up," he says before he starts the Porsche.

"Of course," I yell over the sound of the engine.

Ten minutes after they leave, the gate rings. My heart stops when I look at the security monitor and see Jerry, my formerly beloved pharmacy deliveryman, idling there in his green Camry.

Fuck.

I haven't seen Jerry since I've been back and am immediately jittery and deeply embarrassed. I've been so consumed with Jordan, my husband, and feeling like shit, that I didn't even think about how the meds were going to arrive. When he rings the doorbell, I yell downstairs and ask Maria to get it.

Peeking out the bedroom drapes, I can hear Jerry ask Maria if I'm around. Then I watch him hand Maria a stapled pharmacy bag and I think I see him glance up to my window.

Shit.

"Missus."

I yelp when I hear her voice. I've flattened myself to the side of the window and twisted my neck so that I can watch Jerry's exit but hopefully not be seen.

I'm mortified that she's caught me creepin'.

I read her expression as judgmental as she hands me the bag. Part of me wants to explain that I know better than anyone how ridiculous it is for me to be scared of Jerry and tell her how hard it is to reenter the world after coming back from rehab. The other part wants to tell her to fuck the fuck off.

"Thanks," I say, taking the bag from her. "It's for Jordan," I say quickly, hating myself for giving her an explanation.

But the moment I take the bag from her I know that something is wrong.

It's too heavy.

Carefully I peel open the top, popping the paper open around the staple. As soon as I see the pill bottle, my heart beats faster.

My first pill bottle delivery since my return.

I pull it out quickly and read it so that my brain can understand that it's not Ambien and tell my heart to stop dancing in my chest. The label reads Augmentin, and it has Jordan's name on it. But the other bottle is not a pill container, it is an eight-ounce, graduated, amber-colored bottle with a childproof cap—a cough syrup bottle. I lift it slowly from the bag, trying to recall my conversation with the doctor.

Did I say Jordan had a cough? Did he mention he was sending two meds?

As I turn the bottle so that the label is facing me, I can see the glowing orange liquid inside.

The label reads LAURA ROBBINS.

It's not for Jordan . . .

ONE TO TWO TEASPOONS EVERY FOUR TO SIX HOURS.

TUSSIONEX.

Oh my God.

Suddenly everything stops.

The TV, Maria emptying the dishwasher, the sound of Jordan's sleep breathing, all go silent. Instantly the bottle zooms into focus in my hands, blacking out everything around it. The bottle is heavy, warm, smooth, and full. I want—no, it's absolutely critical that I get to curl up with it somewhere immediately and drink myself into a dreamy, dozy sleep.

I do some calculations in my head.

My husband and Jacob are gone, probably for the weekend.

I've just done my last pee test for the week.

It's possible I could push next week's tests since I have a sick kid.

Maria is leaving for the day in less than an hour.

Jordan is sick and will probably sleep most of the night.

Who would really know if I enjoyed some of the contents of this bottle?

Quickly, I place the cough syrup on my nightstand, fighting the urge to stash it in one of my old hiding places. My whole body is vibrating with trepidation.

What to do, what to do . . .

I start to call my ENT or the pharmacy to tell them they made a mistake. I think to call the woman who just yesterday agreed to sponsor me, or Scott to laugh with him about how fucked-up this is—but I just end up staring at the phone in my hand.

Maybe this is a sign.

I'm not cut out to be sober, to do all of this without help, to work without a net. Maybe, if there is a God, this is his way of saying, "Enough, Laura—you gave it a good try, but you deserve a break." I mean why else would one of my favorite things in the world, second only to my beloved Ambien, have arrived unrequested, on the only weekend in months when I can actually enjoy it?

But what if it's not a sign? What if this is a test?

Isn't it possible that my husband could have arranged for this bottle to be delivered on a weekend when he knew he'd be away with the boys? Could there be some private investigator above our retaining wall right now snapping pics of me with the bottle, or worse, some hidden nanny-type cameras documenting my every move?

Maybe I should call Nancy.

I go check the window again. There's no movement outside our house and the sun is almost gone. An hour later, Maria startles me by yelling up the stairs that she's leaving. Jordan wakes up soon after, and I make him some ramen before giving him the antibiotic. I call his dad and put him on the phone with Jordan, as promised. Afterward, I change Jordan's pillowcase because his head is sweaty, and then go downstairs to wash the dishes.

I'm stalling.

Because even as I take care of my son, my mind is transfixed on that cough syrup. It calls to me, and every single cell in my body wants to answer. I know exactly how it will taste on the different parts of my tongue, the sweet orangyness on the tip, a slight citrusy sourness on the sides, and a hint of bitterness at the back. And I can already feel that delicious warmth that fills my head and neck as the opiated serum enters my bloodstream.

And the relief! Oh my God, I miss that relief.

And the truth was I wasn't addicted to cough syrup, just the pills. So why can't I drink a little?

224

Jordan wants me to read some of his new Percy Jackson book to him, so I get in bed with him and read until he falls asleep again. Afterward, I slip out of bed, grab the bottle, cradling it gently against my cheek. I sniff the outside to see if I can just get a whiff of elixir inside the plastic. When Jordan moans in his sleep, I check his temp before creeping into my closet and kneeling with the bottle clutched in my hands.

Who's going to know?

It's nearly midnight now. I know without looking at the clock because I can hear the fourth rendition of the *Friends'* closing theme song on Nick at Nite. I'm still here kneeling in the closet, clutching the cough syrup, and rocking back and forth.

After a while I get up to pace and stretch a bit. My eyelids are getting heavy, and my knees are carpet-burned. I know I just need to put the bottle away and go to bed, but I can't help but think how much better I'll sleep once I've had a few sips.

Just a few sips.

A couple more laps around my closet and I'm done.

Fuck it.

In an instant, I'm pushing down on the lid and turning the cap. Just as I'm about to make the first rotation I feel hot arms circling my waist.

"Mommy."

Jordan's eyes are glassy with fever and his voice sounds so dreamy, I'm not sure if he's even really awake.

"Mommy, I need you. You weren't there when I woke up."

"I'm right here, sweetie," I say, releasing the bottle and turning around so I can grab him and carry him back to bed.

"Don't leave, Mommy," he says as he snuggles next to me.

"Okay," I say.

I'll just wait until he's asleep and then I'll grab a quick sip and then get back in bed.

But Jordan is sleeping so lightly now that each time I shift even a little bit, he whines and grabs me tighter. He doesn't fall into a deep sleep until after the birds are chirping, and by this time, I'm too exhausted to move. So, despite myself and for the first time in months, I fall into a deep, peaceful sleep.

A while later, I'm awakened by the sound of the house alarm chime, alerting me that the front door has been opened. My husband is walking up the stairs when I stumble-rush to the railing.

"What? Are you still sleeping? It's almost ten. I called and no one answered."

Almost ten o'clock? He called? Oh my God, he probably thinks I'm high.

"We had a long night." My brain feels like it's fogged in, so I try to sound as wide awake and responsible as possible. "He had a hard time getting to sleep. Where's Jacob?"

"With my mom and sister. They came out for the day—it's beautiful out there. How is he?"

He kisses Jordan's forehead and asks him how he feels.

"Did he eat?" he says, looking at me.

"A little ramen. He had some Motrin and took his antibiotic last night."

"Good boy." He's looking at Jordan so lovingly and patiently it makes my heart hurt. He used to look at me that way too.

"Hey, buddy. I just came to get your brother's inhaler, but maybe when you're better Mommy will bring you down to the beach, okay?"

"Okay, Daddy."

A few minutes later down at the door, he asks if there's anything else he needs to take for Jacob. I shake my head no before realizing that there is actually something I need for him to take, but not for Jacob. I dash upstairs and grab the bottle and then run downstairs quickly before I can change my mind and hand it to him.

"Here," I say. "Can you take this please? I can't be in the house with it. It's still sealed, they sent it by mistake when they sent over the antibiotic for Jordan."

I'm handling it as though it's a live explosive, which for me isn't far from the truth.

"What is it?" he says, reading the bottle. "Cough syrup? For you?"

"Yes. But like I said, it's not for me. It's a mistake."

"And you can't be in the house with it . . . ?"

He's inspecting me now like I'm stoned or crazy or both.

"No, I can't."

"Why not?"

"It's just . . ."

I want to explain why, but then I imagine the conversation with Nancy.

"You told him why you couldn't be in the house with it?!" she would yell. "Don't say another word."

"Sorry, Nancy, but I have to get it as far away from me as possible, otherwise I will drain this whole bottle."

"I'd really appreciate it if you took it," I say, moving back inside the house. "I'd better"—I motion up the stairs with my chin—"get back."

The last few months flash before me as I'm walking up the stairs toward my sick son; my seizures, the doctor shopping, and the jittery queasiness from lying to everyone all the time. The painful detox, those plastic mattresses at The Meadows, the absolute agony of being away from my kids. Then I think about the meetings; the humiliation of being new and the embarrassment of counting days and collecting chips. I think about how guilty I feel all the time and how scary it is to be back, to see people, especially the people that love me. And then there are all the relationships I may have destroyed, the marriage that I ruined.

Do I really want to go through all this again?

For the first time since I've been home from rehab something revelatory snaps into focus.

Maybe I want to be sober more than I want to be high.

Maybe it's not just because I'm afraid of losing custody, and not because I'm afraid of losing my house or being poor, but because I worked so fucking hard for this. I realize that all this other shit can be taken away, even my kids. My sobriety is the only thing that no one can take away from me but me, and fuck me if I don't want to hold on to it now.

It seems I'm always counting days.

Five months ago, it was always "How many days until my next refill?" Then four months ago it was "How many days until I have to check in for treatment?" And then three months ago it was "How many days until I can go home and be with my kids?" Now it's "How many days until I'm officially divorced? How many days until I feel normal again?" Days on days on days.

Today I have sixty days sober.

Sixty whole days and nights without anything to help smooth out the edges or knock me deep into oblivion.

I don't know how people do this for real, for months and years.

I look around at the old white people at the meeting today who claim to have all these years, and I want to pull them aside one by one and call bullshit.

"Come on, man, twenty-eight years? You can tell me the real, what do you do? A little marijuana maintenance? A sip of sumpin' sumpin' when no one's looking?"

I mean this is a room full of liars and manipulators, so you gotta figure there's a whole lot of hustle going on. Today there were three anniversaries (ten years, twenty-one years, and thirty-two years), but only two of us stood up for sixty days, me and this skinny white kid, Eric. Eric and a whole posse of teenagers who look like him came in a van from a nearby rehab. His crew clapped it up when Eric got his chip, but the applause decibel level hit the roof when Beth handed me mine.

"Way to go, Laura!" Briefcase Guy shouted. He patted me on the shoulder when I got back to my seat. Last week I asked if he would help me find a sober living for Scott S., and today before the meeting I asked him if he would be Scott's sponsor.

"Temporarily," I said quickly. "Just so he has someone when he gets here."

"Of course. Here's my number, have him call me."

Obviously, the other thing I am counting are the days until Scott arrives—two.

After the meeting this morning I took my newly procured sponsor out for coffee and confessed to her that I had purchased a one-way plane ticket for my rehab buddy (on my secret credit card). The same man I made out with near the ping-pong table at The Meadows, the man I talk to from my car or my closet several times a day. I told her that I've also arranged for him to go to a nearby sober living. A communal home for men to which I've already paid a six-hundred-dollar deposit.

Then I sat quietly and waited for her to tell me I was fired—or whatever it is one says when they're unloading a disappointing sponsee. Half of me was hoping she would fire me so I don't have to keep up this charade of being a "good twelve-stepper." The other half was terrified that she would, as having someone in her position, someone who could go on record and say, "Yes, this woman is working her program," is the third prescription on my list from Dr. Nancy.

Instead, she sighed and looked away. She's only about ten years older than me, but she looks old enough to be the Jewish auntie I never had. Finally, she put her cigarette out, blowing a long stream of smoke out of the side of her mouth.

"Honey, I would ask you if you knew what you were doing, but I know you don't."

The Halls cough drop she's just popped in her mouth fills the air between us with a lemony menthol fragrance.

"You're what? Two months sober? You're still wet behind the ears."

I looked down at my coffee mug and waited for her to rain judgment down on me.

"Hey," she said more gently. "I know two months feels like a long time. But it's just a blip. And he's still drinking, for shit's sake. What about your own sobriety? Think about your divorce, your family. You're willing to jeopardize that? And for that matter, what about him? You want this poor schmuck to leave his home, his kids, and come to LA to do what?"

Instead of feeling guilty or ashamed, I was suddenly overcome with an urge to make her see that it's not like that with me and Scott. That I'd only asked him to come to LA so that he doesn't die or go to prison.

"He's my friend," I started.

She held up her hand as if to say "Spare me," but I kept going.

"And he saved my life."

She made a face.

"He did; I told you my story. I would never have stayed in treatment if it weren't for him. After my kids came, and I thought I was going to die from the pain of having to say goodbye to them, he risked everything to come and comfort me. And driving past that CVS and not picking up the refill? That was only because he was with me. He saved my life. How can I not try to save his life back?"

She took out her compact and applied bright fuchsia lipstick, keeping one eye on me to show that she was still listening.

"And also, his kids aren't even in Utah. They're with their mother in another state. I would never have suggested he come if he had a chance to be with them. He's all alone there."

"So, are you asking me for my advice, or are we just shilly-shallying around?" she said, putting the compact and lipstick back in her purse.

I shrugged as the waitress came to drop off our check. "Anything else?"

"No, thanks," we both said at once.

"I'm not sure what shilly-whatever means, but I'm saying this because I'm trying to be up-front with you," I said, picking up the check. "It doesn't come naturally to me, being up-front, I mean."

"Then I'll be up-front too." She leaned forward, putting her whole ninety-two-pound frame on the wobbly wrought iron table between us.

"You can get loaded on more than just drugs and booze, my friend. Don't make the mistake I did in the beginning and get loaded on a guy."

"You mean you . . . when you were getting sober?"

"Don't change the subject," she said grimly. "I'm talking about you."

"Okay. But it's not like that with me. I'm not getting loaded on Scott S."

"Well, just give this a good think, okay? You've got kids and an almost ex-husband. An ex-husband, I might add, who your lawyer thinks you're currently on thin ice with, correct?"

I broke eye contact with her and studied my empty coffee mug.

"Correct."

"You told me you got sober for your kids, that you're in this battle so that you can keep being a mom to them. I think you have a good shot at sobriety, kid. My advice? Don't fuck it up for someone you barely know."

———

"I'm here."

The two-word voice mail from Scott S. sends me into an adrenaline brownout. Two words that make two emotions, joy and terror, bounce around inside me like a pinball. I haven't seen Scott since August 14, more than two months ago. Hearing his voice on the phone when I first got back from rehab freaked me out so much that I thought I would never speak to him again. Now I'm going to see him in person, and I have no idea what's going to happen.

My husband is leaving for an overnight trip and is saying goodbye to the boys at the front door. I close my eyes and try to calm my jitters before heading out from my closet to join them. He's been kinder to me lately, and I've been trying not to be too suspicious of it. Last night after dinner he caught sight of the sixty-day chip on my key chain and I panicked, instinctively snatching it up and stuffing it in my pocket. It was an act that could be written off as inconsequential, but my energy was like a volcanic eruption of "My sobriety is none of your business, so back the fuck up."

He actually did back up, raising his hands like "I'm out," and shaking his head.

"Congratulations on sixty days," he said before heading upstairs. His voice was empty, like I'd sapped all the fight out of him.

"Thanks," I called up weakly after him.

I'm so sorry.

My body rose as if to follow him, but my feet were stuck to the floor. I spent the rest of the night wondering when divorced people learn how to talk to each other again.

Does a certain amount of time have to pass? Or maybe it's easier when the wife isn't a drug addict recently home from rehab?

Now he's leaving for his overnight, and I think I'm having my first sober panic attack.

Half of my heart is soaring because Scott S. is finally here, and it's taking everything I've got not to book out the door and screech out of the driveway toward the airport. But the other half of my heart is jackhammering its way out of my chest because I'm afraid I've made a really stupid, fatal mistake. By bringing Scott here I know I've crossed a line that can't be uncrossed. This is something I'll never be able to excuse or explain away. If anyone—Nancy, my husband—were to discover that I'd arranged for him to come, then I am so fucked. So now I'm at the door with my husband, desperately trying to appear normal, casual. What's interesting is that the secret of Scott appears to affect my nervous system the same way my pill secret did. Just when I thought I was maybe getting better, balancing out a bit, suddenly I'm this bug-eyed, inappropriately giggly, shaky, imposter again. When I glance down, I catch my hands trembling and clasp them behind my back, but not before he's clocked my shaking too.

Fuck.

He's watching me as he picks up his bag.

"Are you okay?"

Are you high?

"Oh yes, I'm fine. I'm just a little . . ."

Scared, confused, excited, nervous, panicky, detoxy.

"Tired. I'm still not sleeping so well."

He's staring now, like he's not sure if he should leave.

"I'm fine," I say, forcing what I hope is a genuine "you don't have to worry about me" smile and waving him away. "We'll see you tomorrow."

I have ninety minutes to pick up Scott, drop him at a sober living, and get back home before Maria has to leave. And I feel like I'm in one of those video games where obstacles keep popping up to prevent you from reaching your goal. First, as I'm taking my shortcut to the airport, I have to wait for a garbage truck driver to push a dumpster to the side of a back alley.

Are you fucking kidding me right now?

Then there's some kind of power outage near the Burbank airport, so traffic is backed up like twenty deep at Magnolia and Hollywood Way. Finally, just as we get moving, a woman in an old Cutlass cuts me off and then proceeds to go seven miles per hour in front of me while a city bus paces me on the right.

Faaaaaaaaacckkkk!

When I finally make the left onto Bob Hope Drive, giddiness bubbles up and out of my mouth in a yelp, and I can feel sweat dripping under my arms. I check my face in the mirror as I'm rounding the corner to Arrivals and suck lipstick off my teeth.

There he is.

He's wearing a tan, oversize button-down with faded jeans and standing next to a brown roller bag. His broad shoulders are hunched forward as he tosses his cigarette and smiles at me. It's the same slow smile of recognition that greeted me every time we saw each other at The Meadows. The smile that I believe is reserved for me alone.

"Hi," he says once he gets in the car.

As soon as he shuts the door, the car instantly fills with a smell that I've only associated with The Meadows. Now I realize that soapy, smoky, slightly herbal fragrance is Scott S.

"Hi."

"Nice car," he says, looking around the Rover nervously.

"Thanks," I say, trying not to stare at him. His hair is longer, and he's lost some weight, but his eyes are the same. It's still him.

"It's good to see you."

He leans toward me and suddenly I'm grateful for the piece of gum I've been chewing since I left the house. But instead of kissing me, he just buckles his seat belt and winks at me.

A wink? What does that mean? Are we just friends now? Maybe he's nervous? Maybe we were always just friends.

We make small talk for a few minutes.

Me: "How was the flight? Did you talk to your seatmate? Did you sleep on the plane?"

Him: "Thank you for coming to get me. Where do you live? How close are we to the sober house?"

"Um, The Abbey House, the uh, sober living, is only about ten minutes from here," I say during a short silence. "I have to head right back home, but let's get you something to eat before I drop you off, okay?"

I feel so exposed standing next to him at the taco stand.

What if someone drives by and sees us? What if I've been followed?

But I still can't help staring at him while he orders, watching his mouth move, remembering what his lips felt like when I kissed him. I take note of his hands as he pulls out his wallet to pay, remembering how deceptively strong they are, what they felt like on my waist when he pulled me toward him. We stand to the side while we wait for his order. I want to grab his face to convince myself that this is no dream, Scott S. is really, actually here in Los Angeles.

"Um, I hate to ask, but you know they won't take you unless . . . I mean it needs to be three days since your last . . . I had to assure them that you would be . . ."

"I'm sober."

"Oh, okay, good."

———

The Abbey House is a ranch-style four-bedroom home in North Hollywood with a dirt front yard and faded green picket fence that's missing several slats. I'm antsy as we walk up the porch steps because I only have twenty minutes to get home. For the gazillionth time, I'm overwhelmed with the enormity of the probability for error here. Newly sober mom, mid-divorce, risks everything to send for her rehab crush who relocates to some ghetto sober living about seven miles from the home she still shares with her soon-to-be ex-husband and their two young boys.

What have I done?

"Hey, hey!"

Thomas Murphy is wearing a tight muscle tee and enormous headphones that look like mouse ears. He extends his hand toward Scott.

"Welcome, welcome. I'm Thomas, the house manager," he says, shaking Scott's hand then grabbing the bag from him.

"This is the living room," he calls over his shoulder. The small room is dimly lit and smells like the windows haven't been opened for a while. I switch to mouth breathing.

Thomas is fast walking ahead of us. "That's Andrew. He has the room across from yours."

He points to a white guy on a plaid sofa who looks like a short, round Li'l Abner.

"Hey, what's up?"

"Hi," says Scott.

"You're lucky, you won't have a roommate for a while." Thomas is eating a red apple now, which he wiped on his dirt-slicked sweats before biting.

"A few other guys live in the bunk room in the back. Livius, he's at work now but you'll get to meet him tonight. Also, Happy Bob and John."

All at once I'm reminded of how it felt to drop Jordan and Jacob off at their first days of school. Watching them awkwardly meet their new classmates, and me hating to leave them but knowing that I had to.

"Hey," I say to Scott when we round the corner to an empty hallway. "I have to get back . . ."

"I know," he says.

His breath smells sweet and familiar. Tic Tacs or Sprees, I can't tell. My lips are ready for his when he kisses me. But instead of it being like our last kiss, the one where the rest of the world disappeared and it was just his breath, his lips, his tongue, his body pressed close to mine, this one is like our first kiss, the one on the balcony by the cows—tender, chaste, and quick.

I understand how nervous he must be. I know what a precarious position we're in, but if I'm honest, I feel a little robbed.

I was hoping for more.

I wanted to feel his arms around me, to taste that candy in my mouth. But I try to erase the disappointment from my face before he sees it. After all, the guy is sober, probably just a day or two, and now he's in a strange place, away from everything he knows, checking in to this strange house with these strange people. I don't want to add to his stress.

"I'll call you tonight," I say as I'm inching toward the front door. "And then tomorrow I'll pick you up for the meeting."

CHAPTER TWENTY-THREE

Snitch

Jordan forgot his saxophone, and I have to swing home and drop it off at the school before I head to my appointment with Nancy. He's playing a solo in the holiday concert in two months and he's been practicing, if you can call it that, for the last two weeks. It doesn't help that he exudes this next-level joy when he's playing "The Little Drummer Boy" over and over again. I'm a ball of nerves while we all sit next to one another on the family room sofa as his audience twice a day—me, my husband, Maria, and Jacob.

This, him and I being able to sit next to each other, will all be a memory if this thing with Scott blows up. Not to mention that this could be one of the last times we're all together while living under the same roof. This togetherness is ending because of me.

After dropping off the sax, I enter the morning rush-hour gridlock that is Beverly Glen and call Scott. I've been picking him up after I drop the kids off at school for the last two weeks and taking him to Moorpark with me. We have a whole weekday routine; I scoop him up from The Abbey House and then we head to Starbucks for our Americanos. Then we arrive at the 9:00 a.m. meeting early enough to grab two seats together in front. We always stay for the ten thirty meeting and then get lunch together. Afterward, I drop him off at The Abbey House before picking up the kids. When I have a pee test, or some parent association thing, Briefcase Guy works the steps with him in the garden next to the church, and then he gives Scott a ride back to The Abbey House.

I'm getting really good at pretending that Scott's just some guy from the program and we're helping each other stay sober. But it feels so good to sit next to him at a meeting again. I love our little side conversations, whispering about the other newcomers, speaking our secret language in each other's ears. But once we're outside the church, I'm careful. I don't touch his hand or connect with any part of his body in a way that might give someone the impression that he and I are anything other than just recovery buddies. My urges to be with him, to kiss him and hold him, seem to have temporarily taken a back seat to common sense. But I worry that he'll drink again if he doesn't stay busy. I worry that if he relapses, I might be next. I know the bottom line is that if he can't stay sober, I can't have him in my life, and that worries me too.

But now I'm just hoping that Thomas or one of his roommates was kind enough to drive him to the meeting this morning and that's why he's not answering my call.

———

"So," Nancy says, indicating the chair opposite her desk.

"Hey," I say, sliding into the seat. "Sorry I'm late, it's crazy traffic right after drop-off. What's up?"

"Are you having an affair?"

Suddenly the air turns into clear Jell-O. Nancy's face gets blurry and the sound of the copy machine in the next room becomes muffled like I'm underwater.

"I'm, I'm sorry, what? No, of course not!"

My voice sounds like it's coming from far away. I almost look around to see if there's someone else in the room. Someone who had sense enough to deny this accusation right off the bat.

Nancy picks up a notepad and begins to read.

"So you're not attending daily meetings with a tall blond man that you may or may not have met while the two of you were patients at The Meadows?"

A siren's wail slices through my head and splits it in half.

"We're not having an affair . . ."

I'm shouting from the bottom of a well.

"We."

Disapproval clouds her features. "So there is someone?"

She starts reading again, her words cutting through the siren.

"Someone that you are canoodling with at meetings every day."

"Not, um, canoodling, absolutely not. Who's saying this stuff? Who even says 'canoodling'?"

Nancy sets her pad down.

"We'll get to that in a minute. Start from the beginning. Tell me what's going on. Who is he?"

The wailing sound clears, and my brain starts to scramble for a story version that will make the judgmental/disapproving expression vanish from her face.

Option A) I don't know what you're talking about. Whoever told you that is lying.

Option B) Yes, he was at The Meadows but I didn't really know him there. It's just a coincidence that we're both in LA.

Option C) Yeah, we met in treatment, but he's just a friend and he's here visiting.

Option C?

"His name is Scott," I say.

Nancy gives me a look of pure exasperation.

"And it's true," I continue, without looking at her. "He and I were at The Meadows together. I told him to come out here because he drank as soon as he got home from rehab. There are no meetings there, he can't drive. I told him it's like the Cineplex Odeon here for meetings, like one every hour. I never imagined he would really do it, but he came. He's in a sober living in North Hollywood. We're not having an affair. He's never been to my house. He's never met my friends or my kids. I only see him at meetings and sometimes for a quick lunch. But he's my friend."

We're not having an affair.

"And now I want you to tell me who told you about us. I mean, told you about him."

I make eye contact with her again, trying to recall that lightning-strike strength I felt last time I was in her office, but my legs feel like noodles.

"This is the type of thing I've been asking you about. Remember the gas man incident? I asked you point-blank then if there was anyone I needed to know about."

Her mouth is smiling slightly, but her eyes are lasers carving deep slashes all over my face and neck.

"There wasn't, then. I mean, he wasn't here in LA. And he isn't 'someone else.' We're, we're just friends."

"Friends? Laura, what did I tell you back when we started, about male friends? About even talking to anyone who isn't your brother?"

"You said, um, not to."

My voice is small now, like that of a child who's been scolded.

"At the very least, you could have done whatever it is you do in private. You're out with him in public. People have seen you together."

"What people? And we weren't doing anything but sitting next to each other. And we're at a fucking twelve-step meeting anyway. What happened to anonymity?"

"Listen to me," Nancy growls. She's standing now and pointing her silver Uni-ball at me.

"This is fucking us. What did I tell you the day you blew off Harry? You're just out of rehab—strike one. And if that weren't enough, your husband has physical evidence, proof of your past drug use—strike two. And now you're out in public risking everything for some drunk?? Strike three."

Ouch.

"Who is saying these things about me?"

"I have no idea," Nancy says, sitting back down. "But whoever is saying it, it's gotten back to your husband's attorney."

Oh no . . .

"He and I are old colleagues, so he gave me a courtesy heads-up, which is of course really a warning shot. He's letting me know they have the 'W.'"

"The 'W'?"

"The win."

"And my husband?"

"What about him?"

"Does he think I'm having an affair?"

"I don't know what he thinks. But if you're asking if he's heard about Scott, I'm sure he has."

But nothing's changed at home. He's been the same.

Fuck.

"What happens now?"

Nancy smiles slightly and arches her newly tinted brows, reminding me of Cesar Romero's Joker.

"Now? I won't know how this impacts asset division until we sit down with them next month, which means I'll be going in blind. Now we hope that this doesn't impact custody. Now we hope that you don't give him any more ammunition to use against us."

Damn.

"But even if I were having an affair, which I am not, California is a no-fault state, right? I mean it can't really affect custody or assets, can it?"

"You're smarter than that, Laura. Yes, legally a judge would officially deny any custodial requests based on an extramarital relationship. I'm sure your husband has been advised that he can't win on those grounds. But he can win by making you look like an unfit mother. This is why I told you, never, ever bruise the ego. You are a drug addict. You just got out of treatment for said addiction. A treatment center where you met an alcoholic who has now moved to Los Angeles from another state so that he can be near you. Does that person sound like she's stable? Like she can be trusted unsupervised, unmonitored, with her minor children?"

I don't bother to deal with the tears and snot streaming down my face.

I am mortified.

"No, I guess she doesn't."

"Okay. So stop 'not having an affair' with this man. He's not your friend. He's a ticking bomb and he's going to blow up your life and everything we've worked for. It's just a matter of weeks until this is done, so whatever this is, end it right now, do you understand?"

———

I pull over the first chance I get on my way back over the hill.

I have a pee test at one. I'm snack mom for Jacob's soccer game at three. My husband thinks I'm having an affair. I can't see Scott anymore. What if I lose my kids? This is too much.

A dam bursts inside me and tears rain down on my BlackBerry while I'm scrolling for Scott's number. Ten rings until his voice mail picks up. I know I can't speak without sobbing so I click off. A few hours, minutes, seconds later, I try again. Only this time my sponsor picks up.

What tha . . . ?

I double-check the screen and see that somehow I've hit her number by mistake.

"I'm sorry," I say. "I meant to, I mean, I didn't mean to . . ."

Breathe.

"Oh baby, what's wrong? What's going on?"

"Nothing, I'm just . . ."

"Laura?"

"I think—you were right about getting loaded on a guy. I didn't mean to, but I think I'm fucking it up."

"Where are you?"

"I'm pulled over on Sunset. I've got a pee test in forty minutes and then I'm snack mom and . . ."

"Laura, did you drink or use?"

"Me? No, that's not what's wrong. I mean I didn't take anything, and I didn't drink anything."

"Okay then." I can hear her exhaling a stream of smoke. "Then you didn't fuck it up too bad."

———

Is it that guy with the glasses? Is it her? I think she's a producer, she might know my husband. Wait! The meeting secretary was an actor on that hospital show, it could totally be him.

Every meeting for the last three weeks, I've been looking around trying to figure out who it was that dimed on me. And the whole entire time I am hyperaware of the person in the seat next to me. The person that isn't Scott.

Scott drank again.

He drank that day, the day I went to see Nancy. There's a liquor store down the street from Moorpark. He went to the meeting like he'd promised. But before it started, he ran into the store to get a pack of cigarettes and there they were—the point-of-sale vodka bottles. You know, the little ones like they have on planes that they keep next to the register? He bought his cigarettes and then added two POS bottles.

The good news is that he's sober now. And his housemates are taking care of him, taking him to a meeting spot near The Abbey House and keeping an eye on him between meetings.

The good news is I haven't transferred that refill back to California.

But I am on fucking pins and needles at home. Now every time we all take our places on the sofa for Jordan's daily sax practices, every time my husband walks into the room, I am expecting him to confront me about Scott. And every time he doesn't my adrenals dump more epinephrine into my system, making it impossible for me to behave normally. It's then that I realize that I can be just as fucked-up from a drug inside of me as I can from some pill that comes in a bottle.

I'm a mess.

If he hates me, I mean he must hate me, right? Even more than he hated me before. But I just wish he'd say something so that I could explain that whatever he heard was wrong, that Scott and I are not having an affair. Unless you call sitting next to someone, giving them rides, taking them to lunch, paying for their sober house, buying them plane tickets, and phoning them every chance you get and occasionally hoping that they'll kiss you an affair.

I am keeping myself occupied during the day by scoping out these meetings, trying to figure out who it was. What's the connection? Who knows who I am outside of these rooms? Who knows I'm still married? Who knows him well enough that they chose to break our organization's sacred vows of confidentiality and report my movements to him?

"What if your lawyer is right about that gas man being some kind of spy? What if it's someone who works for him?"

My sponsor and I are in the meeting after the meeting (aka the hallway after everyone else has left). My obsession with finding my narc-nemesis has infected her, and now she too has been looking around to see who might be taking an unusual interest in me.

"I mean anyone can come into our meetings, it's not like there's a screening process."

"Could be."

———

The weather snapped cold as soon as November hit, and my sandals and sundresses have been replaced by sweaters and boots. And I lie awake at night after the kids are asleep, protected from the outside chill, wondering how Scott's feeling. Wondering what it would be like to lie in bed next to him, imagining the warmth his body would generate under the covers. I still talk to him for about five minutes every evening, but our all-day-every-day calling each other is a thing of the past. These days he sounds scared, full of shame and humility. He tells me he feels like he's let me down, and I try to make him understand that the best thing he can do is to take care of himself.

"I miss seeing you," he says.

"Me too."

But the risks are too great for both of us. As Nancy always reminds me, my kids are at stake. And as my sponsor reminds me, Scott's life could be at stake.

"If you care about him, you'll let those men at the sober house handle him now."

But knowing that I'm doing the right thing doesn't make it any less painful to be without him. It's different from the pain of my Ambien detox, which is now finally tolerable most of the time. This is an ache not in my body but in my being. An ache that is only satiated when he's next to me. An ache that eases when I hear his voice but doesn't quite go away. It's a constant phantom limb–like pain that makes me crave my former numbness. I want it to end.

This is why people cut themselves. This is why they separate men from women in treatment.

In the middle of the night, sometimes I loop my wrists through the tulle bed drapes and pull them tight with my teeth so I don't call him or the pharmacy or get up and drive to the liquor store or eat the entire red velvet cake in the refrigerator.

It's official. I'm a crazy person.

Mediation is in two weeks, and I am terrified. I am definitely the underdog in this fight and I gotta figure that everyone with half a brain is betting against me. Nancy still seems pissed at me about Scott, my husband is acting as though he's indifferent toward me, and Scott S. is preparing for his own court date in Utah.

He leaves in four days. He borrowed a suit from Happy Bob, and he has a letter from Thomas testifying that he's a sober living resident. Briefcase Guy wrote one as his sponsor, explaining that Scott is attending meetings and working on his sobriety. No mention in either letter, I imagine, of the relapse.

Nancy calls after I've grabbed the boys from school. I stare at the phone for a minute before picking it up. I've never spoken with her in front of the kids. They still don't have any idea that we're getting a divorce. I want to delay telling them until we absolutely have to—we're all just finally adjusting to me being back from rehab. Part of me, though, knows that my desire to postpone the bad news isn't entirely about them. I'm terrified of their sadness. I'm terrified I won't be able to comfort them. What if I'm not enough without their dad?

"Hey, Nancy," I say hurriedly, picking up the phone instead of putting her on speaker. "I'm in the car with the boys."

"Oh, hi, it's Noel."

Phew.

My shoulders drop and my jaw unclenches.

"Nancy just wanted me to tell you that they've scheduled the mediation for nine thirty on December eighth."

Wait what?

"But we'd said the ninth. We can't do the eighth. Jordan's holiday concert is the eighth. He has a saxophone solo. *The* saxophone solo."

"Mom, you're not missing my solo," Jordan calls from the back seat.

"No, sweetie. No one is missing your solo."

"Sorry, it's the only date," continues Noel. "The mediator is leaving town on the ninth. The next date we could get with anyone would be in February."

Fuck.

"Should I see if we can book a February date?"

That's three more months—I won't make it three more months.

"I don't think we can wait until February."

"So I'll confirm the eighth then."

———

At home that night I wait until Jordan falls asleep before heading downstairs to my husband's office.

"So what do we do?"

"I have my guy trying to move it, but if we can't . . ."

"We have to be there. He'll be heartbroken."

"So we'll tell the lawyers we have a hard out. If we leave by two we can make it by two forty-five, which should be just in time. And if we don't get out in time, then one of us will go while the other stays and finishes."

One of us will go. One of us will stay.

I know that the "one of us that stays" should be me. I'm the one who filed. I'm the addict. I'm the one who left him with the kids and went to rehab. I'm the reason we're in this mess in the first place. I'm the unfit mother.

But I really want to be there for Jordan's concert. I want to see him stand up in his new blue blazer and watch him belt out his "Little Drummer Boy" solo on his alto sax. I want to do this for Jordan. I want to show up for my son.

"Okay, one of us will stay."

Before I go to sleep I check my phone to see if Scott has called again. He heads to Utah tomorrow for his court date.

Four DUIs.

I don't know anyone with four DUIs. You would think that anyone with four DUIs would be dead or in prison. Up until I met Scott I always thought that people with multiple DUIs were careless, reckless, and selfish—a danger to society. I never thought of them as sick.

"We are not bad people trying to be good, we are sick people trying to get well," says my sponsor.

And Scott S. is sick. But he is a good person. Maybe the kindest person I've ever met. And now he might go to prison, when maybe for the first time in his life he's in a position to get well.

On impulse I call him and he answers on the second ring.

"Hey."

"Hey."

Silence.

"I just want to say don't forget to call me as soon as you get out of court."

I can hear the smile in his voice.

"Like I ever could."

"And make sure you have your letters and tell him about the recovery community here and how many meetings you go to a day."

"Got it."

"Okay."

"Okay."

Silence.

"Okay bye, I'll talk to you tomorrow."

I lie there in the dark after we hang up wondering if I should have said something more loving. Something more intimate. If he goes to prison tomorrow, I may not get a chance to speak to him again for a long time.

Unable to sleep, I get out of bed and open the photo album I've been working on, one of my many mom-image rehabilitation projects. I figure if I work a little on these albums every week, they might be done by the time they graduate from high school, and hopefully another little piece of my soul might be redeemed. The problem is that while selecting the best photos from each of their life events, I become a teary mess and end up going down a memory lane rabbit hole. Today I am doing Hanukkah 2003. We went to my sister-in-law's house to get gelt for the boys and took pictures with their cousins.

Oh my God, Jacob was so little. Look at those cheeks.

I remember that dress I was wearing. What happened to that dress?

And . . .

Oh shit.

There he is.

There's that muthafuckah who's diming on me.

He's shaved his beard, but I remember him now. He's my sister-in-law's ex-husband's friend. He works in the Starbucks over in Valley Village. I knew he looked kind of familiar, but I thought maybe I just knew him from the neighborhood. He's been at almost every meeting I've gone to for the last three months. That's that muthafuckah right fucking there.

Well, snitches get stitches, bitches. You're going to be fucking sorry you ever messed with me.

CHAPTER TWENTY-FOUR

The Language of Letting Go

"I have news."

I'm smiling as I settle onto Marguerita's sofa. I have a favorite throw pillow. It's soft and bright yellow with a large button in the middle that I can spin around absentmindedly. I grab it quickly and squish it against my stomach.

"Yes? What is this news?"

"Scott S. is on his way back! The judge let him go, after asking him to leave the state of Utah. He said that LA could have him. Can you believe that the judge actually said that? He released him to the care of his sponsor and the sober living. I mean Scott can't drive for a while, which is fine since he doesn't have a car out here, but he's free."

"So, before this was temporary, but now he is moving here permanently?"

"Um, I guess. I don't know. He's just coming here. Maybe it's still temporary."

"I see."

Do you?

"The point is that he doesn't go to prison, and now he has a chance to really get sober."

"I understand."

Unlike my sponsor, Marguerita does not appear to be at all interested in my news on a tabloid level, something which I'm currently finding to be incredibly irritating.

"Look, all I'm focused on right now is the mediation. I need to be as emotionally prepared for it as I can. Knowing that Scott S. isn't getting fitted for an orange jumpsuit is just one less thing for me to worry about."

I'm waiting for that moment of eye contact, that subtle smile that lets me know she understands and possibly approves. I'm waiting for her to be happy that Scott is free. I'm waiting for her to be happy for me.

"So shall we continue where we left off last week?" She picks up her distressed brown journal and opens it.

"Well, I have other news too—about the snitch."

"Snitch?"

"The one who's been talking about Scott S. and me sitting together at meetings."

She puts the journal down and looks up at me, crossing her hands on her lap.

"I figured out who he is. He's a friend of my husband's family and he goes to meetings where I go. I see him like five or six times a week. I found an old picture of a family gathering and there he was and then it just clicked."

"You seem . . . excited."

"Not excited. Pissed. Don't you see? Someone is fucking with my relationship with my kids. And now that I know who it is, I can finally do something about it."

"And what is it that you will do?"

I've tossed the pillow down now and am sitting on the edge of the sofa, poised to stand.

"I don't know," I say, shaking my head. "But seeing him makes me want to flip tables. Thinking about him makes me want to run his ass over in the parking lot, full gas."

"And what does your sponsor say about this, uh, full gas? What does your literature say?"

I'm frowning at her now. *Why is she not getting this at all???*

"My sponsor says that while she totally has my back, resentment is the number one offender for alcoholics, and it leads us straight back to the bottle. I lose my kids if I drink or use again. She says if I want to stay sober that I'm going to need to find a way to let this go."

Marguerita nods and gives me the smile I was looking for moments before.

"Anything else?"

"Um, yeah. She wonders if perhaps some of this anger I feel is misplaced."

"Meaning?"

"Maybe I'm not really angry at this fucker, but at myself. Or angry at my husband. But probably angry at myself mostly for destroying my marriage."

Marguerita hitches up her stretchy slacks and leans forward, putting her large hand on my knee, which has started shaking violently.

"First of all," she says gently, pressing my knee until it stills, "you knowingly entered into a marriage as someone other than your authentic self. This had absolutely nothing to do with him, eh? The truth is, yes, your marriage might have survived if you had continued to pretend that you were happy, but you might not have. You've talked about feeling imprisoned in this life, but how much of this prison do you blame yourself for building? Instead of flipping tables as you say, or hurting anyone, let's talk about finding compassion."

"For him? No, I'll never forgive him."

"I mean for yourself."

I'm surprised by the wave of emotion that swallows me as soon as those words are out of her mouth. Suddenly I don't have enough oxygen in my lungs and just like that, I'm floating outside my body.

Who am I if I'm not the one failing everyone who loves me? Or if I'm not to blame for the pain my kids are going to experience once the divorce is official? How could anyone forgive an unfit mother? How can I forgive myself?

"Your sponsor says this resentment you feel toward him could lead you back to drinking and using, and your lawyer told you that if you drink again you could lose your children. So the question isn't a matter of who's right or wrong, but is this resentment worth the risk? Do you hate him more than you love your children?"

Fuck.

I guess the answer is No, AND.

No, I don't hate him more than I love my kids. Jesus Christ, I don't even know this man. AND I know that ever since I got sober I've had this huge pot of anger boiling inside me, threatening to spill out all over anyone who gets too close. And now this snitch has come along and provided me with exactly what I need—a target. A perfectly justified resentment that I can direct all my unreasonable anger toward. I know what she's about to say, and I don't want to do it. Everything in me is telling me to resist. And yet . . .

I feel betrayed as a tear slithers down my cheek to the corner of my mouth.

"Of course not." I hear myself say.

Marguerita smiles as she hands me a tissue. "Then you have your answer. You must seize every opportunity to let this go."

———

"I'm going to miss you," says Veronica. "But I don't want to see you back here. You stay clean, you hear me. I'll be thinking about you on Monday, praying that you get to keep your kids. You deserve them. You've done an amazing thing showing up here every week."

"Thank you, Vee."

I put my hands on her shoulders and look her in the eyes. As soon as I see the tears there, I feel them in mine too.

"Girl, bye," she says, wiping her nose on her sleeve. "Get out of here."

I leave there with my final urinalysis green slip and butterflies in my stomach. The past three months have felt like mud, like industrial sludge, impossible to get through. And even though I could have stopped a couple of weeks ago, Nancy asked me to go a couple of extra

252

weeks, just so we had the most recent results to show them if they asked at the mediation. This whole time, minutes have felt like hours, hours have felt like days. But now my mind swivels toward December eighth, and suddenly the world feels like I've just gunned the accelerator.

How do people get through this?

When people get dumped by their romantic partner, they meet their friends for drinks. When someone is grieving, they drink alone. When a person wins a bet, or the lottery, what's the first thing they do? Okay, yes, eventually they buy their mother a house, but first they buy everyone in the bar a round of drinks. When someone is getting a divorce and is terrified of losing custody of their beloved children, friends show up with bottles of booze. They drink.

That's how people get through.

Drinking is the only tried-and-true way to do this, and it's the one thing I can't do. I don't think I can face a future that doesn't include my kids.

I can't do this. I won't make it.

I need something.

———

I make fists to stop my fingers from trembling as I idle in the driveway of The Abbey House. I haven't seen Scott since he's been back, and we haven't been to a meeting together for weeks.

It's okay, I'm just dropping a friend at a meeting.

I know that this is a stupidly thin excuse, and I understand what the penalty is if I get caught, but when Thomas called this morning after drop-off and asked if I knew anyone who could drop Scott S. off at Chandler Lodge for his meeting, I jumped at the chance.

"Hey."

I turn the radio volume up slightly instead of down because I'm afraid that he'll hear the hum of the electromagnet pulling me toward him over Alicia Keys singing "No One."

"Hey."

He's wearing the black James Perse T-shirt I got him and fitted jeans with a hole near the knee. There is a tuft of hair sticking up on the top of his head. I want to touch it, to smooth it and run my fingers through it.

"I can't believe this is the first time I'm seeing your face since your court date."

"Me either."

Scott's smiling shyly at me, looking at me from the corner of his eye.

"I missed your face," I say.

He turns to look at me then. "My face missed you."

His gaze is like a tractor beam. I rip my eyes away from it and put the Rover in reverse.

This is a huge mistake. I can't be around him now. What was I thinking? I got that call from Thomas and then it was like something else took over.

Falling in love with someone, I think, isn't a choice. It's more like addiction, or the flu. One moment I was fine and the next I was overcome, feverishly under the spell of it. It's easier to talk to him on the phone, that way I don't have to see those blue eyes, those lashes, those lips. That way I don't have to smell him. Oh my God, the scent of him makes me want to stop whatever I'm doing and inhale him like freshly baked bread. This is why I don't need to see this man until I'm divorced. I cannot be hindered by all of this; the racing heart and the stomach flips—the za za zoo. On the phone we laugh, we joke, we have a good time. But in person, I look at him and start planning a route to the nearest motel. Anywhere to be horizontal with him, to know what it feels like to have his weight on top of me.

I want him to crush me.

"Have a good meeting," I say, as we pull up to Chandler.

There are six or seven white men out front smoking. One of them smiles widely when he sees Scott in the passenger seat.

"Guess I'd better . . ." he says, pulling on the door handle.

"Yeah, you'd better," I say, kissing him near his mouth, but not on it.

"I'll call you tonight."

Twenty minutes later I pull into the parking lot at my Moorpark meeting. I enter quickly and find two seats near the front, taking the aisle seat for myself and putting my purse on the inside seat for my sponsor. As the meeting fills up, people are wandering around looking for any empty chairs. I pull out my Filofax, deliberately keeping my face down so I don't have to look anyone in the eye and refuse them the seat. The look of disappointment on their faces makes me uncomfortable. Also, some of these muthafuckahs are crazy.

At five to nine my sponsor calls and tells me that she's run over a nail and won't make the meeting.

Damn.

I'm about to lift my purse from her seat when I spot him standing in the doorway looking around.

The snitch.

In an instant my insides go from a low simmer to a raging boil. He smiles casually at me and then motions furtively toward the seat next to me.

Oh no you didn't.

Full gas.

The snitch's name is Andrew. He's tall and white (of course) with a light brown crew cut. He lumbers over with an idiotic smile just as the secretary opens the meeting with our preamble.

Muthafuckah, don't you know? I will cut yo' ass.

"Can I?" Andrew whispers. He's hovering, standing right next to me now, poised to slide between me and the row of chairs in front of me.

People are looking over at us. I have two or three brilliant retorts all queued up, but I open my mouth and nothing comes out.

"Is someone sitting here?" He's stooping down now, so as not to block the view of the people behind us.

Andrew, you fucker! You asshole! You're fucking with my family, with my kids! Do you even know how hurtful you're being? Do you know that instead of helping my husband you are destroying our family????

Angry tears fill my eyes and I fall into a vat of angst.

I can't show him weakness. I need him to be scared of me. I need him to be terrified, Friday the 13th *terrified.* Rosemary's Baby *terrified.*

The fireball burning in my throat feels like it's moving into my chest. If I don't do something quickly, I'm going to vomit all over him. I stand up to face him, confront him. I jut my chin out toward him and suck my teeth.

I'm going to tear his ass down right now, right here in front of every-one. I'm going to let them know that he is a true Judas, someone who has abandoned our principles in order to betray me and gain the favor of a Hollywood mogul.

I'm standing chest to chest with him now, and I can feel the fury steaming from my eyes and nose. I'm just about to open my mouth and let him have it. Everything he deserves. Fuck him, fuck the meeting, and fuck recovery. But then I hear Marguerita's voice in my head, and it's like an elephant suddenly sits on my chest, knocking the wind out of me.

Do you hate him more than you love your children? You must seize every opportunity to let this go.

A kerfuffle ensues inside me then.

Let it go? Hell no. He gets to do whatever he wants and no one holds him accountable? He can fuck me over like this and I have to look the other way? Is this some cosmic fucking joke that I have to give this asshole a seat???

But then a small but surprisingly strong voice booms in with reason.

Fair has nothing to do with it. None of this is fair, me being an addict, the pain of the divorce. But this is what's happening now, and I can either get with it or resist it. But resist at what cost? Am I willing to risk losing my kids over this man?

"No one's sitting there," I hear myself say finally. I turn my back to him and move my purse, taking a seat on the inside chair.

"Go ahead."

I see the leader's lips moving after that but hear nothing that's said for the rest of the meeting. My awareness of him is unbelievably loud. Rock-concert-next-to-a-speaker loud. I hear his breath, smell the coffee in his hand, smell the deodorant heating up under his arms.

When we all get up for the prayer at the end, I glare at him, daring him to try and hold my hand.

But instead of leaving it limply by my side as I planned, I feel myself slipping it into his when he reaches for it.

"God, grant me the serenity to accept the things I cannot change . . ."

Mid-prayer, somewhere inside me I feel a glacier melting. I imagine it dripping small puddles onto the floor around me. I am mortified to be thawing right here in front of everyone, in front of him. I wanted to win this. I wanted to hurt him, to make him understand that he'd tried to fuck with the wrong bitch. Now I feel my will dissolving, disarming me, taking away the fight.

"And the wisdom to know the difference."

Fuck.

CHAPTER TWENTY-FIVE

The Concert

My fingers aren't working.

There are ten buttons on my shirt and my nails are too long to put them through the ridiculously small buttonholes. I want to take a pair of scissors and slice these fuckers open, but I can't because this light blue Stella McCartney blouse goes with this dark blue Stella McCartney suit. The suit I bought especially for today's mediation.

Breathe.

"Mom, I can't find my mouthpiece!"

"Basketball or sax?"

"Sax, Mom! For the show today."

"It's soaking in the sink; it was all slimy after your last practice. I'll get it. Do you have your suit?"

"Right here."

My husband is standing on the staircase holding the suit bag.

We've barely spoken over these last couple of weeks and I feel like the air between us is full of all these words that we're afraid to say to each other. I wonder if we'll ever just talk again. I wonder if we'll ever laugh together again about anything.

"Great. Are you taking them or . . ."

"I'll drop them. I have to go to the office first before the thing today."

"Okay."

Jordan is standing in the foyer looking from my face to his father's like he's watching a tennis match.

"But you'll be there for the concert?"

One of us will.

"Yes, of course!" we both say at once. I wonder if my smile looks as strained as his does.

"I'll see you soon," I say, as I kiss Jordan all over his cheeks and forehead. "You're going to be fantastic."

"Make sure you get a seat up front, Mom."

"I'll do my absolute best, sweetie."

For the first time I don't mind the traffic on Beverly Glen heading over toward Nancy's office. I'm not in any hurry to sit down at the conference table. I don't want to face those collated binders and piles of files. I don't want to meet this mediator who's supposed to be so fair. I don't want to sit across the table from his good old boy attorney, knowing that he'll be judging me, has judged me, will continue to judge me long after this is all settled.

The king of Hollywood versus the lowly imposter, Black addict mother.

I wonder what kind of bombs I can expect to be dropped today.

Will they bring up the year of basing, the seizures, and all the pictures of my meds as proof that I'm an addict? Will they bring up dropping out of high school and never going to college as proof that I'm a liar? Will they bring up Scott as proof that I'm unstable and an unfit mother?

After I step off the elevator, I call my mom and ask her to save two seats up front at the concert for me and my husband. While we're talking I watch Nancy and her team gathering outside her office. They look like Theory-power-suit-clad Amazon warriors poised for battle, only with clipboards instead of shields and pens instead of spears. These women have the home-court advantage, and they look like it.

Nancy's offices, Nancy's conference room, Nancy's choice of mediator.

"One ground rule before we go in, okay?"

We're sitting in her private office and I'm squirming in my chair.

My suit pants are too tight around the hips when I sit, and these shoes squeak when I walk. I should have walked around in them before I bought them, but I was in such a hurry. I didn't have anything in my closet that gave off that "don't fuck with me" vibe. I thought I needed this ensemble to be my armor, but now I wish I was in sweats and sneakers.

"What is it?"

"Never speak to him directly during the mediation. You have something to say, you discreetly say it to me and then I'll tell Michael, his attorney, and then Michael will speak to his client."

"His client? You mean my husband."

"Yes."

"That's crazy. I can't talk to him? You know we still live together, right?"

"It's the best way. Michael and I will be able to keep emotion out of it."

Will you?

"So, what? It's some crazy ridiculous $650-an-hour game of telephone?"

"Another thing, while we're in there, lay off the jokes. For him, this divorce isn't personal, it's business, it's contracts. He thrives in that kind of environment, but not you. You've spent the last eleven years raising his children, and he's spent the last eleven years making deals. Just let me handle the business part of this whole thing. Do *not* discuss anything that has to do with the divorce without me present, okay? Believe me, you'll be glad you listened to me when we get to trial."

"I told you I'm not going to trial."

"And I told you that depends on how the mediation goes today."

She and I are facing each other. I try to remind myself that she's not the enemy. I need her. She is the only one fighting for me.

I soften my voice.

"Speaking of that, please remember that we need to be done by two or we'll never make the concert."

"We have the mediator until five. This is a big divorce settlement, lots of moving parts. I don't think we'll be anywhere near done by then."

"We have to . . ."

Pressure is building in the back of my eyes, and I try to calm my voice again.

"We promised him, Nancy. We can't miss his solo."

"You shouldn't have done that."

Nancy is staring at me as though she has assessed my mental capacity and found it to be lacking.

"Okay, get yourself together and let's go in."

The conference room is eerily quiet.

The windows are soundproof and so are the glass walls that separate it from the offices. The main piece of furniture is a large oval mahogany table, framed by several Scandinavian-looking lumbar-supporting swivel chairs. My husband and Michael are on the west side and Nancy and I are on the east, with the mediator at the head of the table. As soon as I sit down I experience a tremendous crisis of confidence and worry that everyone can smell me sweating. We've agreed to work through lunch but at eleven thirty we're not even halfway through. We've spent the last two hours working out what happens if I drink or use again.

"We have a few more items to go over regarding the petitioner's drug use, should that become necessary. Let's turn to page two, item five, post-treatment visitation."

They're preparing for what happens when I use again. Not if, but when. For the sixteenth time this morning I wish I could just disappear.

There are pages and pages of this document dedicated to what happens when I get loaded. So, what? I had a problem and now I'm forever defective? People don't get better?

"The petitioner shall notify the respondent in writing of her desired travel plans . . ."

I can't go anywhere without telling him first? This is bullshit. They're not protecting our children. They're punishing me.

"The petitioner is enjoined and restrained from ingesting any alcohol, illegal drugs, or prescribed drugs in excess of the items in the written statement of her physician pursuant to paragraph B.6 above. In the event that the petitioner fails one drug or alcohol test then the respondent shall immediately be deemed sole legal guardian . . . blah blah blah."

"Do you agree?"

I agree that as the petitioner I am beyond humiliated and mortified and wish I were anywhere else but here.

"Yes, fine," I say, checking my watch. I'm trying to sound poised, but my panic is starting to seep into my voice. "I'm not planning on drinking again."

I see him check his watch and I bug my eyes out at him across the table.

Helpless.

He meets my gaze and then gestures to his watch and shrugs as we move down to the custody.

I've been on the edge of my seat waiting for his lawyer to bring up Scott, the year of basing, my lack of education, even the pictures of my meds, but so far they seem to be shooting straight pool.

"Both minor children shall continue attending the Ashley School. Neither party may change the minor children's school without obtaining written consent . . ."

"How much longer?" I blurt out.

Nancy cautions me with her eyes and places her hand on mine.

I snatch it away from hers and face the mediator.

"It's just that we have to get to our son's holiday performance."

"Well," she says patiently. "I was just about to suggest a fifteen-minute break."

A fifteen-minute break now? It's twelve thirty. Oh God, we'll never make it.

The mediator is white, fiftyish, with thick salt-and-pepper hair and a generous smile. A smile that now flashes in my direction. "Well, if the performance starts at two . . ."

"Three," my husband and I both say at once.

"We have to leave by two to make it by three," he says quickly.

"Then perhaps the two of you might want to use the break to talk to your respective attorneys about the possibility of one of you leaving in time if we're not done by two."

"Just let me handle this," Nancy hisses at me when I look over at her.

"Okay."

In a fog, I make my way down a series of hallways to the women's restroom for some tissues and some privacy. The circles under my eyes are bright red, like I've been rubbing my face with sandpaper. My hair, which was supposed to be in a neat updo, is sticking out in frizzy tufts everywhere. My lips are chapped, and I forgot to bring both lipstick and lip balm.

Look at me. The picture of an unfit mother.

On my way back to the conference room I find myself in an unfamiliar hallway and suddenly have no idea where I am. I start to go one way but find myself blinded by tears. I lean against the wall and then, like in one of those eighties movies, I slide slowly down the wall and hug my knees when I get to the bottom.

I hate this so much. I hate the fighting, the division, the splitting, the fact that my addiction is so conflated with our divorce. And even though we've barely been speaking for months, I hate the fact that we're not allowed to talk to each other now.

"Hey."

His voice startles me. He's standing above me wearing a crew-neck sweater, pants, and loafers.

Next up on the runway, this powerful Hollywood executive is modeling a classic but casual look, perfect for going from a divorce mediation straight to your son's holiday concert!

I open my mouth to say something, but close it quickly and look down again, scared that Nancy might catch me talking to him.

"Are you okay?" he says.

Oh, I remember that voice. That warm, safe voice. The voice of someone who had vowed to protect and love me. That voice that melted me like butter, the voice whose protection I used to seek.

"If I said yes, would you believe me?"

"What are we doing?" he says, sinking down on the floor next to me.

"Getting divorced. I don't know."

"This"—he points down the hallway—"this isn't us. I don't know what this is."

"It's horrible. I think I hate my lawyer."

He smiles. "I think I hate your lawyer too."

I check my watch. Our fifteen-minute break is almost up.

"What do you want?" he says.

"I really want to get out of here so we don't miss Jordan. I don't want just one of us to be there. I want us both to be there. We promised him."

"No, Laura." His eyes are fastened on mine. "I mean what do you want? Just tell me so we can get this whole thing over with."

Oh shit. He's negotiating with me outside the presence of my attorney! Abort, abort!

"We should go back in . . ." I falter.

"Laura, it's me."

There's that voice again.

"What do you want?"

Don't be an idiot.

I can't tell him what I want, he'll use it against me, Nancy warned me against this. He makes deals, he knows contracts. This is his world, and I don't know dick about it. Also, Nancy will be beyond pissed if we come to an agreement without her. And I know that what I want is not enough as far as she's concerned. Also, I don't trust myself to have the courage to stand in my truth.

My conversation with my *Sex and the City* friends comes flooding back to me. What would they say to me now if they saw me sitting with "the enemy" in the hallway sans lawyers? Would they urge me to get what I'm worth? Would they say he's trying to take advantage of me? Or is it possible they might understand that he can't play me right now, because what I really want is to NOT put my kids through a contentious divorce. If there's a chance I can make that happen, then I'm going to fight like hell for it.

For the first time in years I'm not engulfed by shame or fear. I don't want to hide.

The truth is that all I want is to be comfortable, to stay in our home where we've raised our children, to be able to be in the same room with him without arguing about who's the better parent and to maybe, eventually, be able to celebrate our kids' milestones together. That's what I really want.

But what comes out of my mouth instead is, "I don't want a war."

Now his eyes get moist. Instantly I wish that all the pain of the past that led to this moment could be changed or erased. I don't want either of us to hurt any longer.

"I don't either." He puts his hand on my knee. "So, again, what do you want?"

Even though my heart feels as though it's about to explode, I lower my gaze and start talking. I look at my fingers because it's too hard to look at his face while I tell him the truth. I keep talking and when I'm finished, I feel that odd relief that happens after vomiting. I'm empty and hollow, but I also feel lighter, as though I've just released some toxic illness inside me. He chucks me under the chin gently and lifts my face toward his.

"Done," he says. "Let's go tell the lawyers."

———

It's nearly two forty-five by the time we jump into our respective cars and screech out of the parking lot. I'm hysterical as I brake for the stoplight on Avenue of the Stars, smacking my steering wheel with my palm and laughing through a waterfall of tears.

Oh my fucking shit. What did we just do???

Nancy acted like she wanted to have me committed when we walked back in that room together.

"I need a moment with my client please, I need a moment with my client please!"

"No," he said calmly. "We've talked, we've made a decision, and now we just need you guys to draw it up so we can sign and get out of here."

But she was right about my husband.

This was business, this was contracts, the kind of environment he absolutely thrives in. With surgical precision, he brilliantly handled the handlers, ignoring both Michael's and Nancy's pleas for sidebars. He instructed the mediator to draw up everything exactly as we had it written out on a page I'd torn out of my Filofax. The opposite side of this week's grocery list.

"And we need to be out of here in thirty minutes."

"But you're not thinking clearly!" Nancy shrieked. "What exactly did he say to you out there, Laura? This is a joke compared to what you are owed, don't you see?"

I faced Nancy then and placed my hands on her shoulders.

"Nancy, I'm getting the settlement amount we wanted, right? I'm getting more child support than we were asking for. I'm getting my house, and I get to take my boys to school every day and tuck them in almost every night. I give you my proxy to handle all those other details, the residuals, health insurance, the incidentals. But most importantly, if he and I leave right now, we might have a chance to make Jordan's performance."

Nancy looked at me and blinked rapidly. I wondered if she was in shock or if she was trying to hold back tears.

The mediator smiled at me as I sign.

"I hope you make it," she said, squeezing my arm.

Make it to the performance in time? Make it in recovery? Make it as a single mom? Make it on what I'm settling for?

"Thank you."

"And thank you, Nancy," I said, reaching out to shake her hand.

"You're welcome. But I can't and won't take credit for this deal," she said. "And I really hope you don't regret it."

It's 3:05 when we pull into the Ashley School parking lot, one after the other. The parking lot is packed with cars and Danny the security guard waves us up toward the overflow parking lot.

That's three minutes away from here, we'll never make it.

"Fuck it," my husband yells out his window. "Let's just leave them here at the curb, we can move them later."

"But you can't . . ." starts Danny.

Danny's a really nice guy. I've bought him plenty of Starbucks cappuccinos on frosty mornings.

"Please, Danny," I yell out the window. "We're going to miss Jordan. We might have already missed him. He has the solo."

Danny sighs and looks around.

"Leave your keys and come back as quick as you can, okay? Go, go."

I pull up behind my husband's Porsche and we slam our doors, hauling ass up the hill toward the auditorium. I can hear the music coming from behind the closed double doors over the breath in my ears as I run. He's faster than me, especially in these stupid, squeaky heels, so he reaches the doors way before me and tries to open them.

Locked.

What the hell?

I run down to the next set of doors and try them, but they're locked too. He knocks on the center doors lightly with his fists and finally someone opens them from the inside.

"Thanks," he whispers.

The gym looks like Santa's workshop. There is a full-size sled and reindeer suspended over our heads as we run down the aisle, frantically searching for Jordan on the stage.

"Bar-ump-ba-ba-bummm," the chorus sings.

"The Little Drummer Boy"! Wait, did he already do his solo? Did we miss it??

I spot Jordan's new blue blazer as we near the stage. He doesn't try to hide his excitement when he sees us. He chair-dances and smiles. No, he beams, waving his hands wildly as we slip into the two seats in front next to my mother. Moments later, the lights go down as he stands and adjusts the saxophone around his neck.

It's time.

I cover my face with my hands, but it doesn't stop the sob climbing up my throat. Fortunately, the squawk of Jordan's solo drowns everything out. My husband and I both bounce to our feet in fervid applause the moment he's done seconds later.

We made it.

If it wasn't for the pills, I wouldn't be here
But if I keep taking these pills, I won't be here.

Juice WRLD 12/2/1998–12/8/2019

EPILOGUE

Thanksgiving Day 2014

Scottie runs back to put the dogs in the garage before we begin the short walk up the hill. For the fifth year in a row, my ex-husband and his wife are hosting Thanksgiving dinner and have invited us to join. I'm sweating a little in my coat under the weight of the hostess present I insisted on carrying—a large cream-colored votive candle. I used to always bring wine as a gift before I got sober. Now everyone gets candles.

The first year we were invited I was so nervous. I didn't know how to be around my ex in his new home that he now shared with his new wife.

Should I offer to help her in the kitchen? Should I hang out in the living room with my ex in-laws?

Scottie helps, because Scottie always helps. He got sober shortly after my ex and I signed those divorce papers in December six years ago, exactly nine days after we'd told the kids we were getting divorced.

"Hey, buddy, look at us, okay? Your lives aren't going to change. You're going to live in this house with Mom and I'm going to be here every morning for breakfast and every night for dinner, and on weekends I'll take you guys out to Malibu, just like we've been doing."

Once the boys understood what we were saying, it was like we'd slashed them open with knives, one wailed, one bolted, both were yelling and screaming. Sad and angry. Wounded and confused.

I stayed back to comfort the one on the sofa while he took off after the other one. It was the pain that I'd spent all those years hoping to avoid. My heart shattered into a thousand pieces as I kissed his head and squeezed him as hard as I could. This agony would test my sobriety in a way that nothing else had or would. I would have given anything for the strongest of painkillers after we put them to bed that night. I wanted something to make me forget. Trying heroin sounded appealing, and not for the first or last time. I wanted to escape.

But I didn't try heroin. I didn't dull the pain. I called Scott. I called my sponsor. I ate Entenmann's chocolate fudge cake right of the box. I went to bed.

Our divorce therapist had cautioned us that our plan seemed ambitious. She didn't know if it was a good idea for my ex to come to my house every morning for breakfast and evening for family dinner. She advised against us taking our scheduled family trip to Washington, DC, recommending that we do smaller, separate trips instead. She didn't think it would be wise for him to keep his key.

We didn't know either, but we did it anyway.

For two years, my ex came over every morning and evening that he was in town, and for two years I held my tears until after my kids drove away for the weekend with him. When I was five years sober (and five years divorced), my ex moved back to town from Malibu, and I sold my house. Scottie and I, who up until then had lived separately, decided it was time to cohabitate and bought a place together four houses down from my ex-husband. This way, the boys could go back and forth at will, transfers would be a breeze, and a laptop left at Dad's would no longer require an extra, out of the way stop on the way to school.

Three years ago, I started taking writing classes at UCLA Extension, trying to pick up some of the pieces of myself that I'd lost along the way. The classes were hard, harder than I would have ever imagined. Like all my school experiences before, I felt as though I was always a little behind the others. But I reveled in the small victories, faint praise from the teacher, encouraging feedback from the other students.

Baby steps.

My kids are at the door when we get there. I'm pulled inside by one while the other asks me to hold the money his grandparents gave him for his birthday. Someone takes the candle from me and Scottie's coat from him. We're offered wine by the cater waiter, we both ask for club soda with lime instead.

I wonder sometimes if I were to go back to that day in the hallway of Nancy's office, knowing what I know now, would I ask for more? If the world was divided into winners and losers, which one am I? Am I a loser because I should have fought for more money, more property? Or am I a winner because I get to spend almost every day with my kids? Am I a loser because I'll probably never fly private again or live in an eleven-thousand-square-foot house? Or am I a winner because I have a man in my life who loves me just as I am?

My ex spots us and walks over to hug me before shaking Scott's hand.

"Hey, good to see you both, thanks for coming."

We find our places at the table, a sea of expensive-looking accent plates with beautifully calligraphied place cards, each tied with a sprig of fresh rosemary.

Instantly and without envy, I recognize it as her handiwork. Most of the time I find that I'm genuinely happy that he's found someone who effortlessly embodies the type of woman I was trying to become for him. The effort that almost killed me.

We both won and we both lost. We're doing the best we can with what we have, and sometimes that has to be enough.

ACKNOWLEDGMENTS

The writing of this book was at once both an incredibly solo endeavor and a whole "it takes a village" project. I love writing. In fact, if I could just have old sitcoms playing in the background (*I Love Lucy*, *The Mary Tyler Moore Show* . . .) and write all day, every day, that's what I would do. But it was the people in my life who showed up for me before and during the writing of *Stash* that I'd like to acknowledge now.

Let me start by giving love to my parents, Linda Ternoir and Dr. Ronald Cathcart. They have never failed to make me feel loved, beautiful, and worthy. They have been my first call or text every step of the way. It is a thing of wonder to have the two people who created you fifty-eight years ago scream with joy at the sight of your first signed contract or book cover. I love you both so much and I am so very proud to be yours and to call you mine.

Obviously, this book is about my kids. My sons, who were little when I got sober and are now grown men. Every single moment of what I went through was worth it. The greatest gift I've ever experienced is the joy of being their mom. More in love with and prouder of them both I could not be.

Up next is Scott Slaughter, aka Scott S. 412 or "Hon." Who knew that anyone could meet their "person" in rehab? (I bet there's a dating app for that now.) But let me tell you about this man. When I started writing this book, I read him pages night after night after night and he listened and gave me notes. (Good notes too! Hello, first editor!) Meanwhile, he was taking care of me, producing our podcast, building our website, doing ALL the grocery shopping, AND he had dinner ready for me every night when I knocked off "work" at seven (y'all don't hear me though). And as much as I love to write, curling up in bed with him to watch TV is still my favorite thing to do every single day. Oh, my man, I love him so . . .

Stash would not be a book if it weren't for the phenomenal Holly Whitaker. I'd like to pause for a second and have a moment of reverent silence for this sister. In October 2018, she sent me this amazing email about an article I'd written, and somewhere in there, we became friends, aces, sisters. Now I don't remember my life without her. It was Holly who read the first thirty pages of *Stash*. And it was Holly who then sent them to her agent (now my agent too), Rebecca Gradinger (more on her in a minute). Holly wasn't just an early reader; she was THE first reader, and she's never wavered in giving me the real on everything. Holly, I love you fiercely, devotedly, madly.

This is impossible.

How lucky am I that I've had so many people help me that I'm worried you're going to stop reading before I get a chance to thank them all?

I'll start with the bestest, most fiercest lioness agent a girl could ask for, Rebecca Gradinger of Fletcher & Company. You held my hand from the beginning, patiently editing in real time as I wrote, always ready for the next chapter or draft. You are the agent who allowed me to discover my own sense of agency, always encouraging me to find and use MY voice. Thank you for believing in and fighting for *Stash*. Gratitude doesn't begin to cover it.

My editor, Michelle Herrera Mulligan at Atria. You were the one who truly understood what *Stash* was about. And that beautiful letter you sent me? I will treasure it forever. I love that you read my first draft and asked me to go deeper. Because of you, I unearthed photo albums and journals I hadn't read in years. I interrogated my memory and elevated my writing to a level I didn't know I was capable of. I am so proud of what we did together—thank you.

And speaking of Atria, thank you to my publisher, Libby McGuire. When you wrote to me that you'd read every word of *Stash* and couldn't stop thinking about it, I did a happy dance in my office. I'd also like to thank the whole Atria team, with a special shout-out to Alejandra Rocha for making this first-time author feel very well cared for and special.

To the stunning foursome of women who are my writing group, Dana Mich, Riva Lombardi, Amy Bond, and Stephanie Lechner, thank you for your flawless love, friendship, and inspiration. To Emily McCombs, deputy editor at HuffPost Personal—you friggin' ROCK! What would my life be if you hadn't published my "Brave Magic" essay (and the other subsequent eighteen)? You taught me everything I know about what makes an essay publishable along with a bunch of insider terms I'd never heard before. LOVE YOU! To Kelly Karczewski at Fletcher & Co., thank you for all the behind-the-scenes magic. To Tracey Lee Kemble, Sister!! You have never wavered, not once. Thank you for thirty-plus years of friendship and for always, always being there for both me and *Stash*! You have been my eyes when I could not see. I love you.

Karen Brailsford, thank you for your incredible generosity. When I was floundering, your guidance and wisdom were invaluable. Reema Zaman, thank you for being such a loving, patient reader and for encouraging me to keep writing from my heart. Robinne Lee and Keah Brown, thank you for taking my 911 calls when I was at a writing crossroads—I am so grateful. To Cheo Hodari Coker, man—you were always like, "Laura, you HAVE to write this book!" Thank you for seeing so much further down the road than I could.

To my writing teachers, Stefanie Wilder Taylor, Lisa Jakub, and Jessica Ciencin Henriquez:

Stefanie, your humor is so inspiring, and I have incorporated so many of your brilliant notes into my writing over the years. Lisa, thank you for encouraging those of us who took your fabulous class (three times!) to form our own writers' group and then staying connected with us. And, Jessica, thank you for telling me that my best story was yet to come—you were right.

To the inimitable Catherine Gray, who THRILLED ME by including my essay in her fantastic book, *Sunshine Warm Sober*, and even mentioning me in her acknowledgments (eek!), I'm so happy to be able to return the favor.

My brothers: Kenji Hughes, Kofi Cathcart, Jay and Jordan Higgins, and Christopher Young (yeah, we all have different last names, so what?). Thank you for cheering me on, bruhs! To Nora and Lily Slaughter, you are both such remarkable humans! Being your bonus mom is a privilege that I do not take lightly. To my *Sex and the City* friends, Nicole Lamy, Tracey Lee Kemble, Rebecca Gayheart, Ling Chan, and Troy Byer. Our epic text threads, dinners, and lunches have sustained me over these past few years. I don't know what I would have done without you—love you each and all. To Shelly Sumpter Gillyard, for believing in me from day one, opening your heart to me over and over again, and for insisting that this was a book that I both could and should write—thank you. And where would I be without my weekly Black Girl Magic Dog Walk? Lenora Crichlow, Linda Ternoir, and Beverly Mickens Dougherty, you have heard and held all of my *Stash* fears and triumphs over the past three years. I'm not a woman of faith per se, but I have faith in us, in you. To Lilah Hadjinian King (bestie), for constantly calling and texting me for updates on the book, and for always asking, "Can I post about it yet???" I love you so much (also, let the posting begin)! To Désirée Powell for reading this entire book in twenty-four hours so she could give me her corrections before the deadline—thank you! To Sara Dean and Lelia Gowland, thank you for being so genuinely happy for me each time I Voxxed, called, or texted with new news. And, yes, I'm coming to Seattle and to New Orleans! To the Owls, who understood that I needed the space and time to pursue this path, thank you.

And finally, to my ex-husband, who gave me his blessing to write and publish this story, thank you.

ABOUT THE AUTHOR

Laura Cathcart Robbins is an author, freelance writer, speaker, and host of the popular podcast *The Only One in the Room*. She has been active for many years as a speaker and school trustee and is credited for creating the Buckley School's nationally recognized committee on diversity, equity, inclusion, and justice. Her recent articles in *Huff-Post* and *The Temper* on the subjects of race, recovery, and divorce have garnered her worldwide acclaim. A 2022 TEDx Talk speaker, she is also a Los Angeles Moth StorySLAM winner. Laura currently sits on the advisory boards of the San Diego Writers Festival and the Outliers Podcast Festival. She lives in California. Follow her on Instagram @LauraCathcartRobbins and find out more at theonlyonepod.com.